Moral Questions in the Classroom

Moral Questions in the Classroom

*How to Get Kids to Think Deeply
About Real Life and Their Schoolwork*

Katherine G. Simon

Foreword by Theodore R. Sizer and Nancy Faust Sizer

Yale University Press

New Haven and London

Designed by Thomas Whitridge and set in Century and News Gothic types by Ink, Inc., New York. Printed in the United States of America by R. R. Donnelley & Sons.

Library of Congress Cataloging-in-Publication Data

Simon, Katherine G., 1962–

Moral questions in the classroom: how to get kids to think deeply about real life and their schoolwork / Katherine G. Simon.

     p.   cm.

Includes bibliographical references and index. ISBN 0-300-09032-3 (alk. paper)

1. Moral education (Secondary)—United States—Case Studies. 2. High school teaching—United States—Case studies. I. Title

LC311 .S49 2001   373'.01'140973—dc21   2001002809

A catalogue record for this book is available from the British Library.

The paper in this book meets the guidelines for permanence and durability of the Committee on Production Guidelines for Book Longevity of the Council on Library Resources.

10   9   8   7   6   5   4   3   2   1

To my mother,

Anna Shure Simon,

of blessed memory, my first teacher

Contents

Foreword

"THE KIDS ARE COMPLAINING ABOUT THE NEW UNIT," a teacher told us happily. The smile on her face suggested an unexpected contradiction. The unit was on the legislative process, and the students' assignment was to find a bill currently in Congress, to decide whether they should support or oppose it, and then to prepare a presentation that they would make in person to a congressional staffer in Washington.

"Right now, we're discussing the issues behind the issues," the teacher continued, "who will benefit, who will not. The kids are really into the idea that the Congress has to sort out that question, to decide what 'the common good' really is. But they say it makes their heads hurt to think that much!"

Wouldn't it be wonderful to have schools full of such thinking heads? To have students who (as Kathy Simon nicely puts it) "need to practice big ideas by trying them out in their own mouths"? To have teachers with the time and skills to construct such units, to moderate such discussions, and to assess each student's contribution to the project? To have serious questions about the "common good" permeating the curriculum, with activities designed to help students and their teachers learn to discuss such questions?

Kathy Simon thinks so, and in this book she offers much help to those of us who agree with her. (Those who are not in favor of having students who question and who think-until-it-hurts will have to read another book.) She writes of the importance of "the great curiosities and passions of humankind" and the need for schools to provoke students into the habit of an "exploration of existential issues." This goal is a sensitive but critical one, the very heart of a serious education.

Kathy starts by recounting a bit of her own teaching in high school some years ago. Her class was reading *Macbeth*, dutifully "doing" the traditional stuff of Shakespeare study—the vocabulary, the plot's construction, the flow of language, the Elizabethan setting. In time, of course, the class came upon Macbeth's famous assertion that "Life's but a walking shadow, a poor player that struts and frets his hour upon the stage and then is heard no more; it is a tale told by an idiot, full of sound and fury, signifying nothing." Looking back, Kathy realizes that she did not have her students delve deeply into the ideas so expressed; she sees a missed opportunity, or worse, a failure at teaching. What did these words mean to Macbeth? Equally important, Kathy now argues, is the question, what do the ideas that lurk behind this familiar soliloquy mean in the lives of her students? Macbeth speaks to timeless and important issues that should be, in her view, a critical part of schooling. Why did she not make more of them then? Simon now wants us teachers to go beyond the play and to grapple with our students about the issues raised in such a passage, thereby to "invigorate the intellectual and moral life" of high school classrooms.

Over recent years, Kathy observed and tape recorded extensively in a variety of classrooms, and these transcripts are the core of her book. She reproduces critical dialogues taped in real classrooms and follows these with analyses that serve as the foundation of her general argument that the stuff of a deeply intellectual and moral life is embedded in the traditional curricula of American high schools. Issues about the nature and meaning of our very existence do not need their own special, isolated syllabus; they are embedded in all of the liberal arts that make up the core of serious high school work.

Why haven't teachers seized every opportunity to raise and discuss moral matters? That's what her research set out to understand, and she has a number of thoughtful suggestions about why so many teachers seem to come tantalizingly near to moral discussion, and then pull back. She discusses the endless need for time, the determination to "cover material," the demands of standardized testing. She analyzes the compulsion on many teachers' parts to "come to resolution" with the words the students can write down in their notebooks (and be tested on later). She looks at the way moral or existential questions are often relegated to out-of-class assignments rather than illumination in vibrant classroom discussions. She discusses the genuine dilemma of whose values to teach, and in what kinds of formats.

At the conclusion of this carefully measured, analytic, and yet passionate book, she asks us to look into our own English, history, and science curricula for places that provide the setting for consideration of a moral life. She provides us passages of effective moral teaching, ones not intimidatingly perfect (thank heaven) but realistic and powerful enough so that we can be sure that those students' heads, too, were hurting. She provides moral questions that are likely to be compelling to high school students, yet which can only be answered with substantial information and thus require that those students search out what they need. She takes on the thorny problem of how teachers can be passionate believers and yet "pedagogically neutral," how they can acknowledge and curtail their own power in order to let the students, themselves, make up their own minds.

Kathy understands that such educational goals can be neither grafted on to the existing high school regime nor taught by untrained and uncertain teachers. Even as she realizes that students are eager to explore these issues, Kathy knows that moral matters are inevitably explosive in all high schools, and that even raising the prospect of addressing them may cause controversy. Nevertheless, she urges us not to flinch, but to take the time and make the intellectual effort to let all children have the opportunity to ponder the meaning of their lives as something more than being a "walking shadow...signifying nothing" and to plumb the depth of what might be the "common good" until their "heads hurt."

Theodore R. Sizer
Nancy Faust Sizer

Acknowledgments

I WISH FIRST OF ALL TO THANK THE TEACHERS WHO ALLOWED me into their classrooms to watch their work, gave me time for interviews, and provided feedback on my writing in progress. They showed me a warmth, generosity, and trust for which I am very grateful. Because this book criticizes many of the structures and norms of schooling—and because teachers' work in the classroom is the most visible outward expression of those structures and norms—parts of this work may be painful reading for those very teachers who gave me their trust. That thought is sad for me, for despite any of the criticisms I or any other educational researcher could level, these teachers are in the classroom, every day, working to nurture children. I am grateful to have had an opportunity to watch them in action and to think about how the curriculum could be designed to be more engaging for teachers and students alike.

I am also grateful to the many students who let me watch them in class and agreed to talk to me about their lives in school and out. They reminded me regularly why rethinking our educational system is urgent and helped add humor and warmth to my months of fieldwork.

The first version of this book was written as my doctoral dissertation at Stanford University. The members of my dissertation committee—Nel Noddings, Lee Shulman, Arnie Eisen, and Myra Strober—provided encouragement and, through their own scholarly work, inspiration for this project. Myra, my "outside reader," went above and beyond the responsibilities of that position, providing particularly insightful feedback on my dissertation proposal and on the finished work. Arnie provided detailed feedback on my writing, pushed me to try to think clearly about big questions, and, as a father of two school-age children, helped me keep an eye on what my ideas would mean for real kids. Lee helped me early on to articulate my questions in ways that could be researched empirically, helped me see the strengths and limitations of my methodological choices, and regularly connected me with other scholars (from around the country and the world) who were likely to take an interest in my work. Most of all, he believed in my ability to write and think well about important issues, and thereby helped me believe in that as well. Nel has served as a model of the possibility of integrating high-level theoretical work with attention to the most pressing practical concerns of teaching children well. Her work, as will be apparent, provides an intellectual foundation for much of mine. Personally, she was a pillar of support and encouragement throughout my years of graduate school.

I was privileged to meet a marvelous group of visiting professors during my time at Stanford: Jim Astman, Joe Reimer, Miriam Ben Peretz, Isa Aron, Michael Zeldin, and Aryeh Davidson. All of them helped inform my thinking about this project; Michael, visiting Stanford in the few months before I finished writing, read every word of the four main data chapters, providing crucial, well-timed feedback. Much of the dissertation was written with the support of a grant from the Spencer Foundation, which also provided opportunities to meet with a wonderful group of colleagues from around the country.

Several friends and colleagues contributed greatly throughout the many stages of this project. Amy Gerstein, Jenifer Helms, Tom Meyer, and Anna Richert talked through at length the ideas and the incidents described in this study and critiqued various chapters. I am particularly grateful to Denise Pope and Simone Schweber, with whom I formed a writing group, and from whose work I learned much both about schools and about writing. Great editors, powerful thinkers, attending both to big ideas and to matters of style, they helped turn my unfinished drafts into real chapters, providing laughter and encouragement along the way.

Through my work at the Coalition of Essential Schools (CES) and the support of the Shinnyo En Foundation, I have had the incredible opportunity to translate some of the ideas in this book into what we call the "Essential Moral Questions" project. Some of the ideas developed with teachers in this project appear in the Afterword.

Susan Arellano, my editor at Yale University Press, has been enthusiastic about the value of this book and has offered suggestions for revisions in the best tradition of "critical friendship." I am grateful especially for her patience and understanding of my juggling of work, parenting, and writing.

Family members helped out as well. My father and stepmother, Jerry and Yetta Simon, provided invaluable support during the many years of graduate school. My cousins Susan Dworsky, Alan Dworsky, and Betsy Sansby read drafts of chapters, offered editorial advice, and, best of all, got excited. Betsy, in fact, marched off to her daughter Molly's fourth-grade teacher with Chapter 4, asking whether the teacher couldn't incorporate more moral and existential questions into the curriculum. Thinking of that conversation has often provided me with happy motivation to get the book into print.

On my first hike with Inbal Kashtan, I was full of stories from my fieldwork in schools. In the six years since that time, we've done a few other things together—including getting married and welcoming Yannai, our son, into the world. In writing this book, as in all aspects of our lives together, I have depended hugely on Inbal to recognize what matters and to find ways to communicate it well. I could not be more blessed.

CHAPTER 1

The Place of Meaning

IN ONE OF MY FIRST YEARS OF HIGH SCHOOL TEACHING, I asked my students to memorize and recite some lines from *Macbeth*. On the day the assignment was due, one of the students called out the following lines from her seat:

> Life's but a walking shadow, a poor player
> That struts and frets his hour upon the stage
> And then is heard no more. It is a tale
> Told by an idiot, full of sound and fury
> Signifying nothing.

I then did what I understood to be my job as an English teacher: I helped the students understand the definitions of the words "struts," "frets," and "signifying." I asked them to comment on the central metaphor, in which life is compared to an actor. We pounded out the rhythm on our desks, noting that the first, fourth, and fifth lines do not fall neatly into iambic pentameter and discussing why Shakespeare might have departed from his norm for these. We had a passably interesting discussion about the meter and the words.

Neither I nor my students, however, thought to discuss the heart of the passage, the real question being raised here: does life have meaning? I knew that English teachers were supposed to teach about figures of speech and vocabulary, and I knew how to do that. I was neither equipped nor expected to explore questions about what it means to be human. And so our discussion stayed safely out of the realm of morals and meaning. Yet by focusing on the play's external structures rather than on its existential core, I unfortunately ignored the very elements of the play that I myself find most important and exciting and that I believe might have held most interest for my students.

This book arises out of the suspicion that slowly took root in me as a high school teacher, that even as my colleagues and I taught academic disciplines born of the great curiosities and passions of humankind, our classes somehow focused on closed answers, definitions, and formulas rather than on the questions, the sense of wonder, and the yearning for understanding that gave rise to the disciplines in the first place. I suspected that we were not teaching what matters.

This book is an investigation of that suspicion, an investigation into what does matter and what should matter in school, and particularly, into when and how moral and existential issues are addressed in the context of the core subjects of standard high school curricula. In investigating these questions, I hoped to find and to document the work of a number of teachers who, more than I had done in the case of *Macbeth*, were regularly able to integrate the study of moral and existential questions into their courses. I also hoped to examine the notion that students might find exploring these questions fascinating and important—and so discover a sense of purpose and excitement regarding their studies, now so lacking in the daily grind of high school life.

I began with two core assumptions:

- *Moral and existential questions are at the core of the disciplines.* Human knowledge—including that represented by the academic disciplines—has come into existence largely as a result of the pursuit of answers to moral and existential questions. Because of this, study of subjects like literature, history, and science is quite partial and incomplete if it excludes moral and existential questions, and thoughtful study of these subjects inevitably gives rise to further moral and existential questions.
- *Most people find moral and existential questions fascinating.* Moral and existential questions should be addressed in schools both because they are intrinsic to and inextricable from the disciplines and because students are likely to care about them. Study of these questions is likely to imbue students' work with a sense of purpose and meaning.

I began my investigation, in short, with the premise that human beings are occupied with questions of meaning. We want to know if our life has a purpose; we want to connect the meaning of our individual lives to those of other people and maybe even to the universe as a whole. We want to make sense of the pain we endure and to understand the sources of wonder and joy. We are full of questions about our existence. Robert Coles, taking hundreds of interviews focusing on children's moral and spiritual lives, has documented that young people, particularly, are deeply engaged in these questions. He writes: "The longer I've known children, the more readily I've noticed the abiding interest they have in reflecting about human nature, about the reasons people behave as they do, about the mysteries of the universe as evinced in the earth, the sun, the moon, the stars." Coles sees children, like the rest of us, as "pilgrims," wondering "about it all, the nature of the journey and the final destination."[1]

Agreeing with Coles that children actively wonder about "the nature of the journey," I already knew what I believed when I set out to research what was actually happening in schools: Teachers should encourage exploration of moral and existential issues—if only because kids are extremely interested in them. And while they are engaged in questions that interest them, I believed, students would also have opportunities to develop a host of invaluable *intellectual* and moral skills, traits, and sensibilities: a hunger for deeper understanding and the stamina to seek it out, a sense of connection with the human beings throughout history who have struggled with similar questions, the ability to see shades of gray in conflicts and to articulate nuanced opinions, the habit of seeking out multiple points of view, the habit of collaborating to explore complex issues, the willingness to change one's mind when that is warranted, and even the capacity for empathy.

Along with my enthusiasm for the idea that teachers should encourage the exploration of moral and existential issues, I also began with serious concerns about the idea. First, the very terms I was using seemed vague. What constitutes a "moral" or "existential" topic or question? The words are almost infinitely broad, for all human interactions have moral components and all curiosity about the nature of human life can be seen as "existential." If everything is moral or existential in one way or another, what would it mean to focus on the moral and existential in schools? Is there any specific content implied by these words? What would instruction in moral and existential questions look like? Is it a teaching of beliefs, of attitudes? Is it engaging in certain activities? How would I know "it" when I saw it?

Another concern involved the core assumption that moral and existential issues have an important place in *school*. Granted that human beings are moral creatures who wonder about the meaning of their existence, this does not imply that schools must make moral and existential issues their areas of central focus. I, like many others, could easily argue that the primary mission of schools is intellectual; schools are supposed to promote literacy, mathematical skills, and high-order thinking. Anything else, especially given the widespread and daunting lack of success in meeting even those goals, may well be a distraction. This view was supported by Robert Maynard Hutchins, who—in the language of his time—argued that schools should keep out of the business of moral education: "Education deals with the development of the intellectual powers of men. Their moral and spiritual powers are the sphere of the family and the church. All three agencies must work in harmony; for, though a man has three aspects, he is still one man. But the schools cannot take over the role of the family and the church without promoting the atrophy of those institutions and failing in the task that is proper to the schools."[2] I certainly did not want to usurp religious institutions and the family, and I did want schools to focus on helping children learn to use their minds well. Perhaps, I thought, schools should indeed stick closely to the task of developing the intellect.

A third concern focused on the connection, which Hutchins takes for granted, between moral and existential questions and religion. I worried that one could not distinguish moral and existential teachings from religion in a way that would be appropriate in the public schools. Given that many people derive their moral convictions from religious teachings, is it actually possible to address moral and existential questions without effectively teaching religion? Put another way, if teachers became engaged in helping students develop opinions about moral and existential questions, how would they avoid either promoting or negating the teachings of particular religions?

A final concern involved the recognition that many programs of moral education—especially those which seek to please a wide constituency—are quite superficial, transmitting simplistic notions of "right" versus "wrong," and focusing as much on the memorization of terms and regurgitation of facts as some academic courses. There is no guarantee that a course, just because it focuses on moral matters, will be engaging to students, intellectually powerful, or morally sensitive. And I had the sense that simplistic, dull, or heavy-handed teaching regarding moral or existential matters would probably be far more disturbing than simplistic, dull, or heavy-handed teaching about most other things.

Taking my sense that teachers *should* be integrating moral matters into their curriculum together with these concerns, I sought to answer these questions:

- What does the discussion of moral and existential issues look like in high school classrooms?
- How does the exploration of moral and existential issues intersect with more conventional academic work? Do they interfere with each other? Is it possible to do both?
- What about the separation of church and state? How can one explore moral issues without promoting one religious view or another? How can one explore moral issues while honoring cultural and religious pluralism?
- Practically speaking, what might a teacher do to make moral and existential issues more central to his or her curriculum?

To pursue these questions, I spent three months going to school all day, observing classes across the curriculum and interviewing teachers and students. One month was spent at a suburban public high school with a reputation for both innovation and excellence. Conjecturing that teachers in religious schools might have more freedom to pursue moral and existential issues than their public school counterparts, I spent the other two months at a Catholic and a Jewish high school, observing courses in religion as well as English, history, and biology.[3] Through a wide variety of vivid excerpts from classroom discussions, this book reports what I saw and heard in these three schools and explores the implications of these observations for the theory and practice of moral and existential education in the public schools.

The Words "Moral" and "Existential"

As I mentioned above, one of the challenges of this discussion is that the words "moral" and "existential" tend to be used so broadly and vaguely that it is hard to know their boundaries. It will be useful, therefore, to establish some working definitions.

I use "existential" very much as Coles uses the word "spiritual" in his description of children's spirituality, to involve reflection about human nature and the mysteries of the universe, including the meanings of life and death. In addition to these spiritual matters, I use "existential" to include, as the word implies, issues involving the quality of existence—like those regarding health and emotional well-being.[4] Here are some examples of questions I consider existential, as they grapple with the mysteries and meaning of life:

- What does it mean to lead a good life?
- Why is there so much suffering?
- Is there a God?
- What happens when we die?
- Do we have free will, or are our fates determined?

The following, of a somewhat more immediate nature, would also be included in my category of "existential concerns":

- What makes me feel happy and fulfilled?
- Where can I find friendship and love?
- In what ways do I most need to grow and develop?
- How can I nurture my ongoing growth and development?

While existential questions have to do with life and its meaning, moral questions, as I use the phrase, have to do with how human beings should *act* (or should have acted) in situations that involve the well-being of oneself, of other human beings, of other living things, or of the earth. Examples of moral questions that might come up in high school classes include the following:

- Do I have responsibilities toward homeless people in my city?
- Should a shopping center be built where it would destroy a marsh?
- Was the United States right to have dropped atomic bombs on Japan?
- Should someone who is caught using illegal drugs be sent to jail or be given treatment?
- Should I help someone who is bleeding, even though he or she might have AIDS?
- Is it okay to cheat if I think the teacher's grading system is not fair?
- Is violence ever justified?

The boundaries between the moral and the existential quickly become blurred, for, in considering moral questions, people often refer to existential beliefs. One might answer the moral question about homeless people, for example, by stating that "We are responsible for helping all people find adequate shelter, for all human beings are created in the image of God." Moral questions often evoke existential answers, and the reverse is also true. A person pondering the meaning of a good life, for example, might put her existential conclusions into action, thus entering the realm of the moral.

I employ the terms "moral" and "existential," then, while acknowledging that they imply and interact with each other so thoroughly that in practice they are probably inseparable. Furthermore, in common usage, the distinctions are not clear. Some speakers and writers use the word "moral" in a broad sense, to refer to both what I call moral and what I call existential. Many others would use the term "spiritual" for what I call existential. The distinctions are ultimately not as important as the power the terms give us to focus our attention on what Nel Noddings calls "the things that matter most deeply to human beings" and how schools address or fail to address them.[5]

The Educational Context

In the time since I recorded the classroom interactions that form the basis of this book, there has been widespread adoption across the country of high-stakes standardized tests. These tests are typically used both to measure the performance of individual students and to evaluate the work of individual teachers and whole schools. They are known as "high stakes," because, typically, teachers can be censured or fired on the basis of poor test scores on the part of their students, and whole schools can be "reconstituted"—teachers and principals replaced—if they fail to raise test scores a given number of points in a given number of years. For students, failure on the tests can mean being held back to repeat a grade or being denied a diploma.

The best of the standardized tests may in fact assess one or two of the qualities that one might hope to nurture through investigations of moral or existential questions—the ability to analyze a reasoned argument, for example, or to comprehend a variety of points of view. To the degree that standardized tests can help teachers assess progress in these areas, that is for the good. But it is crucial to note that most of the qualities one would hope to develop in students through an exploration of moral issues—or more generally through a rich and rigorous education—cannot possibly be assessed by standardized tests. More important, the development of these qualities is in many cases actually hampered by the existence of the tests and the stakes attached to them.[6]

One of the aims of this book is to question key assumptions behind the testing movement: the assumption that the important outcomes of education are those that can be tested with pencil and paper in a few hours and scored en masse; the assumption that important intellectual achievements of students and teachers can be charted on a bell curve; the assumption that one test will work across a state or a country; the assumption that there needs to be no connection between the intellectual life of a *particular* classroom and the tools that are used to evaluate it.

The truth is that the most important intellectual and moral achievements require the development of habits of mind—such as asking the right questions, seeking out multiple possible answers, knowing when and how to collaborate, knowing where to find more information, thinking "out of the box"—which such tests cannot measure. It is also true that the important intellectual achievements of human beings do not fall out neatly into percentile rankings. If classrooms are intellectually vibrant, if groups of children are allowed to follow their curiosities, they will follow paths of their own, covering different specific content from whatever the test makers might have anticipated. The children in such classrooms may score poorly on standardized tests, while being very smart in every way that matters in life.

The testing movement and the rhetoric of politicians have somehow made it seem that having a high-stakes testing program is equivalent to raising standards. Although this book focuses little on testing per se, I do aim to put a very different spin on what it means to raise standards and also to demonstrate some of the ways education is impoverished when it centers on testable content. As such, this book is an argument for raising expectations for both teachers and students, for believing that it is possible for teachers and students to do much more exciting and substantive work than is now the norm. I seek to paint a picture of what school could be like—including what students' intellectual accomplishments could be—if we explicitly, energetically stopped teaching to tests and made room for a different definition of what matters.

The Social Context

The mid- and late 1990s saw American popular culture brimming with evidence of people groping for moral clarity and spiritual truths. Such works as *The Celestine Prophecy*, a novel promising "insights into the meaning of life," and *Care of the Soul*, a nonfiction piece providing "a new vision of spiritual fulfillment," remained on bestseller lists for years, while *Chicken Soup for the Soul*, a collection of short stories purporting to provide spiritual insight and comfort, spawned more than a dozen sequels. As one journalist described the phenomenon, "If you want to write a bestseller, you've gotta have soul. In the book's title, that is."[7] A compact-disc recording of monks singing Gregorian chants stunned the music industry by becoming a bestseller on the pop music charts; it, too, has given rise to sequels, and now chanters of the Koran and holy Hindu texts are packaged for popular audiences as well. Politicians peppered their speeches with professions of their own religious commitments, chasing what *USA Today* dubbed "the values vote."[8] As the new century begins, talking about, reading about, searching for, and promoting morality and spirituality remain in vogue.

It is likely, though, that the intensity of the search for moral clarity and spiritual insight arises out of an underlying sense of confusion about these matters. Vaclav Havel, like other contemporary thinkers, claims that modern people lack a sense of connection to one another and to the universe, a lack he attributes to the role science has played in shaping modern epistemology.[9]

The dizzying development of science, with its unconditional faith in objective reality and complete dependency on general and rationally knowable laws, led to the birth of modern technological civilization. It is the first civilization that spans the entire globe and binds together all societies, submitting them to a common global destiny.

At the same time, the relationship to the world that modern science fostered and shaped appears to have exhausted its potential. The relationship is missing something. It fails to connect with the most intrinsic nature of reality and with natural human experience. It produces a state of schizophrenia: man as an observer is becoming completely alienated from himself as a being.

Classical modern science described only the surface of things, a single dimension of reality. And the more dogmatically science treated it as the only dimension, as the very essence of reality, the more misleading it became. We may know immeasurably more about the universe than our ancestors did, and yet it increasingly seems they knew something more essential about it than we do, something that escapes us.[10]

Havel's theme has been reflected throughout the past decade in the more mundane prose of the popular media. *Time* magazine, introducing its choice as "Man of the Year" for 1994, explained, "In these days of moral chaos, John Paul II is fiercely resolute about his ideals."[11] Providing a careful rationale for the selection of the pope, *Time* wrote nothing to defend its premise that we live in an age of moral chaos. That idea needed no defense. It had become commonplace by the end of 1994, and remains so.

My study of the possibility of integrating moral and existential questions into public school curricula is situated, thus, in the context of a social paradox: words like "moral," "spiritual," "soul," "virtue," and "values" fill our magazines, bestsellers, and politicians' speeches, while at the same time "something escapes us." As a society, despite our fascination with and increasing dependence on technology, we doubt that science can answer all of our questions. Most of us, however, lack access to or understanding of other sources of knowledge. We seem to have to choose between science as the basis of all knowledge, on one hand, and faddish or highly politicized versions of spirituality and morality on the other.

If society is generally in a moral and existential muddle, it is not surprising that schools' moral missions would be confused as well. It is precisely in times of crisis, however, that people look to schools for solutions.[12] The sense of moral confusion and the pervasive feeling that society is in disarray—along with alarming, regular news reports of teenagers involved in extreme acts of violence—have given rise to widespread calls for moral education in the schools.

These calls rest, quite often, on the claim that a lack of proper moral instruction in the schools accounts for many of the current social ills. Thomas Lickona and a number of other advocates of moral education attribute at least some of the increases in teenage pregnancy, violence, vandalism, and general greed and materialism directly to changing philosophies and practices of moral education.[13]

Schools in the early days of the republic tackled character education head on. Through discipline, the teacher's good example, and the curriculum, schools sought to instruct children in the virtues of patriotism, hard work, honesty, thriftiness, altruism, and courage.... With time, the confident consensus supporting old-fashioned character education began to crumble.

> ... The idea that adults should directly instruct children in right and wrong, or even try to influence students' "value positions," was explicitly rejected.... Teachers didn't see it as their role to teach or foster particular values.... Meanwhile, as society celebrated the individual and schools stayed neutral on values... there was accumulating evidence of a moral decline.

To address the situation, Lickona urges, schools must once again "take up the role of moral teachers of our children."[14] In the context of increasing calls for schools to engage in moral education, this book explores how one can take up the role of "moral teacher" in an intellectually powerful and democratically defensible way.

Moral Questions in the Curriculum

Thanks largely to the work of Lickona and colleagues of his in the character education movement, a number of new curricula have been developed in recent years to teach students certain sets of core values. Districts and states around the country, indeed, have mandated their use.[15] This book focuses not on the implementation of such supplementary curricula, however, but on the moral aspects implicit in the core curriculum, the moral questions that arise, to take my opening example, when an English teacher teaches *Macbeth* or when a biology teacher, for another example, teaches anatomy or ecology. Here are my key findings:

- *Moral and existential questions abound but are barely discussed.* I discovered that though moral questions abound, teachers most often do what I did when I taught *Macbeth*. They focus on structures and definitions and shy away from questions of deeper meaning. The classroom episodes depicted throughout the book give rise to some possible explanations for the sources of this reticence.
- *When moral or existential questions are discussed in depth, students describe these as their best learning experiences.* In the

classes that I observed where teachers and students took time to explore these questions, students repeatedly said things like: "I really enjoy this class just because—it makes you think. It makes you look into yourself, look around at society, look around at what's going on in the world, and how other people think."

- *The moral, existential, and intellectual are intertwined; exploration in one realm often augments the others.* The classroom episodes also show that investigations of moral and existential issues are inextricably intertwined with what might be viewed as the most rigorous aspects of a purely academic or intellectual curriculum. In Chapter 4, I report several classroom anecdotes that suggest that neglecting moral and existential issues robs students of the chance to practice such key *intellectual* skills as marshaling evidence to support their opinions, analyzing alternate interpretations, and reflecting on preconceptions. Chapters 5 and 6, on the other hand, present examples of how discussing moral and existential issues provides opportunities to develop and hone those intellectual skills.

- *Exploring moral questions does not ensure intellectual rigor.* Although a focus on moral and existential issues may invigorate an intellectual program, this is not necessarily the case. We will see some episodes in which moral issues are addressed but are not subjected to intellectual scrutiny, as if it would have been inappropriate to subject opinions on moral matters to rigorous analysis or even fact checking. In other examples, intentional lessons in morality may have actually inhibited intellectual inquiry.

A crucial set of questions arises from these findings. If it is impossible to avoid moral issues, if it is necessary to explore moral questions as part of any rigorous intellectual program, how can this exploration be conducted responsibly in our pluralistic society? Whose values will be taught? In Chapter 7, I propose the notion of a "schoolwide inquiry into values"—a significant rethinking of the mission of schooling—that models democratic practices as it intentionally seeks to put complex moral questions at the core of the curriculum.

Implications for Practice

One might detect throughout this book a kind of double message. That double message is here, so I want to make it explicit. The first message is that teachers can take great strides in infusing much more substance into the curriculum they teach, and they can work to develop instructional strategies that are particularly well suited to fostering in-depth exploration of moral and existential issues. This book, therefore, seeks to be useful to teachers who want to reflect on their work and deepen their craft along these lines. Chapters 4–7, in particular, provide examples of teaching that may provoke useful discussions about effective practice. The Afterword provides some concrete teaching strategies that teachers engaged in this work might want to use in their classrooms.

The second message is that—despite the actual and potential accomplishments of hard-working individuals and small teams of teachers—the problems described in this book are systemic ones. The current situation has not arisen because individual teachers, one at a time, have decided to focus on fairly disconnected facts and formulas at the expense of deeper questions of meaning. It has arisen because all aspects of the system—from teacher education programs to school-bell schedules, from textbooks to tests, from teacher evaluations to the allocation of professional development dollars—mitigate against teachers being able to incorporate discussions of substantive issues into their classrooms. On this level, this book is directed at all those engaged in the policy and practice of schooling—teachers, administrators, parents, teacher educators, textbook authors, policymakers. It is an argument for systemic school reform, for a fundamental shift in what we see as the goals and the content of a valuable education.

CHAPTER 2

What Is Moral Education?

IN THE PREVIOUS CHAPTER, I SUGGESTED WORKING definitions of moral and existential questions. As I use the terms, "moral questions" are those that have to do with how human beings should act in situations that involve the well-being of oneself, of other human beings, of other living things, or of the earth. "Existential questions" are those that involve reflection about human nature and the mysteries of the universe. These two definitions say little, however, about what "moral education" is. What are the purposes of moral education? What is its content?

There are a number of salient schools of thought on moral education, each with answers to these questions. In order to place the argument of this book in relation to them, I briefly outline and critique the central ideas of these schools: what I call "the virtues approach" to character education, "values clarification," Lawrence Kohlberg's "cognitive developmentalism," and "the ethic of care" as articulated by Nel Noddings and Carol Gilligan.

It is worth noting that my approach, based on empirical evidence gathered in classrooms, has a different starting point from much of the contemporary literature on moral education. I ask an anthropological question—what is happening of moral relevance in classroom instruction?—and move to recommendations for schools based on ethnographic data as well as philosophical argumentation. The cognitive developmentalist school of thought, by contrast, asks a question from cognitive psychology—how do individuals' capacities for moral reasoning develop over time?—and moves to recommendations for schools based on experimental findings. Noddings' "ethic of care" asks a philosophical question—what is the basis of ethical human behavior?—and moves to recommendations for schools based on that theoretical exploration.

My approach differs in several additional key respects from the others. First, I argue that moral and existential explorations have tremendous value in the present tense, aside from how they might affect future behavior. They should be incorporated into schools because students are likely to care about them and because of the importance of students' finding meaning in their work. Most of the approaches to moral education reviewed here begin by looking at society's needs and failings, and then ask how schools might produce students who will answer those needs or correct those failings. Whether the desired outcome is order, stability, and safety, as the virtues educators are likely to suggest, or a vibrant democracy, as the values clarification proponents wish, most approaches to moral education see schools primarily as a kind of processing plant; what matters is that the plant's output is respectful, reliable, honest, or possesses some other set of attributes.

My approach, most similar to that of the ethic of care and largely inspired by John Dewey, focuses less on the output of the school, and more on the quality of the time spent within it. Attention to moral and existential issues in schools is crucial, in my view, not so much because society seems to be in disarray, but because it is a scandal that so many millions of children and teenagers spend their days in boredom in classes that systematically avoid questions of genuine interest and importance.[1] I look at a classroom as a parent, and ask, "Is this a place where my child will be intrigued? Will he have the opportunity in a safe, comfortable space to articulate his ideas and think through complicated issues? Will there be a sense of excitement in going off to school, or will I have to push him out the door every morning?" I want students to explore moral and existential issues because I believe time spent in school should be meaningful.[2]

Second, my intent is to explore not moral education as a stand-alone entity, but moral education as it complements, reinforces, and intersects with the intellectual aims of school. My investigation is grounded in the subjects that form the core of secondary school curricula. On the contrary, seeking to "teach right from wrong," the

virtues approach does not promote, in the context of moral education, the questioning attitude that is central to intellectual exploration. Values clarification's extreme relativism—its unwillingness
to pit one view against another based on logic or evidence—shares
this nonintellectual tendency. Cognitive developmentalism, a much
more intellectually grounded approach, rests on discussion of
hypothetical dilemmas or on those that arise in school life. While
these discussions are valuable, the approach does not connect
these deliberations to the study of the academic subjects that make
up the bulk of the school day; it adds moral discussions to the curriculum, but doesn't explicitly focus on the moral dimensions of the
subjects *already* studied in schools.

In this regard, my approach is most similar to that of Noddings,
who, unlike the others, does link her vision of moral education to
students' *intellectual* life. However, her vision of a school set up
around the ethic of care includes a thorough reordering of the curriculum, an abandonment of the disciplinary divisions as we currently know them.[3] My work aims to stay well within the reach of
present realities as it considers how the moral and intellectual
could be linked and enriched.

Third, my approach includes existential questions along with
moral ones as a proper focus for classroom discussion. Most current
discussion of moral education is framed as a way of getting children
to understand "respect and responsibility" or to know "right from
wrong."[4] Because I am interested in thinking about how schools
could be more fascinating places for children (and adults) to spend
time, I am concerned not only with moral but also with existential
questions. As it turns out—because they are fascinating to human
beings and because human beings developed the fields of study that
have become our academic disciplines—existential questions also
underlie most of the academic disciplines. As my brief recounting of
teaching *Macbeth* suggests, and as the classroom episodes presented
in Chapters 4–7 attest, questions about the meaning of life and death,
God, good and evil, and the sources of happiness, for example, arise
as central concerns across the subject areas.[5]

Schools of Thought in Moral Education

A word about terminology. In the mid-1980s, a movement in "character education" was spearheaded by a number of educators including Edward Wynne, Thomas Lickona, Kevin Ryan, and William Bennett. Their approach, which I will describe below, was informed by the Aristotelian tradition and was often embedded in a larger, conservative political framework. In the intervening years, however, the term "character education" has come to refer to a varied array of approaches to moral education and now includes the work of educators of both liberal and conservative bents. The Character Education Partnership—a nonpartisan advocacy group—in fact, describes itself as "a coalition of organizations and individuals dedicated to developing moral character and civic virtue in our young people." As such, it aims to be an umbrella group for all those who believe that schools should be actively, explicitly involved in moral education.[6]

In this new, broader sense, this book is an argument in favor of character education. I do, however, have disagreements with those who founded the contemporary character education movement and with many of the curricula that are being developed under that name. Because the term has become so broad, therefore, I shall shy away from speaking of "character education" by itself, and will refer to the school of thought associated with Lickona, Ryan, Bennett, and their colleagues as the "virtues approach" to character education.

The Virtues Approach to Character Education

Perhaps the most familiar of the approaches to moral education, the "virtues approach" relies on the idea that such traits as hard work, civic responsibility, honesty, generosity, and courage constitute noncontroversial values to which all reasonable people subscribe. There is no need to debate fundamental values; the challenge is to help children internalize what adults of good will know to be right. Adults can help children internalize virtues by teaching them rules, giving them opportunities to practice adherence to the rules, providing good examples, and reading stories with moral messages, such as those contained in William Bennett's collection, *The Book of Virtues*.[7] The theorists contend that when a virtue has been adequately absorbed through these means, it becomes part of one's character and is ready for regular use. A child who has internalized the value of honesty can be counted on to behave honestly; one who has learned about and practiced courage will demonstrate it when called upon.

In his "Defense of Character Education," Kevin Ryan explains that this approach employs several pedagogical methods. "Character development," he says, "is ready to select from many disciplines and use many metaphors—the growth metaphor, the Skinnerian metaphor, the fill-the-jug metaphor." But if one had to choose a single metaphor to capture the spirit of character education, the "fill the jug" metaphor would probably come closest.

In fact, some proponents of the virtues approach define what they do as "benign indoctrination." Linking the virtues approach to "the great tradition" of moral education, the late Edward A. Wynne explained that it is natural that adults, who know more than children, should indoctrinate them: "Of course indoctrination happens. It is ridiculous to believe children are capable of objectively assessing most of the beliefs and values they must absorb to be effective adults. They must learn a certain body of 'doctrine' to function on a day-to-day basis in society. There is good and bad doctrine, and thus things must be weighed and assessed. But such assessment is largely the responsibility of parents and other appropriate adults." In Wynne's view, "appropriate adults" agree on the basics of beliefs and values; adults know more than children; it is therefore the responsibility of the adults to teach the children what they know— what "the great tradition" has taught—in this realm.[8]

Advocates of the virtues approach describe the method as a means of getting back on course, returning to our better selves, rediscovering truths our society has known all along. William Kilpatrick, author of *Why Johnny Can't Tell Right from Wrong*, articulates this concept of "return" quite explicitly, explaining that what he calls traditional character education is "an old alternative, to be sure, but a large part of our education consists in rediscovering things we once knew to be true but forgot. In looking at them again, we often see that, however demanding they may be, there is really no alternative to them. The traditional character education model seems to be one of those basic forms to which we must always eventually return."[9]

As I mentioned in Chapter 1, the call to return to old truths implies that new approaches to moral education have led us astray. While admitting that complex factors have led to current social problems (such as drug abuse, violence, and teenage pregnancy), advocates of the virtues approach tend to blame what they see as society's general moral decline on the decline of character education in schools.[10] The virtues approach to moral education, and by implication social stability, is portrayed as having been dethroned by other, misguided approaches to moral education, chief among them the theories of "values clarification" and "cognitive developmentalism."

From my perspective, the major strength of the virtues approach is that it recognizes our collective need for order, reliability, and safety. We need to trust that everyone will always stop at red lights. We need to trust that store clerks will give us the right amount of change. As teachers or students in the classroom, we need to trust that no one will hit us or insult us or walk away with our backpack. In these days, shockingly enough, we need to trust that no one will fire at us with a gun at school. We need, in short, to trust that everyone will follow the rules, at least most of the time.

Given such needs, I agree with the virtues approach that there are certain codes of behavior that need to be taught, without a lot of wiggle room. "I do not want you to throw that fork," I tell my toddler. "There will be no negative comments about anyone's appearance in this classroom," I told my high school students. As adults, we set rules and we model appropriate behavior. Perhaps most important, we seek to engage children in *wanting* to live in a way that will help all of us meet our needs for safety and respect. All of this is a certain aspect of moral education, and I am in favor of it. As I hope to demonstrate, however, the virtues approach in itself is an extremely limited view of moral education. For in much of life, moral questions are more complicated than learning a set of virtues or following rules.

From the perspective of the ethic of care, there is an additional, serious problem with the virtues approach. First, virtues educators, in their nostalgia for the past, tend to be alarmingly uncritical about the messages sent by the honored texts of the "great tradition." In the section on loyalty in his *Book of Virtues*, for example, William Bennett includes the story of Penelope's Web from Homer's *Odyssey*, introducing it as follows: "Penelope's long wait for her husband's return from the Trojan war may be our ultimate tale of fidelity. The Ithacan queen's patience, resourcefulness, constancy, and love make her one of Greek mythology's most memorable characters." Penelope *is* memorable, but Nel Noddings, for one, would not like her children to take Penelope, "totally unproductive—weaving and tearing out, weaving and tearing out, day after day," as a model.[11]

In a more extended discussion of Homer's Telemachus and other authors and characters that are part of the "great tradition," Noddings starkly claims that many texts central to the Western canon reinforce the "*evil* enshrined in a culture that does not really want to forsake it." When read in light of an ethic of caring, the story of Telemachus, typically treated as a heroic coming of age tale, depicts a young man of uncommon viciousness. "When we treat material of this sort in the classroom," says Noddings, "we should address the great themes of torture, cruelty, and misogyny in some depth."[12] Clearly, this is not what virtues educators typically have in mind when presenting this or other classic heroes. What is virtuous in the eyes of some is cruel in the eyes of others. The virtues approach offers no guidance in exploring these differences, no guidance in recognizing when heroes, rules, or practices that have been enshrined by tradition require critical reexamination.

Values Clarification

"Values clarification," popular during the 1970s, has largely fallen out of favor as an educational movement. Nonetheless, because of the vehemence with which the other schools of moral education continue to react against it and because individual values clarification exercises remain in use, its echoes remain strong. Credited to (or blamed on) popular books called *Values and Teaching* and *Values Clarification: A Handbook of Practical Strategies for Teachers and Students*, the values clarification approach posits assumptions very different from those of the virtues educators.[13]

Far from holding that there is a noncontroversial list of virtues to which all good people subscribe, proponents of values clarification assert that there is no consensus about moral values. Explaining why the tenets of character education are not viable, they write: "The direct inculcation of values works best when there is complete consistency about what constitutes 'desirable values.' But consider the youth of today. Parents offer one set of shoulds and should nots. The church often suggests another. The peer group offers a third view of values. Hollywood and the popular magazines, a fourth. The first grade teacher, a fifth. The seventh grade teacher, a sixth. The President of the United States, a seventh.... and on and on."[14]

For the proponents of values clarification, the existence of a wide range of competing value systems is incontrovertible. Even if the teacher were to present a very clear set of values, an unequivocal list of "do's and don'ts," the students still would know that there are other options. They would still have to *choose* values from among various claims. Proponents of values clarification contend, furthermore, that a value must be freely chosen, otherwise it is not a genuine value, but simply a by-product of coercion. The educator's duty is to help students make free, considered choices.[15]

In this model, then, the teacher must avoid declaring one set of values superior to another; indeed, the "particular content" of the teacher's values "holds no more weight than would anyone else's."[16] The *process* of coming to hold values rather than the *content* of the values becomes primary. Students are to be given practice in choosing values through values clarification discussions on a wide range of issues, which may or may not be tied to the content of the regular curriculum.

One fairly typical values clarification lesson, called "Values Voting," proceeds as follows: The teacher reads aloud a set of questions. Those who wish to answer affirmatively raise their hands; those who wish to answer negatively point their thumbs down; those who are undecided fold their arms; those who want to pass do nothing. The list of seventy-three sample questions ranges from "How many of you watch the Super Bowl every year?" to "How many of you feel free to discuss sex with your parents?" The teacher participates, but holds "his vote until a split second after most of the students have committed themselves to a position" to avoid influencing students' decisions. After a list of such questions is read, the teacher may open various items up for class discussion.[17]

The attraction of this approach is simple: it provides strategies for teachers to discuss matters of moral weight with their students while avoiding what might feel like moralizing and while honoring a diversity of opinions and backgrounds. Despite these strengths, values clarification provides no criteria by which a given moral judgment or action might be deemed better or worse than another. Allowing students to emphatically and freely state their views, the approach does not give students the tools to analyze their beliefs, to assess their likely consequences; nor does it promote the necessity of diligently gathering information to inform those beliefs. It promotes, in a nutshell, the forming of uninformed opinions. This is a very serious shortcoming. I argue that an approach to moral education in schools must serve the academic aims of the school; it must complement and nurture students' intellectual growth.

Cognitive Developmentalism

The cognitive development approach of Lawrence Kohlberg, informing the work of scores of students and colleagues and spurring the work of critics, has dominated the research literature on moral education since 1965. Given the enormous scope of Kohlberg's project, seeking the integration of psychology, philosophy, sociology, and education "into an integrated theory and practice of moral education," given its voluminous incarnations in the work of many different theorists, and given the developments in Kohlberg's own thinking over the three decades of his career, it is impossible for me to do more than to gesture here at the guiding motifs of cognitive developmentalism.[18]

Studying seventy-five American boys at three-year intervals from early adolescence through young adulthood, and then replicating the study in a number of other countries, Kohlberg found and named three levels of moral thinking, each of which contains two stages.

I. Preconventional level:
Stage 1: *The punishment-and-obedience orientation*
Stage 2: *The instrumental-relativist orientation*

II. Conventional level:

Stage 3: *The interpersonal concordance or "good boy–nice girl" orientation*

Stage 4: *The "law and order" orientation*

III. Postconventional, autonomous, or principled level

Stage 5: *The social-contract, legalistic orientation*

Stage 6: *The universal-ethical-principle orientation*[19]

Kohlberg's stages distinguish between the content of a moral judgment (for example, "to lie" or "to tell the truth") and what he calls the "structure" of the moral judgment—the reasoning behind it. Instead of focusing on the *content* of a virtuous character, Kohlberg emphasizes the *process* of moral deliberation. Kohlberg points out that situations demanding a moral choice often involve conflicting values from the virtues educators' list. One cannot be brave, courteous, humble, cheerful, honest, et cetera all at once, certainly not in a situation that demands decisive action.[20]

Further, such lists of virtues tend to reflect social convention—stage 3 and 4 thinking—rather than any higher moral principle. At the sixth, highest stage of moral development, deliberations are governed not by what he would call conventional virtues such as "honesty" or "bravery" but by what Kohlberg—based on Kantian theory—considers the universal principle of justice.

Given this framework, the moral educator seeks to nudge students up the ladder of moral development by confronting them with moral deliberation at one stage higher than their current tendency, using the vehicle of hypothetical moral dilemmas, such as the well-known "Heinz dilemma."[21] Later work by Kohlberg, heavily influenced by Dewey, focuses less on the power of discussing this sort of hypothetical problem and turns instead to the possibility of fostering a "moral atmosphere" in the school more generally. To this end, he and his colleagues set up a number of "just community" schools, where he hoped that democratic discussion of "real-life moral situations"—the ones that emerged from the regular operation of the school—"would stimulate advance in both moral reasoning and moral action."[22]

I share with the cognitive developmentalists the observation that simply stated values, like "courage" and "hard work," do not provide much guidance in real-life situations, and I share an emphasis on the importance of deliberation about moral issues. For me, a central gap in this school of thought is that in its focus first on hypothetical dilemmas and then on living together in a just school community (a very laudable goal), the cognitive development approach has not cracked the wall between the academic subject areas and moral deliberation. It still separates out moral work from intellectual/academic work, as if they belong to different spheres.

Ethic of Care

Carol Gilligan's *In a Different Voice* articulates a theory of women's moral development in direct response to Kohlberg's version of cognitive development. Gilligan rejects two of the key claims of the Kohlbergian scheme—first, that the stages of moral development are universal, and second, that operating according to a principle of justice is the highest aim of morality. She notes that Kohlberg's original sample included only males, and so his schema for the normal course of moral development was of necessity a schema of male moral development. On the face of it, this might not seem to be a problem—it seems that morality should transcend gender categories. But then, how can one explain the finding that while mature men, on average, are at stage 4 in their moral reasoning, mature women measured on Kohlberg's scale tend to exemplify stage 3 kinds of thinking? Gilligan claims the problem lies in the inadequacy of the theory, not in the inadequacy of women as moral agents.[23]

Girls and women, she shows, focus their attention on preserving human connections, regardless of what principles might be at stake. This attention to human connections constitutes the "different voice" that Gilligan claims women bring to moral deliberation. Without spelling out the direct implications this different voice has for conceptions of moral education, Gilligan does present an alternate vision of moral maturity. Rather than a thinker who is governed by abstract, universal principles, the mature adult might be one who bases her actions on the particular needs of those to whom she is connected.[24]

Whereas Gilligan bases her claims in psychological theory and empirical work, Nel Noddings provides philosophical grounding for an ethic of care and much more fully elaborates its implications for schooling. The "good," in Noddings' view, is not to be found in Kohlberg's principle of justice, which uses reason to abstract one from one's particular circumstances, but in caring relationships, prototypically found between mother and child. Acting morally entails striving toward the sort of caring and being cared for that human beings universally recognize, Noddings says, from that primary bond. Furthermore, because human beings are defined in relation to one another, one cannot be moral alone. As Noddings puts it: "How good *I* can be is partly a function of how *you*—the other—receive and respond to me. Whatever virtue I exercise is completed, fulfilled, in you."[25] This moral interdependence puts a special weight on moral education—it is not just a matter of a teacher teaching students to be good. The teacher's own goodness depends on the students' growing ability to care and be cared for.

What exactly does it mean to care? Noddings consciously avoids a "systematic exposition of criteria for caring," preferring to give a sense of "how complex and intricate, indeed how subjective caring is." But the core of caring seems to be "apprehending the reality of the other."

> When my caring is directed to living things, I must consider their natures, ways of life, needs, and desires. And, although I can never accomplish it entirely, I try to apprehend the reality of the other.... To be touched, to have aroused in me something that will disturb my own ethical reality, I must see the other's reality as a possibility for my own.
> ... We also have aroused in us the feeling, "I must do something." When we see the other's reality as a possibility for us, we must act to eliminate the intolerable, to reduce the pain, to fill the need, to actualize the dream. When I am in this sort of relationship with another, when the other's reality becomes a real possibility for me, I care.[26]

With this description of the ethical ideal, Noddings departs from the parameters kept by the other approaches to moral education.

The other approaches, grounded in different disciplinary perspectives, all seek to answer a question of this sort: "How can a human being be educated to make moral choices consistently?" Noddings' approach replies more to a query like this: "How can a person most completely fulfill her human capacity for connection to other people and the world?" For Noddings, a person who is fulfilling her capacity for connection can be trusted to make moral choices.

Noddings' project, touching on the fulfillment of human capacity, goes beyond morality, narrowly construed. Noddings in fact evokes religious philosopher Martin Buber to describe an essential feature of caring, "engrossment": "When one cares, there are active moments of caring in which the engrossment must be present. In those moments the cared-for is not an object. In Buber's words: 'He is no longer He or She, limited by other Hes and Shes, a dot in the world grid of space and time, nor a condition that can be experienced and described, a loose bundle of named qualities. Neighborless and seamless, he is Thou and fills the firmament.'" Buber, to be sure, yearns ultimately for an I–Thou relationship with a transcendent, immortal Thou, while Noddings steadfastly grounds her ethic of caring in interpersonal relationships, without taking "recourse to notions of God."[27] But even when the relation is between human beings, the quality of engrossment, of letting one "fill the firmament," goes beyond the realm of morality implicit in other approaches to moral education—the realm of right and wrong judgment and action—and moves into what I would call a matter of the spirit. It links morality to existential longing and a conception of a human ideal.

A school that takes caring seriously would have to rearrange fundamentally many elements of school structure. As Noddings puts it, moral education is "not only a form of education that concentrates on producing moral people, but also an education that is moral in purpose, policy, and methods." Noddings would alter the ways that teachers and students are grouped, allowing teachers to stay with students over a number of years. And she would alter the curriculum and the school day so that it could be set up not around the traditional disciplines but around "centers of care": care for "self, care for intimate others, for associates and acquaintances, for distant others, for nonhuman animals, for plants and the physical environment, for the human-made world of objects and instruments, and for ideas. Within each of these centers, we will find many themes on which to build courses, topical seminars, projects, reading lists, and dialogues."[28] A school that met "the challenge to care" would both provide an environment in which students could be truly cared for and also give students room to connect themselves in caring relationship to the matters they study.

I share with Noddings the notion that "moral education" is by its nature broader and deeper than learning right from wrong or making choices about behavior. It is connected to deeper questions of meaning. I share the idea that moral education—like education generally—should not be defined solely in terms of outcomes. A good general educational program and a good moral education program are ones in which students' passions are engaged. And I agree with her that fundamental change in basic school structures is essential to building intellectually vibrant and morally sound educational programs. If my suggestions for change are less radical than hers, I hope they are also more practical.

Beyond the Moral Education Literature

Because I seek to consider existential questions in education, the literature on moral education alone provides inadequate background. There are a few works in moral education that do explicitly examine existential or spiritual issues in public education—most notably Noddings' *Educating for Intelligent Belief and Unbelief*, David Purpel's *The Moral and Spiritual Crisis in Education*, and James Moffett's *The Universal Schoolhouse: Spiritual Awakening Through Education*. Purpel, arguing that school curricula should include questions of meaning, notes that consideration of moral and spiritual questions exercise the reflective, intellectual powers that schools are intended to develop:

> We educators have for the most part been able (willing) to
> separate our concern for education from our discussion of our
> most serious and profound matters. What is the meaning of life?
> How do we relate as a family, nation, people? What is a just and
> fair way of distributing rights and responsibilities? How do we

make appropriate moral choices? The irony here is that such questions are quintessentially reflective ones—areas that require knowledge, insight, understanding (i.e., an educated mind). However, we tend in our fragmented and highly differentiated society to equate education with particular institutions and processes which are, if at all, only vaguely linked to deeper social, cultural, economic, and political matters.[29]

Moffett, similarly advocating a deeper connection between what is studied in schools and what Purpel calls "profound matters," adds the notion that existential questions lie at the foundation of the academic disciplines: "Questions about the nature of the world and the purpose of life should undergird education just as they underlie our routine activities. Whether avoided or confronted, these are not only issues, but *the* issues. Our lives are profoundly affected by these questions, whether we feel we have laid them to rest forever or whether we cannot rest for lack of answers. Humankind's greatest mental efforts have been exerted in science, philosophy, and literature to try to illuminate them."[30] As one can glean from these passages, Purpel and Moffett support my project of considering existential issues crucial to the curriculum, along with the moral and the intellectual.

Rather than pursuing their theses in greater depth, however, I turn instead to a theologian for help in building my argument about the importance of these issues. I claim no expertise in theological literature; there may be others who speak to these points equally well, or who link their arguments more directly to education. But I turn to Joseph Soloveitchik because nothing I have read captures better for me the peculiar difficulties and attractions of addressing existential and spiritual questions in the modern age than his book *The Lonely Man of Faith.*

I cite Soloveitchik here with some hesitation, because I recognize that by invoking the work of a theologian I open myself to the following criticism: although Soloveitchik's thinking may be wise, *religious* contemplation has no place in policy considerations of how to run public schools. I hesitate further because Soloveitchik was an Orthodox rabbi, and many of his starting assumptions— from the fact of God's existence and the sanctity of the Hebrew

Bible to the imperative of developing a relationship with God—are far from the starting assumptions of many of my readers. Nonetheless, and perhaps precisely because he lived his life in opposition to many of the assumptions that predominate in the academic and policy worlds, Soloveitchik provides a good starting place for thinking about existential and spiritual questions and how they might have a place in schools.

Soloveitchik's Conception of Human Nature and Spirituality

Soloveitchik suggests that the two versions of the creation of human beings recounted in chapters 1 and 2 of Genesis refer to "two types, two representatives of humanity," each of them a component part, to a greater or lesser degree, of each human being. (Soloveitchik refers to each of them as "Adam" and in the masculine gender, but both Adams are meant to be understood as human archetypes, male or female.) Adam the first, one of the creatures brought into being in the plural with the lines "man and woman God created them," is told to "be fruitful and multiply, and fill the earth and subdue it, and have dominion over the fish of the sea, over the fowl of the heaven, and over the beasts, and all over the earth." Adam the first is "made in God's image" in the sense that he or she, too, is a creator and master—culture builder, inventor, artist. Adam the first is blessed, as Soloveitchik says, with a "great drive for creative activity and immeasurable resources for the realization of this goal, the most outstanding of which is the intelligence, the human mind, capable of confronting the outside world and inquiring into its complex workings." Possessed of creative urges and a desire to "dominate the elemental natural forces and to put them at [human] disposal," this Adam asks one complex but eminently practical question: "How does the cosmos function?"[31]

This Adam wants to know how things work and to get his or her hands on them. Imagine a chemist, an architect, a deep-sea diver, a doctor, a farmer, a psychotherapist. Not limiting him or herself to the purely practical, Adam the first is a culture builder in all senses. Seeking self-actualization, to use contemporary terminology, Adam the first finds joy in all of his or her creative powers, and so dances ballet, builds rocket ships, writes novels, and, perhaps most important, begets children. Naturally inquisitive, energetic, sociable, and creative, Adam the first would be almost anyone's model high school student—our elite academic schools, indeed, are designed for him and her.

According to Soloveitchik, God creates Adam the second, by contrast, alone, of dust, by breathing "into his nostrils the breath of life, and Adam became a living soul." The text suggests an intimate relation between this singular, soulful human being and God, a literal sharing of breath. Adam the second, born in intimacy, remains primally aware of the possibility of relation to a greater being, but also recognizes his own limitations, his own humble origin in dust. While Adam the first revels in his powers, Adam the second reminds one of Hamlet, who recognizes what happens to our worldly pride: "Imperious Caesar, dead and turned to clay / Might stop a hole to keep the wind away." While Adam the first establishes partnerships for the practical purposes of "being fruitful" and building civilization, Adam the second yearns for I–Thou relationships.[32] Indeed, God creates a soul-partner *not* for Adam the first, but for Adam the second, for in his or her case, "It is not good for Adam [a human being] to be alone." Recognizing his or her own createdness, and yearning for relation to the cosmos, Adam II asks metaphysical questions, contrasting sharply with those of Adam I. Adam II wants to know:

> "Why is it?" "What is it?" "Who is it?" (1) He wonders: "Why did the world in its totality come into existence? Why is man confronted by this stupendous and indifferent order of things and events?" (2) He asks: "What is the purpose of all of this? What is the message that is embedded in organic and inorganic matter, and what does the great challenge reaching me from beyond the fringes of the universe as well as from the depths of my tormented soul mean?" (3) Adam the second keeps on wondering: "Who is He who trails me steadily, uninvited and unwanted, like an everlasting shadow, and vanishes into the recesses of transcendence the very instant I turn around to confront this numinous, awesome, and mysterious 'He'?"[33]

Though Soloveitchik's Adam II uses lofty diction, Adam II, like Adam I, is quite recognizable. Adam II is one of those spiritual "pil-

grims" Coles finds within most children, one of the multitudes of
human beings throughout time whom is deeply concerned with
"the meaning of life, the possibility of gods, birth and parenting,
sexuality, death, good and evil, love, happiness."[34] If we have lis-
tened, most of us will have heard the voices of Adam II in our classrooms, around the dinner table, and within ourselves.

How is Soloveitchik's conception of these two types of humanity—embedded in each person—useful in thinking about existential concerns and the role of schools? One of the things that strikes
me about these two types is that although Adam II remains recognizable, Adam I has undoubtedly gained ascendancy in our times.
We might say that our society is almost all Adam I, with very little
Adam II. As we saw earlier in the words of Vaclav Havel, modern
people know how to ask technical, how-to questions, but we do not
know how to ask spiritual, why questions. In fact, as Stephen
Carter has argued in the contemporary American context, our culture trivializes such questions and dismisses those who explore
them within the framework of religious traditions. "The consistent
message of modern American society," Carter charges, "is that
whenever the demands of one's religion conflict with what one has
to do to get ahead, one is expected to ignore the religious demands
and act... well... *rationally*." To combine Soloveitchik's idiom with
Carter's, Adam II does have concerns besides "getting ahead," and
those concerns are hard for Adam I—the dominant mentality of our
culture—to understand. For Adam I, to whom "rational" discourse
excludes questions that are beyond human ken, Adam II seems
helplessly irrational.[35]

Soloveitchik's work helps me argue that the kind of vulnerability,
questioning, and yearning for intimacy symbolized by Adam II must
not be ignored. It is a fundamental part of what it means to be
human. For this reason alone, it makes sense to make room for
Adam II in schools. If one cares to take the argument a step further,
the types of Adam I and Adam II also provide a lens for looking at
society. It seems possible that our devastating social and environ-
mental ills can be attributed not so much to people who do not
know "right from wrong" but at least partly to our collective adula-
tion of Adam I over Adam II. At least some of the "moral chaos" we

face might be attributed, in other words, to our collective habit of honoring our creative, technological, masterful sides over our humble, vulnerable, intimacy-seeking sides. If this is true, and if what happens in schools can have a positive effect on the broader society, it makes little sense to follow Hutchins' advice to keep school out of the realm of moral and spiritual education. It makes sense, instead, to build schools that redress this imbalance by nurturing Adam II even as they give tools to Adam I.

Spirituality and Physicality

One unfortunate aspect of Soloveitchik's work as described here is that it tends to reinforce the idea that "spirituality" should be understood in opposition to "physicality." As has been documented by feminist theorists, this dualism pervades Western thought. It is encoded, indeed, in our dictionaries, which define "spiritual" as "of the human spirit or soul, *not* physical or worldly." This kind of dualism, these theorists argue, is neither necessary nor for the good.[36]

Madeleine Grumet, for example, has claimed that knowledge gained through our bodies can be a sacred kind of knowledge and can be a guiding force for reenvisioning curriculum. To make her point, she tells of relating, at an academic conference, an intensely personal, physical moment: "There is one moment I would remember, the day following the birth of my daughter, my first child, when my skin, suffused with the hormones that supported pregnancy, labor, and delivery, felt and smelled like hers, when I reached for a mirror and was startled by my own reflection, for it was hers that I had expected to see there. Over and over again we recapitulate and celebrate that moment, even as we struggle to transcend it." This sort of writing does not usually find its way into academic papers nor into school curricula. Grumet, in fact, reports feeling intensely uncomfortable reading about such private feelings at a professional conference. She felt that she had to share them, nonetheless, because by "withholding information about that [private] relation from the public discourse of educational theory we deny our own experience and our own knowledge.... we become complicit with those theorists and teachers who repudiate the intimacy of nurture in their own histories and in their work in education."[37]

Grumet's words and actions suggest that the intensely personal, physical world and the transcendent experiences that are related to physicality have a place—along with the sort of metaphysical questions that haunt Adam II—in school curricula. In this work, I use the word "existential" rather than "spiritual" partly to highlight the physicality of some of our most powerful experiences and questions. As will become clear in the classroom excerpts, some of the most important existential questions that I saw arise in classrooms involved such earthly, physical concerns as pimples and fertility cycles.

The Empirical Research Context: Studies of Schools with Intellectual, Moral, and Spiritual Aims

Along with the theoretical work on moral education and on the nature of spiritual or existential knowledge, other empirical studies also provide context for this study. Of particular interest are studies of schools that explicitly articulate a mission of integrating moral, intellectual, and existential or spiritual education.

Alan Peshkin's *God's Choice* describes "Bethany Baptist," a fundamentalist Christian school whose teachers and administrators would agree wholeheartedly with my premise that intellectual, moral, and existential/spiritual education belong together and should be pursued in an integrated fashion. In fact, as Peshkin reports, "Fundamentalist Christian educators commonly use the term 'integration' to designate their need to merge Scripture and subject matter in their daily classroom routine. Whatever the subject and activity, they are urged to integrate to the fullest extent possible."[38]

What does this integration look like in the fundamentalist school? What happens if the demands of moral and spiritual education seem to be at odds with intellectual work? Peshkin describes how the attempt at integration plays out in practice: "Several teachers expanded their observations about spiritual goals to include the academic. 'It's not separate, you know,' explained a teacher. The spiritual dimension 'is woven in with everything because all subjects are taught in the light of God's word.' For those who teach literature, growing in the Lord and growing in literature are one and the same: 'I like to teach all kinds of truths and philosophy and it all pretty much agrees with the Bible. If it doesn't, I just don't teach that part in literature,' says an English teacher."[39] The point needs no belaboring: things proceed smoothly when spiritual and intellectual aims overlap; when, on the other hand, a potential piece of curriculum seems to conflict with the school's spiritual teachings, it simply does not get taught. "Integration" remains a goal only as long as the integration does not make waves. In fact, Bethany Baptist's brand of spirituality—perhaps better called religiosity—requires that its spiritual teachings win out against academic inquiry every time.[40] One of the questions underlying my study is whether public schools could adopt a different approach to existential and spiritual issues—one that would engage rather than suppress intelligent inquiry.

Another researcher, David Schoem, studied a Jewish supplementary (afternoon) school in California and found a persistent, troubling "confusion of purpose in the classroom" that reflects the apparently competing claims of the intellect and of religious teachings. Schoem's description of a few moments of classroom discussion will serve to illustrate the point.

> In what was a typical classroom lesson, a seventh grade teacher asked the students to describe in what ways the Sabbath differed from the other days of the week. In response to a student's answer that "on the Sabbath we pray," the teacher said, "But you pray every day." In this case not only was the teacher's response completely detached from reality, but the student who answered was also speaking in theoretical terms. Many of the students in the class had not been to a prayer service on the Sabbath for up to six months or more. When the teacher, who managed a restaurant Friday evenings [that is, on the Sabbath], then began to speak about "why we don't work on the Sabbath" students giggled incredulously because of the question's absurdity. Clearly, this lesson that was being discussed in first person terms, was, in the students' minds, about a people that was far removed from their own reality.[41]

This is not a case of a powerful spiritual belief overruling intellectual inquiry, as we saw at Bethany Baptist. We have here, according to Schoem, a teacher who does not find particular meaning in Jewish religious practice. But in an effort to protect a version of spirituality she thinks she is supposed to believe in and to teach, she refrains from raising the *intellectually* honest question: "Our tradition teaches us to keep the Sabbath, but none of us does in fact keep the Sabbath—so what is going on here?" Believing that the observance is silly, outmoded, or irrelevant, she also refrains from raising honest *spiritual* questions: "Is there a way for us to begin finding meaning in these practices, which now seem so irrelevant?" Or, "Are there other practices that will help us access the spiritual power that the Sabbath has seemed to have for our people?"

The students understand that the questions that are being asked are not genuine, and they are not urged to develop their spiritual awareness or to explore what might be attractive in the tradition's teachings. Perhaps worse, they are left without an opportunity to think deeply about the discrepancy—of which they are well aware—between the tradition and their community's practice. Rather, potentially powerful exploration of spiritual matters and clear-eyed intellectual inquiry have both been waylaid by a reluctance to speak truth about the students' and teacher's shared knowledge and experience. A "correct" lesson is delivered, but intellect and spirit, teacher and students, all lose out.

Having discussed in Chapter 1 the difficulty of talking about, let alone living, a life of the spirit in our age, one can empathize with the challenge facing the teacher. It would be challenging to discuss the discontinuity between the tradition's teachings that she felt it was her duty to support and the real lives that she and her students were living. One may well wish, however, that education did not have to be like this, that we could design honest encounters between intellectual, moral, and spiritual/existential questions and teachings. This book investigates that possibility.

My Approach for Observing Classrooms

As I have attempted to show here, intellectual, moral, and spiritual/existential educational goals do not necessarily fit neatly together. Intellectual inquiry, for example, may neglect or dismiss the importance of moral or spiritual questions. Education in moral matters may neglect critical reflection and tend toward indoctrination. Spiritual teachings may contradict other sources of knowledge. Therefore, as I watched classroom interactions unfold, I wanted to inquire simultaneously into the intellectual, moral, and spiritual/existential integrity of those moments. I was interested always in the interplay and interactions between these elements.

When moral or spiritual matters arose in classrooms, I wondered whether the following key features of a well-functioning, intellectually focused course would remain in place.

- *Pedagogical coherence (order):* How do the topics addressed in a given class fit into the larger picture of the course and the educational program as a whole? What connections are made between "small pieces of information" and "big ideas"?
- *Intellectual honesty (depth):* Are class activities designed to encourage thinking processes that are used by skilled adults in similar fields in non-classroom contexts? Does the material seem reduced to rote or oversimplified?
- *Critical reflection (use of evidence and alternate interpretations):* Is there respect for and training in the marshaling of evidence and the consideration of alternate interpretations? Is credence given to doubts and dissenting opinions? To what degree does the teaching encourage students to notice, reflect on, and revise preconceptions? To what degree does the teaching facilitate the finding of common ground between apparently divergent opinions?

On the other hand, when intellectual or "academic" questions were at the fore, I wondered whether any attention would be paid to their moral or existential elements. As markers of the moral and existential, and informed by Soloveitchik, Grumet, and Noddings, I looked particularly for the following elements:

- *Queries connected to how human beings should act*—including discussions of the past, present, and future effects of individual and societal actions on the well-being of other human beings, other living things, and the earth.
- *Queries into life's meaning and the human place in the world*—including discussions of such things as the goals of a

good life and the relations between people and the natural world.

- *Queries into the unknown*—including discussions of things beyond our ken like the sources of life, the sources of evil and suffering, the possibility of gods.
- *Exploration of universal existential concerns and ways of knowing*—including discussions of such concerns as beauty, health, death, friendship, and love, and nonintellectual kinds of knowledge such as "body knowledge" or "knowledge of the heart."

I was interested, in short, in the balance among the intellectual, moral, and existential elements of a discussion. If existential questions about the unknown were being asked, I also looked for research into the known or the knowable. If, for another example, a class was asked to learn scientifically based information, I also looked for any inquiry into the implications of that knowledge for moral action. When and where were the intellectual, moral, and existential elements complementary? When were they at odds with one another? When were they inextricably linked?

Before sharing excerpts from my classroom observations, I turn to a brief explanation of how I chose the sites I studied and to several notes on the ways the study evolved in the field.

Three High Schools and a Researcher

THIS CHAPTER DESCRIBES HOW I CHOSE TO STUDY
the schools and classrooms that I did. It also describes some of
the theoretical assumptions, practical considerations, and personal
predilections that influenced the study design, and outlines important changes in my conception of the study as the work unfolded.
Further details of research methods and methodological concerns,
such as the validity and generalizability of the study, can be found
in the Appendix.

Schools, Subjects, Teachers, and Students

Because my chief interest was to consider how moral education
could be conducted well in public schools, I necessarily wanted to
include a public school in my study. But I also assumed that American public schools, constrained by the United States Constitution
and by their mission to serve diverse student populations, would
place less emphasis on and would be less innovative in the investigation of moral and existential questions than some religious
schools. Religious schools, while facing constraints of their own,
are considerably freer to engage in explicit moral and spiritual education.[1] It seemed to me that, as a result, religious schools might
have something to teach public schools about these areas. I decided,
therefore, to study three schools—one public and two religious.

School Selection

I sought schools and classrooms where I would have a chance to see the ways moral and existential issues arise in the context of the core curriculum, in the care of talented teachers. I sought, therefore, a public school recognized for its quality, yet not significantly unlike most public high schools in its size and structure. I assumed that schools involved in certain kinds of reform efforts—those whose charters explicitly called for such things as addressing the "whole child"—would be most open to thinking of education as including moral and existential dimensions. After soliciting a variety of recommendations from school reform organizations and visiting a number of schools and classrooms, I chose the school I call Frontier, regarded as a regional leader in school innovation.[2] Though located in a fairly affluent suburb, its student population features considerable economic and ethnic diversity. Slightly more than half the students are white; just over a quarter are Asian-American; 11 percent are Hispanic, and 5 percent are African-American.

My choice of religious schools was guided by my hope that their practice of moral and spiritual education would be instructive to public schools. Given this purpose, I sought religious schools that resemble public schools in many respects. I sought religious schools that aim to imbue their students with moral and spiritual insight while fully honoring the use of critical intellect, not those that train their students in a clear, indisputable version of the truth with regard to moral issues. I also sought religious schools that serve students of the diverse class and ethnic backgrounds that characterize student populations in public schools.

With these criteria in mind, I chose to study one Roman Catholic and one Jewish high school. Diocesan Catholic schools seemed suitable both because of their enrollments of a relatively large number of students throughout the country and because of their long history of practice in the field of moral education.[3] Further, many Catholic schools hold a strong commitment, like that of the public schools, to serve a wide variety of students, including the urban poor. Although some Catholic schools have nearly all-Catholic student bodies, others enroll up to 50 percent non-Catholics. And even in schools where almost all the students are Catholic, the Catholic population is quite diverse, including students with origins on every continent.[4]

I chose to study a non-Orthodox Jewish school for a different set of reasons. Progressive Judaism seeks to balance participation in a tradition of revealed truth and personal relationship to God with simultaneous participation in the modern, Western, skeptical, rationalist tradition. A progressive Jewish school, negotiating the tension between these two traditions, seemed particularly well situated to provide insight into the questions I was interested in with regard to the public schools: How is a school to navigate the common ground and the conflicts between rational and spiritual or existential kinds of questions and knowledge? Or, as I would put it based on the discussion of Soloveitchik in Chapter 2, how does the school attempt to nurture both Adam I and Adam II? It also seemed to me that a Jewish school would offer instructive contrasts to the Catholic school, for basic assumptions about where one turns for moral guidance differ strongly between progressive Judaism and Roman Catholicism. Further, unlike the well-established diocesan system, non-Orthodox Jewish day schools are a fairly recent phenomenon in America, and thus are in the process of inventing themselves.[5]

I was also drawn to studying a Jewish school for more personal reasons: I am Jewish, have taught in Jewish schools, and have an interest in the quality of American Jewish education. Beyond that, studying a Jewish and a Catholic school seemed methodologically interesting: it would be an intriguing way to experience the differing kinds of access, insights, and feelings that might go along with researching as an "insider" in one of the religious schools and as an "outsider" in the other.

Having decided to study a Catholic and a Jewish school, I set about looking for specific sites. In each case, I wanted a school that had a good reputation with regard to thoughtfulness and innovation in curriculum and pedagogy. I also sought schools that had several teachers in three core subjects—American literature, U.S. history, and biology—who saw themselves as moral educators at least to some degree, and who were willing to let me observe their classes and interview them. Ultimately, I chose the schools that I call Saint Paul and Agnon for their relatively diverse student populations, for the amount of student participation in discussions in the classes I visited, and for the emphasis each of the schools seemed to place on a combined moral, spiritual/existential, and intellectual mission.

Subject Selection

I chose to focus in each school on three courses—American literature, U.S. history, and biology—that cover the ground of the core subject areas generally required in high school (with the exception of mathematics). Additionally, in each of the religious schools, I observed the religion courses that seemed most likely to focus heavily on moral and existential issues. At Saint Paul, these courses were called "Morality" and "Social Justice"; at Agnon, they were "Foundations of Jewish Law: Ethics and Practice I and II" and "Introduction to Jewish Thought." At Frontier, I looked for elective courses and other special programs that might similarly highlight moral and existential issues, and found a course entitled "War and Peace." I also regularly visited two special programs at Frontier, the "Anchor Program" for at-risk students, and a newly formed interdisciplinary course called "Science, Technology, and Society." When I had an unscheduled period at any of the schools, I visited a variety of other classes whose teachers were recommended to me. These courses included world literature, drama, foreign language, and psychology.

Selection of Teachers for Class Observations

For each of the subjects, I received recommendations from principals and vice principals at each school about which teachers might be most likely to devote class time to the discussion of moral and existential issues; in several cases, I was able to get recommendations from department chairpeople and students as well. The teachers studied are among the most widely respected, well-liked, and experienced at each of the three schools. The pseudonyms for the teachers chosen, along with their course names and some demographic data about each school, are included in Table 3.1.

Once I had chosen the teachers and solicited their participation in the study, I spent approximately four nonsequential weeks in each teacher's class.

Table 3.1 **SCHOOLS AND COURSES STUDIED**

HIGH SCHOOL	TYPE	LOCATION	ENROLLMENT	POPULATION	%	TEACHERS OBSERVED	COURSES OBSERVED
Frontier	Public	Suburban	1,760	White	55	Atlas, Carlson	U.S. History, American literature
				Asian-American	26	Morgan	Biology
				Hispanic	11	Carlson	War and Peace
				African-American	5	Morgan	Science, Technology, Society
				Pacific Islander	2	Andrews	Anchor Program
				Native American	1		
Saint Paul	Catholic, diocesan	Urban	1,110	White	41	Manning	U.S. history
				Asian-American	26	Masters, O'Brian	American literature
				Filipino	16	Carver, Rivers	Biology
				Hispanic	13	Davis	Drama
				African-American	4	Yearly	Morality
				(Catholic, 80%)		Castle	Social Justice
Agnon	Jewish, non-denominational	Suburban	250	—		Gilman, Hayes	U.S. history
						Williams	American literature
						Greene	Biology
						Putnam, Sherman	World literature (9th)
				(Jewish, 100%)		Katz, Ross, Singer	Jewish Ethics & Practice
						Katz, Singer	Jewish Thought
						Orloff	Psychology

Researcher Bias and the Experience of Researching

Recent work on qualitative methods, especially that influenced by feminist theories of scholarship, has emphasized that the researcher is inevitably influenced by his or her assumptions, allegiances, and life experiences. There is no possibility of "controlling" for these personal factors. Indeed, some theorists posit that there is no reason to control for them; they can be a wellspring of insight. Shulamit Reinharz argues that, at the least, "Research reports should contain a vivid description of the experience of researching. In these reports the value positions of the researcher should be faced squarely and addressed fully."[6] In the spirit of Reinharz's remarks, I would like to reveal some of the "value positions" I hold relative to this work, and also to share some of my experiences of researching that do not appear explicitly in later chapters.

In Chapter 1, I mentioned one of my experiences as a teacher of high school English, and the influence that work had in raising the questions that became the core of this study. Thus, while I began this research open to the possibility that seriously addressing moral and existential issues was beyond the realm of public schools, I certainly already leaned toward the position I hold now: public schools would be greatly invigorated, morally and intellectually, by attending more fully to these issues. The reader must judge whether this early bias limited or enlarged my ability to understand and interpret the events that I describe.

In addition to drawing me to include a Jewish school in the study, my being Jewish also played a role in the fieldwork itself. When I was at Agnon, the Jewish school, several of the students and teachers I spoke to asked me early on if I was Jewish, and I answered them. I believe that the sense that I was in some ways an insider—though I had never been at the school before—may have affected the things people at Agnon told me. There was an assumption that I valued Jewish education and understood at least some of the obstacles Jewish educators face. The feeling of comfort went both ways: fluent in Hebrew, familiar with traditional Jewish texts and practices, I was immediately at home at Agnon and found my place quickly in what might otherwise have been fairly incomprehensible discussions of ancient texts, interspersed with Hebrew terms. Having grown up in public schools and then having taught and supervised student teachers in several public schools, I was also a relative "insider" at Frontier.

Conversely, I felt less at home at Saint Paul. Although the words and symbols of Catholic life were not completely unfamiliar to me, they were not resonant with warm childhood memories or current practices; perhaps because of that, I was more aware of small things, which may blend into the scenery for insiders—the crucifixes on the walls, the garb of the nuns and priests, the sounds of the Lord's Prayer uttered in unison. Some students (but no teachers) at Saint Paul asked me if I was Catholic; it is hard to know how the response that I am not Catholic might have affected their openness with me. I know that my Jewishness made me prick up my ears with special alertness when I heard discussions of Jews, Israel, or the Holocaust at the public and Catholic schools I visited. Most important to me is whether my Jewishness made me more judgmental and critical at Saint Paul than at Agnon. On the other hand, I recognize that my stronger stake in excellent Jewish education could well have had the opposite effect, of heightening my judgment at Agnon. In any case, as with the other areas of the study, I try to present enough of the context and the actual words of the participants in the scenes I describe to allow readers to question my analyses and to devise their own.

There is another factor that informs all of the writing here, though it goes otherwise unstated: I found the overall experience of sitting in high school classes for five to seven hours a day, five days a week, exhausting and often tedious. I found myself slipping into patterns I had only dimly remembered from my own high school experience—doing such things as watching the second-hand on the clock, mentally urging it onward, and slipping to the vending machine at ten o'clock for a pack of M&M's that seemed necessary to make it through the day. I noted some of these feelings impressionistically, during the fieldwork itself.

> Sitting in Ms. Castle's class, as the students work on finding definitions to the terms for their final exam, I have a few moments to reflect. I'm not so happy. I'm overcome by the boredom, by the rigidity of the structure. Part of my method

here is to put myself through the paces of the school day—
without the stresses the kids have of being quizzed on things
they might not know—but physically to live out the day, moving
from one little desk to another, sitting quietly in it. It's true that
I'm lacking the great redeeming feature of school—I have no
beloved friends here whose lockers I can visit and drop notes
into.... As I write, Ms. C. interjects to say, "If you are sitting on
this side of the room, and you'd like to quickly go get a drink of
water, or go to the bathroom, you may do so at this time." It's
infantilizing. It's hard to see these kids in this context as
responsible types. There's Allison across the room—I have
friends who hire her to take care of their four-year-old and their
infant son. Here, she needs permission to go to the bathroom.

I put myself through the paces of school and it's physically
exhausting as well as passive-making. My fate lies in someone
else's hands, and the path of least resistance is to let it blow over
me. It's hard to describe the feeling, but I have it, even though I
feel I'm engaged in meaningful work doing this research. A kind
of double-consciousness. The quiet sitting begins to feel
excruciating, or soporific, like a day of television.

I include these reflections both because of the window they provide into my work as a researcher and because of their relevance to
the larger argument of this book. Investigating genuine questions of
my own in a project of my own design, and thereby interested in
almost every interaction I saw and heard at school, I nonetheless
felt numbed and enervated by the routines of the school day. One
can see from their behavior that students find those routines
extremely trying as well. In this light, the central argument of the
book—that the substance of school work must be connected to
things that genuinely matter to students—becomes all the more
important.

The Role of Researcher

The principal of Frontier High School, before he would grant me
access to his school as a study site, questioned me rigorously about
what the teachers and students at his school would get out of the

research. I answered, at first, with a fairly standard reply along these lines: teachers and students often find the process of being interviewed quite interesting, and teachers might enjoy having an outside observer in class for the opportunity it provides to be more self-conscious and reflective about their work. The principal was not satisfied. He wanted to make sure that the results of the research, the written product, would be of interest to the teachers at his school.

The principal's concern reflects the unhappy history of relations between university researchers and school people. School teachers and administrators have found academic writing about schools to be remarkably unrelated to their concerns, published in dissertations and journals never intended for their use. Writing about the "stunted sense of community among educational researchers and practitioners," Larry Cuban notes: "The notion that professors and practitioners are engaged in the same enterprise, sharing common purposes, has been shredded into finely chopped specialties, distracting dichotomies such as theory and practice, and an abiding hunger for higher status by increasing the distance of scholars from public school classrooms. We are known for our degrees and our publications. In being known, we have gained a crippling rigor in our research and kept potential colleagues at arm's length."[7]

The principal was right to worry that a study acceptable in the world of university researchers and academic presses might have little relevance to the teachers and students who gave their time to make the study possible. I could not promise that my study would be useful to the people at Frontier; I could only assure him that I hoped so, that I had moved from teaching to research with the desire to contribute to changing how schooling is conceived and practiced. Over the course of this study, I have thought often of the principal's concerns. Trying to stay true to what I observed while constructing a work that would pass muster in the academy *and* be of use to teachers, I used the principal's question as a guide. I repeatedly asked myself: how can I report what I have seen, even if it is somewhat painful, in ways that teachers will find provocative and meaningful? Whether I have succeeded in that, of course, remains to be seen.

Researcher Reciprocity

As Cuban's remark suggests, there is a long history of alienation between university researchers and school people. If I could, in retrospect, change one aspect of the design of this study, I would push it much closer to a relatively new model of collaboration and reciprocity between university researchers and teachers, of the sort described, for example, by Suzanne Wilson, Carol Miller, and Carol Yerkes, in which teachers and researchers jointly design research questions and methods.[8] Although the questions underlying this dissertation interested all the teachers I worked with, they were *my* questions. Further, the number of teachers and students involved precluded my developing close relationships with them and limited the amount of reciprocity that was possible.

In a few cases, I was able to give something in return for the generosity with which I was greeted. I shared, for example, my teaching files on the novel *The Bean Trees* with one of the English teachers in the study, and offered technical and writing help to students while I observed them in the computer lab.[9] I also gave many of the teachers an opportunity to reflect on episodes from their teaching through early drafts of my writing, and incorporated their comments into the text. Nonetheless, in this book, I subject their work to analysis and critique, while *my* work is critiqued by a different audience. The main offering I have for the teachers who allowed me to observe their work, therefore, is the completed writing; in the future, I look forward to designing studies that are more reciprocal and collaborative throughout.

Evolution of the Study

Like other qualitative studies, this one underwent significant changes as it unfolded. Three of those changes were key.

Speaking of "Existential" Rather than "Spiritual"

When I first conceived this project, I described one of the realms I wanted to study as the "spiritual" aspect of schooling. It did not take me long to realize that the word "spiritual" was more of a stumbling block than an asset to the inquiry I wished to conduct.

While some teachers at the religious schools use the term, most teachers at the public schools I visited simply do not use the word comfortably with regard to their work; they by no means see themselves as engaging in "spiritual education." This is not surprising, given the contemporary sense of alienation from things spiritual explored by thinkers such as Havel and Soloveitchik. Indeed, this non-spiritual orientation made finding a public school that paid explicit attention to spiritual matters—as I had originally hoped to do—nearly impossible. As James Moffett, author of *The Universal Schoolhouse: Spiritual Awakening Through Education*, whom I asked for advice in finding such a school, wrote to me: "Ironically, the kind of case you seem to want to make through your research, and which I tried to argue in my book, would provide just the rationale to permit schools to experiment legally with spiritual education. Proving the case, however, makes for a kind of Catch 22 whereby finding the school may depend on the case already being made." Moffett had no suggestions of schools that might already be pursuing such an agenda. One high school principal with whom I spoke told me explicitly that he found the word "spiritual" off-putting and confusing. He was certainly interested in students' moral and intellectual development, but spirituality was not his concern.

Even if no public school that I could find would describe its mission as partly spiritual, I knew that those kinds of universal concerns about which Havel and Soloveitchik write must come up in the context of schooling. Finding that the word "spiritual" got in the way of studying the ideas that mattered to me, I decided to refrain from using it (at least in the public school setting) in describing my research. Instead, I began to use the word "existential" to capture the questions and ideas I had originally intended to capture with "spiritual." While I still like the phrase "spiritual exploration" for its sense of being connected to the deepest yearnings of the human spirit, "exploration of existential issues" does convey a similar interest in questions of ultimate meaning. In some ways, as I suggested in Chapter 1, "existential" even improves on "spiritual," for it can also include questions involving more immediate concerns, such those regarding friendship, beauty, or health. The first key change in the study, then, was mostly one of semantics. Now an investigation into how schools treat existential questions, the study still focused on how schools address issues of vital, universal, and ultimate concern to human beings. I continue to use the word "spiritual" when citing works or responding to the dialogue of others who use that word.

A Shift in the Unit of Analysis

Originally, I thought that I would be looking at three *schools*. I thought I might walk away with a sense of how Agnon, Frontier, and Saint Paul "do" moral and existential education and that I would be able to understand and describe the approach of each of the schools as a whole. I supposed, for example, that all of the classes in a school would be significantly affected by their presence within a school with a given approach to moral education. An English class at Agnon would be different from an English class at Saint Paul which would be different from Frontier, and so on throughout the disciplines. I found, however, that aside from differences in the sizes of the classes (Agnon and Saint Paul tended to have smaller classes than Frontier) and their physical facilities, it was hard to tell the same courses in the different schools apart from one another.

What became more interesting to me, therefore, were the kinds of issues that tended to come up in each of the core disciplines, across schools, and how individual teachers tended to handle them. Rather than looking at the schools as wholes, my unit of analysis became the classes I observed within given disciplines. In the analysis that follows, I look at several high school English, history, and biology classes across three schools, and religion courses at two religious schools. I do not attempt to compare the whole school programs to one another, nor in any way to compare between Catholic, Jewish, and public schools more generally.

A Focus on Explicit Aspects of the Curriculum

When I conceived this study, I recognized that the moral lessons of school are just as often implicit in the way schools and classrooms are managed as they are explicit in the curriculum. Moral matters inevitably permeate all subject matters and all moments of the school day. Making sense of these influences, however, requires considerable interpretation. What are the moral implications of a half hour spent taking a quiz in biology class? Is this a time when students are being taught the values of hard work and concentration or of cold competition and successful cheating? What are the moral implications of giving all students the same amount of time on a quiz? What are the moral and existential implications of the content of the quiz or of the teacher's demeanor during it? Does she answer questions? Does she monitor against cheating? Should she? There is a long list of morally relevant questions to be asked regarding even such bland, everyday events in school. This is to say nothing of the moments of powerful human interactions that are more difficult to capture, but also laden with moral import—lunchroom conversations, interaction on the playing fields, late-night rehearsals, and so on.

I knew that the educational research world does not have a clear idea about how to study the moral aspects of schooling.[10] If one believes, with many theorists, that all aspects of schooling contribute to the moral and spiritual education a child receives, it is not clear exactly where a researcher should focus her gaze.[11] I wondered how I would elicit the moral implications from the everyday acts of school. Would I focus on the interpersonal or the structural? The content or the process? The explicit or the implicit? I knew that I would have to answer these questions as I spent time in schools and began to think and write about what I saw.

As I sat in classes and hung out in the quads of the schools I studied, I felt awash, as I have described, in the varied elements of schooling that have been called the "implicit curriculum" and what Philip Jackson called "the daily grind"—the predictable patterns of teacher questioning and student response, the desks arranged in neat rows, the rigidity of the schedule, with bells propelling everyone to another task, the fresh-fried junk food sold at brunch and lunch, the tardy slips and hall passes, the endless negotiations and warnings about points and grades and cheating.[12] It was clear to me that all of these are significant factors in the moral life of a school.

Although these matters impinged themselves on me quite strongly, I chose not to write about them. Partly, I did not know what I could say that other researchers and school reform advocates have not already said quite persuasively about the questionable aspects of these elements of school organization.[13] There is consensus among these theorists that the ways time, space, and people are distributed in schools deserve rethinking, for both moral and intellectual reasons; and happily, there are several current restructuring efforts that attempt to engage schools in such rethinking.

Less clear, though equally important, is the following idea, explored in this book: even if the structural elements of school were rearranged so that the days were less fragmented, so that teachers and students could come to know one another well, so that students demonstrated their learning through exhibition rather than through pencil and paper tests—even these considerable, necessary improvements would not ensure that the content of each course would be worth studying. What is trivial, boring, or lacking in connection to issues of ultimate concern would remain so, even if class periods were longer or teacher-student ratios smaller. Hoping to contribute to current discussions on school reform and concerned that, in the rush to restructure, the substance of school subjects may be neglected, I chose to focus mostly on the *explicit* curriculum in the classes I observed. I shifted an original concern with the moral *environment* in which students and teachers do their work to a focus on the intersection of *course content* with moral and existential concerns. The next chapters describe what I saw.

"We Could Argue About That All Day"

Missed Opportunities for Exploring Moral Questions

W HEN RESEARCHERS HAVE CLAIMED THAT ALL SCHOOLING inevitably involves moral education and that all teaching must be seen as a moral endeavor, they have generally referred not to course content but to the "implicit" or "hidden" curriculum, the inescapably moral implications of day-to-day interactions and of the structural aspects of school.[1] In this chapter, I claim that in addition to what happens implicitly in the structural or interpersonal arenas, the *content* of high school classes regularly—even daily—includes matters of moral and existential concern. This is because the explicit curricula of the core subject areas abound with moral questions. Given the truth of this claim, important implications follow for the ways we design many aspects of our educational system—from lesson plans to bell schedules to teacher education programs.

This chapter traces the most common trajectories of moral and existential issues as they rise and fall in classroom discussions, and analyzes what happens along the way. As shown in the representative examples from more than 240 fifty-minute periods of classroom observation in the subjects of English, U.S. history, and biology, the following pattern held true almost uniformly:

- Although moral and existential issues arise frequently, they are most often shut down immediately;

- If moral issues are not shut down completely, they are often relegated to assignments for individuals, rather than explored in
public classroom discussion; and
- When time *is* devoted to discussing moral issues, such discussions are surprisingly uninformed by evidence from textbooks or
research.

These moments—when moral or existential issues are dropped
from the public forum of the classroom or are discussed in an uninformed way—represent missed opportunities in both the moral and
the intellectual realms. And these moments are frequent: fewer
than 2 percent of the class periods I observed (aside from religion
classes, to be discussed in Chapter 6) included discussions of
moral or existential issues which were sustained for more than five
minutes, which included more than a few students, or in which students had opportunities to speak more than a few words at a time.
The infrequency of such discussions of moral and existential issues
suggests that in a wide variety of classrooms across the curriculum,
there exists an unfortunate partition between these issues and
what is considered the intellectual content of the subject matter.[2]

One might wonder why I focus so much on discussion and do not
include other pedagogical strategies, such as the telling of stories,
for example, which might be used toward moral aims. I assume that
even when using a method such as storytelling, a good part of the
learning comes from analyzing the story or parable, discussing its
various interpretations or applications. I assume, in short, that
there is something crucial about talking for learning.[3] Storytelling
followed by discussion of the story's moral or existential components would certainly have been included in my tally; stories told
and left unexamined were not.

Individual Snapshots
with Implications for School Reform

I opened this book with a brief scene from my own high school
classroom, describing how I taught *Macbeth* without discussing—
beyond the confines of the plot itself—anything to do with human

nature or the sources of evil or the significance of life. There have been many other similar incidents in my own teaching that I might have chosen. In this chapter, I describe at some length the scenes I observed in which other teachers likewise neglected important moral and existential issues, dwelling rather on what I see as less important information. I also try to explain why I see the information as less important.

I hope the transcripts in this and the following chapter will be useful to teachers as they struggle, very practically, with issues of pedagogy. What should teachers do when an important question arises that they were not expecting, have not researched, and have not allotted time for? When should the teacher stay on course, and when should he or she throw the lesson plan out the window? How does one deal with potential controversy or parental disapproval? When should one insert one's own opinion, and when should one remain "neutral?" Although this chapter does not answer all these questions (I address them further in Chapter 7), it does provide rich material for discussion.

In many cases, I fear, the teachers described in this chapter end up looking quite clumsy. While I do think there was room for these teachers to make different pedagogical choices, I hope the cumulative weight of the examples presented will lead to a different level of analysis. This is not a story of lots of individual teachers making mistakes. This is a story of individual teachers acting rationally and competently within a system that does not value the particular thing that I set out looking for: in-depth discussion of moral and existential issues. When I brought draft versions of many of the scenarios depicted in this chapter to teachers in two of my school sites, the teachers agreed with me in almost all cases that there had been some kind of missed opportunity, but they quite often felt that the depicted teachers' choices were highly constrained by structural issues: the length of the class periods, the size of the classes, and the demands of mandatory assessments.

As Theodore Sizer has shown persuasively, the structure of schools regularly forces teachers to compromise between what ought to be done and what can be done. Lee Shulman similarly argues that "when practitioners are observed to behave in a manner that appears irrational, silly, maladaptive, or just plain foolish, we [must] ask what would make their choice of behavior sensible."[4] Often, Shulman asserts, teachers' apparently nonsensical actions reflect a "wisdom of practice"—an understanding of a wide range of contingent factors and potential repercussions—which cannot always be deciphered by an observer in the back of the room.

Linda Darling-Hammond describes one of the mechanisms of school administration that limits teachers' flexibility and actually fosters the kinds of missed opportunities I shall critique:

> In addition to highly prescriptive curriculum and testing policies … the prescriptive policies for teacher evaluation that exist in many states actually impede teachers from teaching responsively and effectively. One such policy, adopted in several states, requires that teachers be rated as "ineffective" for engaging in practices that take into account the needs and interests of their students. Despite research that suggests the importance of linking classroom work to students' personal experiences, the Florida Performance Measurement System (FPMS) codes as "ineffective" any teacher questions that "call for personal opinion or that are answered from personal experience." The coding manual notes that "these questions may sometimes serve useful or even necessary purposes; however, they should be tallied here [in the ineffective column] since they do not move the classwork along academically."[5]

Even if a state does not use the particular evaluation system described by Darling-Hammond, teachers may be wary of leading class activities that are not clearly designed to "move the classwork along." From my own teaching, I know that both my students and I felt we had not been really "doing English" if we took an hour out of English class to explore a question about life, even if it was a question that was prompted by our readings.

In this context, the most meaningful follow-up question to scenarios I present is not "Why do teachers drop the ball so often?" but rather "What is it about the way school is conceived and structured that tends to drive the exploration of moral and existential issues out of the curriculum?" As I noted in Chapter 1, this book is ultimately an argument for rethinking the ways that education is conceived and structured. The scenarios that follow give a sense of why this project is so urgent.

As a reference, Table 4.1 provides an alphabetical list of the teachers referred to in this chapter, along with their number of years of experience, their school, their course taught, and a range for the number of students usually in attendance.

What Happens When Moral Issues Arise?
Common Cases of Missed Opportunity

This chapter is organized not by subject matter but by three genres of missed opportunity, in which moral or existential questions are (1) raised by the teacher, but the teacher does not foster their discussion; (2) raised by a student, but the teacher cuts off their discussion; and (3) raised by the teacher or a student and then discussed, but in an uninformed or superficial manner. Each of these three sections is broken into subsections, in which I document dif-

Table 4.1 **TEACHERS AND COURSES IN THIS CHAPTER**

TEACHER	YEARS OF EXPERIENCE	SCHOOL	COURSE	APPROXIMATE ENROLLMENT
Ms. Andrews	35	Frontier	Anchor Program	8–12
Tom Atlas	32	Frontier	American literature	60 (team taught; sometimes split into groups of 30)
Larry Carlson	32	Frontier	U.S. history	60 (team taught)
Ms. Carver	10	Saint Paul	Biology	25
Ms. Gilman	14	Agnon	U.S. history	15–20
Mr. Greene	8	Agnon	Biology	25–30
Ms. Halinan	—	Saint Paul	Drug education (in Morality class)	20–25
Ms. Hayes	5	Agnon	U.S. history	15–20
Mr. Manning	3	Saint Paul	U.S. history	25–30
Ms. Morgan	3	Frontier	Biology	25–30
Ms. Putnam	12	Agnon	World literature	20–25
Ms. Sherman	—	Agnon	World literature	20–25

ferent kinds of "derailers" of the potential discussions—such as the teachers' apparent reticence to talk about controversial issues or their decisions to provide quick, "right" answers. I turn first to one such common discussion derailer, a tendency to stress the learning of facts rather than the exploration of moral or existential issues.

The Teacher Raises a Moral Issue, But Does Not Foster Its Discussion

EMPHASIZING THE FACTS. Sometimes, a teacher raises an issue of moral or existential importance, but then quickly moves on to other matters. Such interludes may fly by in just a moment. In the middle of a unit on the 1920s, Ms. Hayes, for example, introduced her eleventh-grade United States history class at Agnon, the Jewish school, to production techniques initiated by Frederick W. Taylor. She explained that Taylor designed new, more efficient shovels for the workers in his plant, and that he therefore was able to reduce the number of workers he needed. Taylor further promoted efficiency, she said, by measuring each worker's output and firing the least productive. Ms. Hayes then led the following brief discussion.

Ms. Hayes: If you were a worker in Taylor's factory, how would you feel [about his strict management techniques and his laying off of workers]?

Jason: I would not like it if I got fired. I would not like being treated as a slave, with a stopwatch held over me.

Sorayah: If the workers are lazy without a stopwatch, then someone needs to supervise them.

Ms. Hayes: When you start your business, remember Taylor.

With this admonition, Ms. Hayes turned back to her lecture notes and began speaking about a new topic.

By asking the students to imagine themselves as workers in Taylor's factory, Ms. Hayes raised a question of central importance to the economic history of the United States. Abstracting and generalizing it a bit, her question might be read: "Is increased manufacturing efficiency worth the suffering caused by new production standards and the laying off of workers?" Replace "Taylor's factory" in her question with "AT&T," "Coca-Cola," or "Boeing," and the question would have resonated strongly with contemporary discussions of "downsizing." But Ms. Hayes closed off the discussion, seconds after it began, and moved on.

The students and I were left without a clear understanding of Taylor's relevance. What is the legacy of Taylor's practices? Is there a connection between Taylor and contemporary disputes between management and labor? And most important, from a moral point of view, we were left to wonder about Ms. Hayes' final comment. If we should remember Taylor, is it for better or for worse? Is he to be emulated? Is it wise to choose efficiency at the cost of jobs? Is it good? Outside of the wider social and moral context implied by these questions, it is hard to see the value of knowing simply that Taylor innovated.

Ms. Hayes had other material to cover. One can understand much of teachers' reticence to explore moral issues in depth by understanding the great pressure they feel to get through their textbooks in the course of the year. If one is to cover the history of the United States in a year, one cannot spend much more than a week or so on the 1920s—and many things besides Taylorism are important to know about the 1920s.

In this case, however, like many others, the circumstances suggest that the need to forge ahead with the curriculum did not play a key role in Ms. Hayes' decision to move on. When Ms. Hayes opened class the following day, she explained that there was "extra time," because this period's class had gotten ahead of one of her other classes. To use that extra time, and displaying creative pedagogy, she asked the students to break into groups of four or five and to come up with a pantomime for a scenario from the 1920s that she would give them. One group performed a pantomime of Taylor timing his workers with a stopwatch as they shoveled, and then throwing half of them out of work. This pantomime, like the others, took approximately forty-five seconds to enact. Neither it nor any of the other pantomimes were followed by discussion. The skit reinforced the factual—that Taylor had succeeded in increasing productivity and reducing the number of workers—while leaving relevant moral questions unexplored.

Avoiding discussion of moral questions is not an idiosyncratic oversight of Ms. Hayes alone; high school history is overwhelmingly taught in this way.[6] To put it simply, the apparent conception of history represented by this example reflects a widespread conception of what history, or at least "high school history," is. High school history is about learning the names of important figures, what they did, and the dates of their deeds.

But in stripping moral considerations from historical actions, history lessons like this one promote "learning history" (its names and dates) without learning *from* history (its consequences and implications).

The impulse to review factual material at the expense of deeper issues can be overwhelming in English classes as well, even when the teacher explicitly aims to explore moral and existential issues. One of the reasons Tom Atlas, a literature teacher at Frontier, chose to teach Barbara Kingsolver's novel *The Bean Trees* (1988), he told me, was that he hoped it would engage the students on a personal level, bringing up issues of relations between men and women, of relations between mothers and daughters, and of a young adult acting independently in the world. He expressed this hope when he introduced the novel to his students, handing out a list of study-guide questions for the first couple of chapters: "One tip—use the questions to guide your reading. We're going to study this novel, not just read it. I'm very hopeful that you will have a personal reaction to this. On the other hand, I'm your English teacher, and I'm interested in getting beyond plot. I want depth of thought, I want you to go into this novel and find all the stuff that's there.... Use the study guides."

On one hand, Tom wanted his students to respond emotionally to the text; on the other hand, as he put it, he wanted them to "find all the stuff that's there," using the study guides he had created. (He invites his students to call him by his first name, and most of them do, so I follow suit in describing his classroom here.) The study guides generally asked ten to fifteen questions per chapter, while the chapters average around thirteen pages. Chapter 2 in the book is ten pages long, and Tom's study guide for the chapter had fifteen questions. In each case, the study-guide questions pointed the students to a striking literary technique, a plot detail that would resonate later in the novel, or a telling bit of characterization. Here are a few examples:

Why did Lou Ann believe that the period after Angel's accident was "their best time together"?

At Jesus is Lord Used Tires, how does Mattie treat Taylor that contrasts to how Mrs. Hoge treated them?

Why does Taylor say, when she notices that Mattie was watching her, "I missed Mama so much my chest hurt"?

I know of no formula that dictates the appropriate proportion of study questions to pages of text. But imagine having to answer about 230 such questions during the course of reading a novel about 230 pages long. Even if the questions are thought-provoking and relevant—which I find these to be—the process might well have the effect of fragmenting the reading experience, rather than helping one to find overarching meaning or simply to engage in the aesthetic experience of reading.

My class observations suggest to me that the study-guide questions had this sort of distracting effect. Almost daily during the unit on *The Bean Trees*, Tom gave his students time to meet in small groups to talk about their responses to the novel or to discuss a major theme he had pointed out to them. One such day, Tom suggested that the students discuss an important issue at the end of the novel: whether Taylor was right to adopt Turtle, despite the illegality of the adoption.[7] The question touched on an even larger one, of potential moral and existential interest to seventeen-year-old students: under what circumstances, if any, is it right to break the law? On that day, like many others, as I visited the small groups, I saw students filling in answers on their study guides, rather than discussing the question. I heard them say to one another, "What did you get for number 3? Number 8? How about 11?" The numerous questions on the study guide—reflecting Tom's desire that the students "get all the stuff that's there"—seemed to crowd out discussion of the more central issue. When Tom or his teaching partner visited a small group, the students would turn briefly at his prompting to the larger question; when he left, in my observation, they would return to their pursuit of the answers.[8] The students had good reason to answer all the questions on the guides, rather than the larger, thematic one, as Tom frequently reminded them that "eighty out of a hundred questions on the final exam" would ask about *The Bean Trees*, and he intimated that knowing the answers to the study-guide questions would prepare them well for the test. It was not as clear how having grappled with the larger issues would benefit the students.[9]

I know that Tom teaches *The Bean Trees* because he believes that it touches on matters of moral and existential importance to teenagers, and that he provides the study guides chiefly as a way of ensuring that students will understand key points in the novel and so be able to think about it more deeply. I know, further, that many of his students were touched and moved by the novel. Several students told me as much, and some of their journal writings reflect engagement with the novel and its characters.[10] Relatively little of that enthusiasm met the eye in class, however, where students' attention was dominated by the need to "get the answers" to the scores of questions thrown at them.

What to do? Study guides are often useful in getting students to do the reading, without which, of course, there is no way they could grapple with the meaningful issues in the text. So it is not the study guides per se that are the problem. It is, to borrow the metaphor, that the forest gets lost for the trees. Students come to believe that the study of literature *is* the memorization of details of plot.

One of the strategies Tom used to allow his students to respond personally to the novel was to ask them to keep a journal. Larry Carlson, Tom's teaching partner in this combination English and history class, told me about written dialogues he and Tom were able to have with students in the context of their journal entries about *The Bean Trees*. Larry told me, "When you read the journals, many of them talk about a sense of wanting to be a Taylor, a little concerned they're a little too much like Lou Ann, and they are wanting to be strong, and admiring people who are being strong. It gives us an opportunity to write back to them, feed back to them some things: 'You say that, but I really see you as a very strong person, and as capable of really having a lot of power in your life.'"

This kind of dialogue seems likely to have a strong, positive impact on students. Their responses to student writing clearly help Tom and Larry build a tremendous rapport and sense of trust with their students. But these journal conversations, powerful as they are, do not seem to leak into the regular life of the classroom, which remains very focused on getting the answers.

Teachers like Tom are in a tricky situation. At the end of the semester, they have to grade each of their students, rank them on their performance of the study of literature. This means, it would seem, that at the end of each unit, teachers have to grade each student, rating and ranking their knowledge of the particular book. Teachers thus strive to create objective ways of evaluating student performance. In this context, study guides and the corresponding short-answer tests gain great prominence in the life of the classroom.

This scenario raises a set of questions that must be explored in further depth, the answers to which would affect the very way we conceive of English as a discipline in high school. We must ask: what is it that we want a student to get out of reading a novel in English class? Let us imagine that this answer includes, in addition to some basic facts about the novel, things like "a sense of empathy with characters from another time" or "insight into some of their own human relationships" or "inspiration to act against injustice." Then, as teachers, we must ask: How would we know if students had received these things? Are we prepared to rank the students on these kinds of knowledge? If so, how? If not, what do we do about the obligation to grade the students?

Without attempting to answer these questions at this point, I hope the questions help to show how appropriate Tom's work is within the current system. He provides as many outlets as possible "off-line"—through journals and outside conversations—for kids to respond to the novel personally. But in the public forums of class, he does what we think of as "teaching English," pushing the students to find and copy the answers onto the study guides. It would take a different system, one that rewarded students when they developed empathy or insight or found inspiration, to make real room for a different kind of teaching English.

RELEGATING TO PRIVATE FORUMS. The practice of using journals as the outlet for exploration of morally or existentially significant issues is fairly widespread in English classes. I found this public/private divide in biology courses as well. At Frontier High, Ms. Morgan regularly seeks to have her students connect the issues they learn about in her biology class with their lives and with wider social issues. In an assignment I found innovative and exciting, she asked her tenth graders to read a piece of science-related fiction or nonfiction and report on it briefly for the class. Many of her students liked the books they had read and took great interest in discovering scientific concepts outside the biology textbook. I saw Steve, for example, give a report on John Robbins' *Diet for a New America*. Steve was clearly moved by what he had read, and the class paid good attention to his report. Here are a few of Steve's words: "Robbins talks about what humans do to animals and how animals have feelings, too. He says the food industry is trying to make money and they don't really care how good the food is for people.... The dairy industry has a contract with McDonald's—they sell them tons of milk, and then make posters about nutrition. So basically when you were in elementary school learning about nutrition, you were basically being lied to.... He also said that America's breast cancer rates are linked to diet." Ms. Morgan, who clearly had also read the book, volunteered some comments and questions, reinforcing Steve's report. She asked, "Didn't he also say that the average American woman's breast milk would not pass the FDA, because it's so contaminated?" Steve responded, "Yes—the farmers get so annoyed with flies that they spray insecticide on the cows and feed it to them." Steve then read aloud a passage from the book and concluded, "I'm kind of worried about my children's generation, that they won't have as much as I have had." At the end of his five-minute report, both Steve and Ms. Morgan recommended the book highly to the other students, and the class moved on to study a chart about the differing body structures of vertebrates and invertebrates.

Despite Steve's heartfelt report and Ms. Morgan's supportive response to it, the structure of the assignment made it clear that the book—and the social, moral, and political issues it raised—were not central to the course. There was no time in class to bring good scientific scrutiny to bear on the questions arising out of Steve's report: Are animals really mistreated on a widespread basis in the agricultural industry? Do the nutrition charts in schools really reflect commercial interests rather than accurate biology? Is the breast milk of most American women really horribly contaminated? If these claims are true, what is to be done? And, as Steve wondered aloud, how are future generations being affected by today's actions? There was no time for a collective consideration of the scientific or moral questions at hand. This is not a criticism of the assignment—which I admire—but a reflection of how peripheral to high school courses such morally rich assignments tend to be.

What if, instead of merely being exposed to the questions raised by Steve's brief report, the whole class took the time to investigate them thoroughly? It would be a different course, clearly, and one that would step on to controversial political terrain. But we must ask whether stepping on that terrain might not be worth trading away, for example, what the students learned that week about the structure of vertebrates and invertebrates. I raise the question sincerely, and hope that biology teachers and curriculum writers will consider it. Bone structure is worthy of study, too. As it stands, though, I am concerned that because consideration of moral questions was relegated largely to the private realm—Steve's private encounter with a disturbing book—his worry about his children's generation remains a kind of special interest of his, a private uneasiness.[11] Bone structures, it seems to me, might be studied in private. Hugely vexing questions about conflicts between capitalism and environmentalism, on the other hand, cry out for collaborative, public thinking. We must face the irony of what we are doing when we stick to the facts at school and leave the hard questions to be pondered alone.

It is also extremely important to note that if students were to explore questions like those raised above—is the breast milk of American women really contaminated, and if so, what should we do about it?—they would have to learn a lot of important biological facts. The choice is not between teaching facts and raising big moral questions. The choice is between learning facts disembodied from big questions or asking big questions and then doing the research—uncovering the facts—required to address them. In the scenarios below, I will explore more examples of exciting ways that asking big questions could provide context and motivation for "getting the facts."

GIVING THE RIGHT ANSWER. Teachers do sometimes raise big questions regarding moral issues connected to the curriculum. However, in my observations, the teachers who raised such questions often also *answered* them, giving the "moral" of the story, so to speak, in a fairly closed way. I take an example from Ms. Gilman's eleventh-grade United States history class at Agnon. Her students had been reading about the Gold Rush from their textbook, and they had just finished taking a ten-question quiz, written by the publisher, on the reading. As Ms. Gilman was reviewing the answers with the class, she lingered for several minutes over question number 2, which read: "Outnumbering all other groups of gold seekers, _____ tried to drive the Californios from the gold fields."[12]

One of the students provided the correct answer, "Anglos," and another asked what "Anglo" means. Ms. Gilman answered that question, then introduced the idea of bias in historical writing and asked the students to infer the bias of the author of their text. Here are Ms. Gilman's comments and the ensuing conversation, worth following at some length.

Ms. Gilman: So "Anglo" refers to Anglo-Saxon, which refers to a mix of Irish and British, which we really aren't, but because there is no other race to—everybody who's not another race gets called Anglo. By the way, before we go any further with this. There was a bias in this section. And one thing you have to do, also, when you are reading through history, is not just read for the facts, but read for an underlying point of view. I think the author's point of view was very clear here. Was he only giving you facts about the Gold Rush? What else was he trying to accomplish? He was trying to get something else across. It was really quite blatant—

Jonathan: Oh!

Ms. Gilman: Jonathan?

Jonathan: The mistreatment of some of those—smaller groups.

Ms. Gilman: By?

Jonathan: By the Anglos.

Ms. Gilman: Almost every other sentence there are these monster Anglos, taking advantage of what other groups?

Parvin: Chinese, Native Americans—

Ms. Gilman: Chinese, Native Americans, Hispanic Californios—that may have indeed been true. But was that the only thing that went on during the Gold Rush? It may have been—what else in this particular section—Had we written this section about the Gold Rush, what would you have wanted to know that was not there? Kim?

Kim: Well, they should have gone more in depth about the problems the native people had and what the native people felt.

Ms. Gilman: Well, no, that was pretty clear. The native people weren't real thrilled, and they were being abused and used as peons. When the Anglos would come in, they would take away the native person's claim. It was very interesting information—

Kim: No, but like their point of view.

Ms. Gilman: Well, we know what their point of view is—they don't like it. Jonathan?

Jonathan: I think—like the white point of view.

Ms. Gilman: Right! That's right. Maybe the Anglo point of view.

Jonathan: Maybe there were some who helped out other people.

Ms. Gilman: Right, that's right. There may have been some real good Anglos that may have set up shops in the mining towns, and may have given Indians and blacks credit; you know, who may have said, "We haven't really struck it rich yet, but could we get some shovels from you, and we'll pay off when we can." Maybe there were some real good Anglo doctors or teachers that went into mining camps and took care of some of their kids. The bias in this section—I have not noticed it before in other parts of the book—but the bias in this section was absolutely incredible. Horrible Anglos, going in and taking all this money, and stealing claims from every other ethnic group. Well, what else, besides that, would you have wanted to know about the Gold Rush that was not in this section?

Student: [Inaudible]

Ms. Gilman: That's right. And it's almost as if—"Oh, the Indians were involved in an aggressive war—so we won't go into this too much, because we don't really want to say anything bad against the Indians." It's almost as if all the bad details are reserved for the Anglos.

Mimi: It seems like every section we read, we look really bad. We take over land—

Ms. Gilman: Yeah, I know. It's like the only thing we ever did that was good was the Declaration of Independence and the Constitution.... Yeah, basically, so far, that's the only two good things that we do. Is that wrong? I don't know. I'd like to be prouder of American history than that. It is true that much of the country is built on this move westward, and doing things like Andrew Jackson did, taking the Indians, and saying, "I don't care if you march and die with your children, we need your land." There are many, many black marks. Maybe the goal of American history books in the future is to kind of try to point out some of the good things that we have done—even in the midst of taking Indian land.

Jack: Then they are going to come out and say, "Well, that's biased for the white people."

Ms. Gilman: It's a real problem now. It used to be easy in my day, they just figured all of the Anglos were heroes, and they wrote from that point of view. So it was almost as if anything bad that we did didn't get in.

Jack: Everything's biased, when you think about it. Like if I even say, "I like basketball," that means I'm a basketball fan, I'm biased towards the basketball team.

Ms. Gilman: Okay, let's finish this grading. Number 3?...

Ms. Gilman then finished the grading, quickly answering the remaining quiz questions.

Ms. Gilman began this conversation by opening two quite fascinating and important issues of moral import. First, she asked students to be aware that all writing about history has a bias—that historians will tend to take some historical subjects' accomplishments and suffering more seriously than others—and she asked them to ferret out this particular writer's bias. A sophisticated understanding of history requires realizing that all authors, even authors of textbooks, dispense not Truth, but a version of the truth based on their own backgrounds, political leanings, and access to source materials. Ms. Gilman pushed her students toward this realization. Asking students to detect this particular writer's bias, as Ms. Gilman did here, invites them to think and read critically. Second, Ms. Gilman opened the question of whether the history of the white European settlers in the United States is, on the whole, a proud or a shameful one. This is certainly an important, relevant, even a brave question. Indeed, one can imagine building a fascinating course around this question alone, looking squarely at both the stunning achievements and the inhumanities in American history.

And yet, for all the power of Ms. Gilman's questions, this classroom exchange failed to live up to its potential. For while Ms. Gilman asked thought-provoking questions, she seemed determined that the students get what she saw as the right answers, and so allowed little room for them to think or talk the questions through. When Kim ventured that she would have liked to see more from the point of view of the Native Americans, Ms. Gilman told Kim that the text contains enough of the Native Americans' perspective, and took an answer from Jonathan, who provided the answer she was looking for.

One might argue that Ms. Gilman is certainly a better reader than Kim, and it must be that Kim really has missed the overwhelming bias of this passage; Ms. Gilman is simply correcting Kim's misreading of the history text.[13] Even if Ms. Gilman's interpretation of the text would be widely agreed upon, my pedagogical concerns remain: There was little room here for students to express opposing points of view. They were not encouraged to use the tools of critical thought and argumentation. This would have been a wonderful opportunity, it seems to me, for Ms. Gilman to have encouraged Kim to return to the text, to cite passages supporting her claim that the Native American point of view was missing; the teacher might have encouraged Jonathan, with whom she agreed, to do the same.

With regard to the question of whether the history of the United States is essentially a shameful one, Ms. Gilman similarly answered it, albeit somewhat tentatively, herself: "Maybe the goal of American history books in the future is to try to point out some of the good things that we have done—even in the midst of taking Indian land." Is there anything wrong with Ms. Gilman answering her own questions? Not categorically; indeed, the "wisdom of practice" might suggest the value of this technique in many circumstances. One must always ask, however, what is lost when efficiency is gained. Grappling with the question of whether American history should inspire pride or shame or careful shadings of both would be a worthy year-long project for eleventh-grade students of American history. The quick answer from the teacher, I fear, closes off further investigation. Or, to put it another way—the ready answer from the teacher suggests that engaging with these difficult questions is *not* a primary goal of the course—the course requires the students to get the facts, not to struggle with the ambiguities.

Again, while this scenario is specific to Ms. Gilman in the particular points she chose to emphasize, it represents a very general phenomenon: high school history courses are mostly about answers, not about questions. What if history curricula and pedagogical strategies were conceived so that they put struggling with ambiguities at their center? One can imagine, in this case, how such an orientation might have opened up an opportunity for students to delve deeply, marshaling facts to support their opinions.[14]

One might object that ambiguity is not such a great thing. Sometimes, especially with regard to moral issues, students need to be told the right answers. Opening up everything for discussion creates the danger that all truths will be seen as relative, or at least that some students will walk away having missed the point that the teacher wants them to understand—in this case, that the text was biased against the Anglos. A teacher may understandably want to correct what he or she sees as a mistaken belief or understanding on the part of the students. I agree that there must be moments when teachers give unequivocal answers. Deciding which moments demand unequivocal answers is of great importance.[15] In this case, though, it is hard to see the danger that would have resulted from asking students to gather evidence rather than quickly giving them an answer.

One might wonder, at this point, what my critique has to do with moral education; I have been suggesting ways that the discussion might have been more rich *intellectually*. Ms. Gilman might have had the students gather more evidence from the text to support their conjectures; she might have prompted them to analyze competing points of view. These are sound intellectual practices; they are widely promoted as elements of "critical thinking." Of course, it would be better if critical thinking were required more regularly in more classrooms. But critiquing this classroom episode as if the problems are peculiar to *moral* education is not necessary; it can be adequately critiqued on intellectual grounds alone.

I want to address this point here, because it is one that might be raised at several points in my analyses, and it underscores a key claim of this book. At the very moment in this scenario that a question of moral import was not pursued or was answered summarily—at the very moment that a rich-in-potential moral discussion failed to materialize—an opportunity for intellectual development was lost as well. My central critique of the teacher in this moment does have to do with the *moral* realm: although she raised exciting, rich moral questions, she answered them quickly herself, and so did not promote moral deliberation. At the same time, it is clear that a rich discussion of the moral issues—has the author treated the white settlers fairly? is the legacy of white settlers in America a proud one?—would also have held great intellectual potential.

The conjunction of the intellectual and the moral in this case is not coincidental: questions of moral import usually demand rigorous intellectual examination. The point might be put in the reverse, as well: rigorous intellectual work is inspired by grappling with difficult, important questions—and many difficult, important questions are moral in nature. Nel Noddings expresses this point: "We talk perennially about teaching critical thinking but, too often, we settle for critical thinking as a bland (if powerful) set of techniques. *We forget that critical thinking is induced by tackling critical issues*—issues that matter deeply to us."[16] Looking at opportunities lost in the moral realm, we uncover a whole species of deliberation also given *intellectual* short shrift in schools.

Whereas the two morally charged questions discussed so far were raised by Ms. Gilman explicitly, another highly significant moral question remains beneath the surface in this passage. From the start, Ms. Gilman associates the people in the classroom with the "Anglos" in the text. When Mimi comments, "It seems like in every section we read, we look really bad," Ms. Gilman picks up the "we," and continues to use it unproblematically in relation to the whole sweep of the history of white Europeans in America. "We" are the "Anglos." Without getting into the genuine problems of this equation—especially given a classroom of perhaps 25 percent first-generation immigrants, many of Middle Eastern origin—the subtext of Mimi's remark opens up several important issues for all history classrooms: When a group of American teenagers of varied origins studies United States history, is there a "we" and a "them"? What are the benefits and dangers of using those terms to identify participants in the story? Is the current generation—of whatever origin—to identify with the triumphs and be held accountable for the cruelties of a previous generation? Who will or should identify with the oppressed groups in the story? By adopting the language of "we" and "they" here, Ms. Gilman gives implicit answers to those questions—without opening them up for potentially fascinating moral and intellectual exploration.

Students Generate a Question of Moral Import —And It Is Dropped

So far, I have reviewed cases in which a teacher introduces a question of moral import and in one way or another moves on without prompting a thorough, public examination of the question. Even more fascinating cases arise when *students* bring up questions of moral import. I turn now to examples of these.

BEING CAREFUL: STEERING CLEAR OF HOT TOPICS. Ms. Putnam's ninth-grade English class at Agnon was studying Pearl Buck's *The Good Earth* in October. The teacher asked the students to brainstorm and take notes about the "role of women" in the novel. Introducing the activity, Ms. Putnam remarked, "We're talking about old Chinese culture—girl children were just another mouth to feed, of no value. Some people even killed the girls. For girls in O-lan's position, there were few choices—they might be killed at birth, or they might be sold into slavery or prostitution." Students then called out things they had noticed about O-lan's role vis-à-vis her husband. Together, the students generated the following list.

- O-lan carries things that are heavy
- She takes care of her husband's ailing father
- She walks behind the man
- She's expected to bear sons

After the class generated this list, Tom raised his hand and initiated the following exchange, reacting to Ms. Putnam's opening comments.

Tom: If sometimes they kill the girls, that seems stupid, because if they kill the girls, they won't have anybody to be the moms.

Ms. Putnam: Be careful, we're talking about an old Chinese culture; it seems cruel to us, but it's a different culture.

Tom: It's not only cruel, it's just not sensible.

Ms. Putnam: If they were impoverished, it might be the kinder thing to kill her.

Ms. Putnam then asked the students to turn to their copies of *The Good Earth*, announced a page number, and started reading aloud. The students took turns reading aloud from the novel for the remainder of the period.

Ms. Putnam was in a delicate situation. She did not want, it appears, to express a blanket condemnation of traditional Chinese culture's treatment of women, and for good reason. Thousands of Chinese parents cannot simply have been cruel. Given what they saw as their choices, it is possible that their decision to kill some of their female babies could indeed have been considered "the kinder thing." Especially in this postmodern age, when we sense that value judgments about other cultures are extremely tenuous, I feel for Ms. Putnam's reluctance to delve into the question of why the Chinese people portrayed in this novel acted as they did. But I am drawn, nonetheless, to thinking of the conversations that might have followed Tom's good, hard question.

Tom phrased his remark, as he himself insisted, not as a moral question, but as a practical one. While Ms. Putnam was right to hear its moral overtones, one approach to unraveling the question's complexities might have been to begin by pursuing its practical angle. Indeed, if significant numbers of female babies were being killed, how *were* there enough women to be mothers—or wives? Would it be in anyone's interest for wives to be in short supply? How, in this situation, was it feasible for some men to have many wives? Which men would go without wives? We need not follow this line of questioning very far to see that if it were pursued, one might come to understand some of the interactions of gender and class in the Chinese social system. Given her choice of themes for the students to follow, Ms. Putnam clearly wished them to examine these issues. Following the implications of Tom's practical comment might have fostered that examination.

Ms. Putnam might have chosen, alternatively, to take Tom's comment as she seems to have heard it, as a moral one—wondering directly how parents could be so cruel as to kill their babies. The teacher might have asked, on one hand, for students to come up with the very best, most humane rationales that they could glean from the novel (and perhaps even from other sources) for this apparently cruel behavior and then to analyze whether and to what extent those rationales could indeed be considered "humane." Such prompting might have led students to a deeper understanding of the tragic choices human beings sometimes face, and to a consideration of which human tragedies are an inevitable part of life and which could be alleviated through social action. On the other hand, as several teachers reviewing this case in focus groups suggested, Ms. Putnam might have pushed students to consider whether there are any parallels in our own culture to this seemingly incomprehensible and cruel behavior in another. In either case, rather than the condemnation of the Chinese that Ms. Putnam apparently feared, pursuing these questions had the potential of fostering deeper empathy and understanding.

There is yet another alternative: Ms. Putnam might have asked the students to think through the problem with which she herself was apparently grappling—is it fair to condemn aspects of another culture? Under what circumstances? What would one have to know first to be able to judge another culture? Are there actions that are wrong no matter what the context? What are the dangers of saying that we cannot judge another culture? What are the dangers of saying that we can?

These scenarios of "what might have been" are not completely realistic, given all the current constraints of a normal high school class. Indeed, I can imagine a whole high school course devoted just to the six questions in the above paragraph. And Ms. Putnam unquestionably did have other goals to accomplish. But there is a great loss in shutting down a genuine question from a student. The loss feels especially grave when the issue at hand—in this case, whether or not "sense" can be found in the traditional oppression of women—is so very important and so unhappily relevant. I do not fault Ms. Putnam at all for finding the question vexing. It would be inspiring, though, if teachers felt empowered to share their own moral quandaries with their students. Instead of "Be careful... it seems cruel to us, but it's a different culture," one might ask, openly, "How should we react when aspects of another culture seem cruel to us?" The words "be careful," in themselves, imply a core idea of this chapter: in many classes, moral and existential questions are simply too hot to handle.

Even so, some students do persist in bringing up moral and existential questions. In one session I observed, Mr. Manning, of Saint Paul, reviewed with his eleventh-grade U.S. history class what he saw as some key aspects of the Civil War. He read aloud from an overhead projector until he was interrupted by Bryan.

Mr. Manning:... The North had the economic advantage. They were able to produce war products and the nation's railroad. The Union was able to move troops and supplies at will. The South, however, had excellent military leadership. Most Southern victories resulted from battles of skillful Confederate officers. Among the ablest of southern military leaders was Robert E. Lee.... By the end of 1861, the Union had more than 527,000 soldiers. The Confederacy had more than 258,000 soldiers.... Had the Confederates pursued the Union forces, they might have captured Washington.

Bryan: Was the South using slaves for war?

Mr. Manning: No.

Ian: But the black soldiers in the North weren't treated right—they didn't get shoes or anything.

Mr. Manning: Well, eventually they got it.

Ian: Eventually, but they were basically mistreated.

Mr. Manning: Well, we could argue about that all day—but they were still better off fighting for their freedom in the North than being in slavery in the South. Which would you do?

Ian: But they weren't treated as well as the white soldiers.

Mr. Manning: But they were still better off, that's what I'm saying.

Mr. Manning turned back to the overhead, and continued to read.

Mr. Manning: The North had three things in mind: (1) Capture Richmond, (2) Gain control of the Mississippi River, and (3) Naval blockade of the South.

Having completed this section of his lecture, Mr. Manning put the students to work with partners, answering factual review questions for an upcoming test.

I read Mr. Manning's "we could argue about that all day" as an implicit acknowledgment that the question Bryan raises is actually quite thorny. It would be easier (for Northerners, at least) if, during the Civil War, the North stood unambiguously on the side of justice, and the South stood wholly on the side of oppression. But the truth of that story—like most everything in history—is more complicated. The "good guys" had their share of racism, and the "bad guys" probably had some shares of compassion. A fascinating discussion might be held in a class that took time to confront this complexity.

Mr. Manning, in what I and other teachers reading the case heard as a dismissive gesture, asked Ian what he would do if he had to choose between North and South. What if Mr. Manning had taken Ian's comments more to heart, and had asked his own very good question in a way that opened up discussion: "Would you rather have been a soldier in the North, risking your life in a gruesome war, or would you rather have been living as a slave with a relatively humane master?" The intellectual potential of pursuing this morally important question seems great. The class might have considered whether the idea of a "humane master" is an oxymoron; it might have considered how discrimination in the North differed from the institutionalized slavery of the South. To investigate these questions, students might have turned to the writings of slaves and African-American Union soldiers and other primary sources for insight.

What matters, it seems to me, is not so much exactly what path should have been taken to pursue Ian's comments, but rather that (1) a student's question be given weight in directing the course of inquiry and (2) frequent opportunities be taken to explore difficult moral issues. Mr. Manning's remark that "we could argue about that all day" sent the message, most likely, that history class is not supposed to be about wrestling with complicated reality—it is about getting the facts. If a discussion will not help anyone "get the facts," it is seen as futile. And again, as in other cases we have seen, both moral inquiry and rigorous intellectual work lay victim to the ceaseless pressure to cover material. In such circumstances, all but rare students—like Ian, perhaps—are likely to surrender their curiosity and sit passively.

Although all the teachers with whom I discussed this case in focus groups found Mr. Manning's apparent tone troubling, some of them also found my critique unrealistic. Part of a teacher's job, they argued, is to keep the class on track, to cover certain subjects.[17] A teacher has no obligation to stop and deal at great length with a student's question, even if it is interesting. Furthermore, just because Mr. Manning did not stop for the particular question cited here does not mean that he *never* stops to pursue good questions. A teacher can't stop at every good question. Finally, Ian's comments were off the subject. Mr. Manning was lecturing about Southern military strength, and Ian wanted to talk about black soldiers in the North.

These objections have merit. A teacher does have an obligation to keep a course on track. My purpose here is not to suggest that a teacher should always drop all plans for the rest of the hour just because a student has asked a good question. But I do argue that we need to examine what it means for a history course to be "on track," and also that good questions do merit attention. Students need to know that asking questions is a mark of intellectual vitality and rigor, that part of their job as they listen to a rendition of history (or any other subject) is to ask probing questions, that one of the marks of a skilled historian, in particular, is that he or she asks questions rather than accepting any particular version of history as the whole truth.

Unfortunately, the joy in asking questions—characteristic of both skilled historians and healthy toddlers—has been squeezed out of many children by high school, or at least is squeezed out of them while they are sitting in high school classes. John Dewey suggested that students may even begin to feel happy enough to do busywork rather than to be genuinely inquisitive, for children get used to having little expected of them.

> We get used to the chains we wear, and we miss them when removed. 'Tis an old story that through custom we finally embrace what at first wore a hideous mien. Unpleasant, because meaningless, activities may get agreeable if long enough persisted in. *It is possible for the mind to develop interest in a routine or mechanical procedure if conditions are continually supplied which demand that mode of operation and preclude any other sort.* I frequently hear dulling devices and empty exercises defended and extolled because "the children take such an 'interest' in them." Yes, that is the worst of it; the mind, shut out from worthy employ and missing the taste of adequate performance, comes down to the level of that which is left to it to know and do, and perforce takes interest in a cabined and cramped experience.[18]

Questions like Ian's have the potential to animate students and to liberate them from what Dewey refers to as the typical "cabined and cramped experience" of school. It is natural that raising morally complex issues could reinvigorate students and schools, for these are the issues that animate the disciplines themselves.

The following scenario presents more evidence that good, hard, morally complex questions are routinely underexplored. Ms. Hayes' eleventh-grade U.S. history class had been studying the New

Deal and had just completed an article and a worksheet about the Civilian Conservation Corps and the Tennessee Valley Authority. The worksheet, based on the reading and published by a textbook company, contained the following five questions.

1. How did these two agencies contradict the notion of *laissez faire*?
2. Which phrase from the Preamble of the Constitution might justify these government activities?
3. Economists have described such activities as "social engineering." Explain in your own words the meaning of that phrase.
4. Name some government activities today that might be classified as social engineering.
5. Do you consider social engineering a valid function of government? Explain your reasoning.

A brief analysis reveals that questions 1 through 4 demand reading comprehension, knowledge of some definitions, and a bit of interpretive skill, as follows:

1. Reading comprehension; definition of *laissez faire*
2. Reading comprehension and quick interpretation of Preamble
3. Reading comprehension
4. Knowledge of current events; drawing an analogy

The fifth question, however, is of a different order. It demands making a judgment about the proper role of government—it is a political and moral question.

In class, Ms. Hayes went over the above questions, asking different students to share aloud the answers they had written for questions 1 through 4. After a few members of the class had answered question 4, Ms. Hayes said she would now continue lecturing on the "Second New Deal." David noticed that they had not finished going over the worksheet, and the following brief discussion ensued.

David: Hey, we missed number five!

Jon: Yeah, let's talk about it.

Ms. Hayes: That's the one question that comes up in so many contexts in history, that we are just going to let it alone now.

Ms. Hayes then began to lecture about the key political figures of

1934, writing on the board their names—Dr. Townsend, Father Coughlin, Al Smith, Huey Long, President Roosevelt—and briefly outlining their platforms.

Ms. Hayes does not dismiss question 5 as unimportant; her words, in fact, imply that it is very important. Her decision to ignore the question, however, sends an implicit message that although definitions and reading comprehension cannot be skipped in history class, questions of moral judgment are optional. I observed her class for only part of the year, so I cannot say that the class never got to the question of the value of "social engineering." I did, in fact, observe a subsequent class, to be examined below, in which students debated in the context of current events a proposal regarding the establishment of orphanages for children whose parents could not support them. The topic of government responsibility was addressed, to some degree, in that discussion.

But if, as Ms. Hayes tells her students, the topic recurs in U.S. history, why not give it sustained attention, especially in the context of the New Deal—certainly the paradigmatic example in U.S. history of widespread efforts at social welfare. This is another example of a trade-off between engaging in discussions of perhaps unresolvable, morally laden questions—regarding which Mr. Manning might say, "we could argue about that all day"—and rather superficial information delivery. As in the lesson on Taylorism, Ms. Hayes here seemed to want the students to be able to recognize terms and names (like "social engineering" and Father Coughlin) and to know one or two key facts about them. But she relates the terms and historical figures covered in her lectures neither to ongoing themes in history nor to contemporary social debates. When the historical questions are "What happened to whom, where, when?" they receive considerable classroom attention. When the question has to do with what is valid and good, like question 5 in this example, it is easily passed over.

IGNORING THE QUESTION'S MORAL OR EXISTENTIAL DIMENSIONS. The unexamined question discussed in the previous example, regarding social engineering as a valid function of government, clearly inquires into justice and proper human social relations, and thus obviously has moral import. Other questions that come up in class may not present their moral or existential elements quite so baldly. A moment in Mr. Greene's tenth-grade biology class at Agnon provides a good example. The students had been studying the human reproductive system for one week and had just completed a ten-question multiple choice quiz. Here, to give a sense of the kind of knowledge the students were expected to have by that point, are questions 3, 4, and 8 from that quiz.

3. Fertilization in human females occurs in the...
   a) alimentary canal
   b) Fallopian tubes
   c) uterus
   d) ovaries
   e) placenta

4. The male hormone responsible for secondary male characteristics at the time of puberty is...
   a) estradiol
   b) testosterone
   c) vasopressin
   d) progesterone

8. Semen is composed partly of fructose which enters the system from...
   a) the epididymis
   b) seminal vesicle
   c) cowper's gland
   d) prostate gland
   e) none of these

After the students finished the quiz, Mr. Greene quickly gave out the correct answers. He then turned to the blackboard, drew a sketch of the female reproductive system, explained the meaning of "ovulation," and traced the two- to three-day trip an egg takes from the ovaries, down the Fallopian tubes, and into the uterus. As he spoke, Marjorie raised her hand and asked, "So there's only two to three days when a woman can get pregnant?"

Was Majorie's question a moral one? On the face of it, it was not. It was a factual question, a scientific question, a simple clarification of the lecture, on the order of the questions that were asked on the day's quiz. And yet, Marjorie was a sixteen-year-old girl, and the question was likely of far more than academic concern to her. Possibly its answer could have informed her present or future decisions about her own sexual activity. It is possible, even, that the answer would have brought her relief or fear regarding sexual decisions already made. This was a question unlike any of those on the quiz. It had potential implications for Marjorie's and her classmates' behavior and peace of mind. The answer Marjorie received, in short, might have had significant practical and moral repercussions.

Mr. Greene answered Marjorie by saying, "I'm going to answer that at more length, later," and continued his lecture about the development of the fetus in the amniotic sac and fetal respiration. In a certain context, Mr. Greene's answer is understandable: that day's lecture was about fetal development, not about conception or contraception. It makes sense to address questions in a pre-planned order. Moreover, the question deserved more than a quick "yes" or "no" response; one can imagine wanting to answer it when one was adequately prepared.

Both of these are reasonable considerations, and would make perfect sense if the question were seen as merely factual, if it had been a question about, say, the function of the epididymis. When one thinks of Marjorie's question as having implications for her own life, when one thinks of it as a moral or existential question, however, the necessity of answering it immediately becomes more apparent.

In Mr. Greene's place, in addition to the above concerns, one might fear that Majorie's question would lead to a flood of others, shifting the unit from the fairly tame "human reproduction" into the potentially controversial ground of "sex education." While I can certainly understand wanting to steer clear of controversy, it is striking to me that it is possible even to conceive of a distinction between "human reproduction" and "sex education." The subtle difference in the way the material is labeled underscores the problem here: we manage in high schools to frame even subjects that might fascinate students in ways that separate the students from the subject matter. "Human reproduction" is delivered in a way that makes it seem like it has nothing to do with the kids in the room—and is therefore much less controversial than "sex education."

Nel Noddings writes that "when we consider those things that matter most deeply to human beings—the meaning of life, the possibility of gods, birth and parenting, sexuality, death, good and evil, love, happiness—we may well wonder how the standard set of subjects became our curriculum."[19] More narrowly and pointedly, here, I would say, "when we consider those things that matter most deeply to human beings, we may well wonder how the origin of the fructose in the semen (quiz question 8) comes to supersede in the curriculum information about the possibility of getting pregnant."

This case fits as part of an unfortunate pattern in the way school curricula are constructed and enacted. The "things that matter most"—ways of approaching material that connects the students' lives to the subject matter and vice versa—are regularly relegated to "later." (I should note that although Marjorie's question came up on a Monday, I had not heard Mr. Greene answer it directly even by the following Friday.) If education is to hold any meaning for students, teachers must be actively supported in engaging potentially controversial topics, and they must be released from the bondage of being required to cover everything in the book.[20]

All teachers will recognize in the following scenario from Ms. Carver's biology class at Saint Paul the exuberant participation of students when they sense a juicy tangent in reach. This scenario might seem a bit out of place in my argument because again, strictly speaking, the questions the students ask are not of a moral nature—they are biological. I am drawn to include this case, however, because it was so striking in its context. This brief tangent about skin troubles, in the midst of a unit on cell structure, unquestionably drew more student excitement and participation than any other moment that I observed in Ms. Carver's class over two weeks. The classroom was simply abuzz. And yet, what does the scenario have to do with moral or existential education? I describe the scene, then examine its place in this discussion.

Ms. Carver's tenth-grade biology class was studying the parts and functions of animal and plant cells. Ms. Carver showed an overhead projection of an animal cell and a plant cell, and reviewed such terminology as "plastid" and "chloroplast." In a seeming non sequitur, but in a reference to a lab they had done in which the students had scraped cells from their inner cheeks for examination under the microscope, Amy then asked a question that evoked an animated discussion.

Amy: Okay, I have a question, because like, when me and my friend were playing when we were little, we used to rub our hands together, to like watch our skin peel away. Is it just dead skin, or could you like actually wear away all our skin, and then would you just die?

Ms. Carver: Well, the skin is always replacing itself with new skin. So it pushes it out. When you guys get a scab, you know, when you cut yourself, why do you eventually get a scab? Why do you get healed up?

Angela: Look at my finger, I cut it with a knife—is the skin dead?

Several kids leaned over or turned their heads to view the wound she displayed, responding with "oohs" and "ahs."

Ms. Carver: Basically, I don't think your skin died, unless you have a scar. That's why when you have a scab, you don't want to keep on picking it. Eventually, the new skin is going to push it out and replace it.

Ramsey: Why do you get scars then?

Ms. Carver: A scar sometimes, depends—especially when kids get pimples, they tell you not to squeeze the pimple—because you have a little indent. What happens if you keep squeezing it and squeezing it?

Nick: You'll have more.

Ms. Carver: You can have more, and it can scar.

At this point, Michelle pointed out some scars on her face and explained, "I had chicken pox really bad, and I had to go to the hospital for a few months. And I had really really bad scars. They had to sand them down." Ms. Carver mentioned some other cases she knew of scarring and said, "People can do a lot with makeup and different things—yours are really tiny." The talk of scars got a big reaction from the students. Many of them started talking among themselves, and several hands shot into the air.

Ms. Carver: Okay, one more question.

Nan: My weirdo cousins—they live down by, like, some cow town in Fresno. And one of them has this really weird skin. I mean, it looks like craters, but does it have to do with the heat, because like it's really hot?

Beth: It's really bad acne.

A lot of other students jumped in to speculate on this, and laughed. Somebody else said, "It is not funny."

Ms. Carver: What's not funny is that many of you guys don't have a lot of acne now, but you may have it after high school. You know, there are some kids, especially the ladies—ladies may not even have any acne until after their first child, because of the hormonal changes. You can have it right after you have a child. You don't know these things. Ask your mom about it.

Several hands remained in the air. I heard side conversations about various skin concerns—what are stretch marks? what does it mean to sand down a scar? what does sunburn do to the skin? Ms. Carver waved down the hands and proceeded.

Ms. Carver: Okay, I have less than fifteen minutes, and there are some things that I really need to cover. Page 92...you know that the nucleus is the brain of the cell.... The nucleus contains DNA, and the nucleolus has proteins and RNA.... Know your definition of mitochondria and chloroplasts.... You need to know endocytosis, phenocytosis, phagocytosis...

Class ended with Ms. Carver's admonition to remember about "carrier proteins" and "facilitated diffusion" and her assurance that the students have it within their power to do well on the upcoming quiz.

Given the context of schooling, including the students' imminent subject-matter exams for college entrance, the brevity of the class periods, and the need to keep different classes on the same page to avoid having to plan separately for each class, I understand Ms. Carver's decision to close down the students' questions and get back to the subject at hand. Nowhere in this example, further, is there anything that can be called a moral issue, except perhaps in the exchange about the "weirdo cousins" and laughter about their acne. But without digging too much, we can find issues here of nearly universal concern about beauty and attractiveness: How do I look? Am I attractive enough? What do I need to know to keep myself looking good? What do I need to know to keep my skin healthy? Ms. Carver picked up on these concerns when she assured Michelle that her scars were "really tiny" and that "people can do a lot with makeup." The importance of these concerns to kids—relative to the tangential place they are accorded—suggests the need to rethink the organization of the curriculum.

If schools were conceived as places in which to explore universal existential questions, the discussion about skin might be seen as more than an entertaining, time-killing tangent. It would be part of, and explicitly connected to, a larger, interdisciplinary conversation about beauty, which might include such topics as historical conceptions of beauty, social constructions of beauty, connections between health and beauty, the study of nature as a source of beauty, and the connection between science and aesthetics more generally.[21]

It is not that there should be no time in school for the names of cellular metabolic processes and such. It is that students—like most other human beings—care more about beauty than about terminology. And the truth is, no matter how far scars and pimples and scabs seem from the normal stuff of high school biology classes, these topics are connected to straight-up science. What if students did biology and chemistry labs examining the components and functions of the various creams and soaps they put on their face and hair? What if they had to investigate what it means to "sand down" a scar? What if they studied skin pigmentation, social perceptions of suntans, and the effects of the sun?

Without placing scientific concepts like cellular metabolism in a broader context of existential concerns, the scientific concepts are likely to be forgotten the day after the quiz. Even bits of terminology, like those Ms. Carver taught, exist within that broader context of things that kids care about. But because schools are not conceived as places to explore existential questions, conversations that might speak to students' hearts and minds give way time and again to the hurried, ephemeral memorization of terms like endocytosis, phenocytosis, and phagocytosis. We need to reconsider the goals and the curricular design of biology classes in a way that would enlist such terminology to the service of important questions.

DEFERRING TO AN OUTSIDE MORAL AUTHORITY. In the above two cases, students generate questions that the teacher does not acknowledge as of moral or existential importance. In the following cases, students generate questions that the teacher does acknowledge to be morally or existentially important. In these cases, however, the teacher closes down discussion of the questions by deferring to an outside moral authority.

In one such case, Ms. Sherman's literature class at Agnon was reading Elie Wiesel's *Night*, a memoir of the author's experience in a Nazi concentration camp. Ms. Sherman had asked the students to look for the themes of "denial" and the "father-son relationship."[22] After a few minutes of discussion about the relationship between Wiesel and his father, Gary raised his hand.

Gary: How can Wiesel still believe? How is it possible for anyone to believe in God after the Holocaust?

Ms. Sherman: That's an important question. You really should bring it up with the rabbi in your religion class.

Ms. Sherman went on to point out symbolism in the novel, noting, for example, how Wiesel's use of the phrase "no light in the world" represents his loss of connection with the Creator. The class had a few minutes at the end of the period to continue reading.

The emphasis in this English class was clearly on recognizing and being able to name themes from the text, not on grappling personally with those themes. The teacher likely expected that the students would be able to write an essay explicating Wiesel's experience along these lines: "Wiesel confronts the dissonance between his childhood beliefs in an all-powerful, good God and the nightmare reality of the concentration camps." The teacher did not see it as her role, however, to discuss in a more personal way Gary's and Wiesel's implied questions—why is there evil in the world? what does this imply about God? what does it mean for me, as I wonder about whether there is a God? what does it mean for me as I try to have a relationship with God? English class is a forum for analyzing literature, not for examining one's own beliefs. That was to be done with the rabbi.[23]

English teachers neither have special training nor consider themselves experts, I would guess, in the problem of evil in the world; it is not surprising that an English (or other subject area) teacher would be reluctant to tread this ground. We must examine, though, what is lost when we attempt to separate the spheres of knowledge so starkly. As penetrating as Ms. Sherman's essay topic is, it does not go deep enough into the core of literature as a discipline. Human beings, throughout the world and throughout history, have wondered about and struggled with the existence and nature of God and the gods, good and evil, and life itself. Indeed, they have written memoirs, novels, poems, epics, fables, and myths to articulate those and other such wonderings, and we call these collected wonderings "literature." Outside school, people read these works in order to share in the wondering and the struggle. Our task is to find a way to conceive of English-as-a-high-school-subject so that English teachers—in their capacity as thinking, feeling human beings with a love and understanding of literature—could feel comfortable engaging themselves and their students in these questions, rather than referring them to experts.[24]

It is not only clergy members who serve as the experts to whom moral questions are deferred. In the case that follows, rather than grappling more directly with a moral question, the teacher appeals to the legal system as a moral arbiter. Ms. Halinan is a drug educator who travels among various Catholic schools to give one- to five-hour presentations on drug and alcohol abuse to each of the classes. I observed her working with eleventh graders for three days in Mr. Yearly's morality class at Saint Paul. She began by reporting the percentages of adults who are "social drinkers." She then stated emphatically, twice, that teenagers, for whom drinking is illegal, could never be considered social drinkers. Here is her statement, followed by reaction from students, and Ms. Halinan's ensuing responses.

Ms. Halinan: Actually it's about 32–33 percent of adults [who drink socially]. And you do notice that I have written "adults" down here, and the reason for that is very simple. The next statement I'm going to make, I acknowledge, is a very, very strong statement: No young person can be considered a social user. No young person can be considered a social user. There is no such thing.

Karen: Just because it's not legal, how does that mean it's not social?

Ms. Halinan: There you go. When a young person says "social," Karen, I understand that what they are usually referring to is in a social setting, with friends, at a party. But in fact, Karen, anything that is illegal is inherently antisocial, as in anti-society. It goes against society's laws and mores. So, I understand what a young person means when they say to me "social" as in "social setting." But I've never ever, ever, ever heard someone who was able to explain to me how one moderately, responsibly, breaks the law....

Patrick: You were saying, like, it's illegal and that means it's antisocial?

Ms. Halinan: Yes.

Patrick: Does that mean that the law is right? Like, for example, Southern society in the 1800s—it, like, endorsed slavery. In German society—like, anti-Semitism and all that.

Ms. Halinan: Yes, absolutely. Patrick, I understand completely what you're saying. But, you know, people give the same argument about why should motorcycle drivers have to wear a helmet, people give the same argument about why should the speed limit be fifty-five, people give the same argument about why should people sixteen and under have to stay in school.... But the reality is, Patrick, that we have the law.

At this point, two other students jumped in to respond, both disagreeing with the idea that it is always antisocial for teenagers to drink. I skip ahead to Danny's comment, just before the close of this particular point.

Danny: I was just going to say that I think when you talk about drugs and alcohol or whatever, you have to distinguish whether or not you are talking about it from a legal aspect or a practical aspect.... I don't think it's very practical to tell us that you know none of us can be responsible and use alcohol or drugs, because practically, I think that's very incorrect. We can be responsible. I mean—you have to make the distinction.

Ms. Halinan: I would absolutely, totally disagree with you, Danny, for a very simple reason. When you talk about somebody breaking the law, you may not want to face the legal aspect, but the reality is, when somebody chooses to break the law, they are being irresponsible. Now, they may morally feel just fine about their decision. But they are not being responsible.

As one can sense from the transcript, there was life in this conversation. Ms. Halinan made a provocative statement, and she elicited strong reaction from the students. Karen, Patrick, and Danny all were eager to explore a very powerful question—can we really equate "illegal" with "immoral" or "antisocial"? Patrick made the point that sometimes laws are wrong, and he cited two salient examples.[25] Ms. Halinan did not acknowledge the power of Patrick's remark; she did not concede that some laws are unjust. Rather, she seemed to suggest that there are quite a few laws that people gripe about; this is no reason not to follow them. Perhaps she feared that if she acknowledged that some laws are indeed unjust, she would have created room for the students to contend that the prohibition of underage drinking is an unjust law. As I interpret it, Ms. Halinan did not want to discuss that proposition; she wanted the students to learn that it is bad or "irresponsible" for them to drink. She closed down the conversation by simply reiterating her point until the students gave up.

I understand wanting to communicate to teenagers that drinking can be extremely unhealthy or even deadly. But appealing to the law as a moral authority that cannot be questioned defies our historical knowledge and good sense, as Patrick tried to point out. Aside from the historical examples of immoral laws, many of the students' regular experiences must contradict Ms. Halinan's claims. Certainly some students drink a little wine on special occasions, for example, with the permission of their parents, who are actively modeling drinking responsibly and moderately. Far from engendering respect for the law, Ms. Halinan's stand opened the law to scorn. (I heard students after class say that the law against underage drinking is "stupid.")

Most important, by locating moral authority in an "expert"—in this case, the law—Ms. Halinan lost the opportunity to exercise what I believe should be part of a teacher's role: the modeling of deliberation on moral matters. Very practically, and still within the framework of encouraging the students to obey the law, Ms. Halinan might have asked them to weigh the perceived virtues of underage drinking against its dangers and the potential consequences of breaking the law. Beyond that, this conversation might have been a conduit to an exploration of a whole range of important and fascinating questions: How can one tell whether one's drinking is responsible or irresponsible? How should society balance the protection of the common good with the demands of individual freedom? How can one tell when a law is just or unjust? Who is responsible for deciding what the law should be, and what means are available to protest unjust laws? Just as the prior case suggested reconceiving the role of the English teacher, the task at hand is to conceive even a role like "drug educator" in a way that would enable a teacher to engage her students in moral deliberation about such questions.[26]

A Moral Issue Is Discussed in Class in an Unfocused Way

Not all discussions of moral and existential issues are quickly sidetracked or closed down in one of the ways described above. Sometimes they are discussed in class. Before I examine, in the next chapter, several examples of discussions I found particularly powerful and successful, it will be useful to look at a couple of ways such discussions—though pursued—can go awry.

DEBATE WITHOUT DELIBERATION. I think of one genre of discussions gone awry as the "unmoderated radio talk show." Everyone gets a few seconds to call in and state his or her opinion. Rarely does anyone seek recourse in solid data, and no one seems to listen to others except for the purpose of finding weak spots to attack. These sorts of talks, when they happen in class, generate some excitement among students, and I prefer them to situations in which students do not talk at all. Like most call-in radio shows, however, these discussions seem neither to build common ground nor to facilitate deeper understanding.

A good example is a discussion from Ms. Hayes' U.S. history class, as it responded to a *Scholastic* magazine article reporting on a congressman's recent suggestion that orphanages be set up for youngsters whose parents are unable to support them. Here is the discussion, beginning with Ms. Hayes pointing out how the legislator's "orphanage" idea differs from orphanages in the past.

Ms. Hayes: One thing that's different in the new proposal is that these aren't true orphans—the parents are alive—the idea is that these are parents who can't support their children.

Moussah: It might be a good idea to put them in orphanages.

Holly: Maybe, as long as the orphanages are nice. Once the parent can support the kid, they could go back.

Jerry: They should not call it an orphanage, it should be a temporary home environment. It's one thing if you [a parent] are on the street, but you shouldn't put your kids there [on the street]. Also, sometimes foster situations are really bad.

April: They shouldn't call them orphanages. It could be like "Boy's Town" or something. The foster home of the girl in the article is no good. She should go to someplace like an orphanage.

Ms. Hayes: I think this article does a disservice to foster homes—there are many very good homes.

Lisa: I think unless a parent sexually abuses or hurts a child, they should not be taken away. No matter how good an orphanage is, you would never feel at home. The government should not take away a kid just because the parent can't support it.

Alan: I think that it is really important that the government gets involved with poor people by having orphanages where the kids would go if the parents can't pay for them.

Parvin: The orphanage should be used as a way to encourage parents to get their life together. Like—they give the parents six months or twelve months to get their act together, but then if they don't do it, the kid stays in the orphanage.

Ms. Hayes: That is like the current system of foster care.

Ivan: But wouldn't that wreak havoc with the kid, if he doesn't know where he's going to live?

Parvin: You don't tell the kid—if he goes back, he goes back.

Ms. Hayes: There is something to be said for the idea that it's difficult for kids to live with uncertainty.

Moussah: But there are so many people without a job—

Parvin: Trust me, if you really wanted a job, you could get one.

At this point, no more hands being raised, Ms. Hayes directed the conversation to another article the students were to have read, this one about welfare, and the class turned to it.

The discussion transcribed here has many merits: Ms. Hayes made room for the students to talk about an issue of overt moral import; she neither gave a definitive "right" answer herself nor rushed through the subject in order to cover more material. Several students joined in the discussion, and they clearly felt comfortable expressing different views and challenging one another. Most striking, Moussah seemed to make some movement toward a deeper understanding of the issues, starting out supporting the idea of orphanages for the children of poor people, and intimating at the end that too many adults are unemployed to make it reasonable to send all their children to orphanages.

Notice, however, how many questions were at play in the discussion: Should children be taken away from parents who cannot support them adequately? If so, where should these children be put? And if so, what effect would this have on the children? Would the threat of a system of orphanages help parents "get their act together?" Is the current foster care system adequate? How would a system of orphanages compare to the foster care system? Are there adequate employment opportunities for everyone who wants a job?

While the issues raised here are related, having all of them on the table at once made for an unfocused, superficial discussion. The discussion cries out for a clearer enunciation of a problem to be addressed and a systematic approach to thinking about it. It demands, further, a marshaling of evidence to support the opinions expressed. There are data, after all, that could be brought to bear on the claims that "there are many very good foster homes," and "wouldn't that wreak havoc on the kid, if he doesn't know where he's going to live," and "if you really wanted a job, you could get one."

Given that classrooms are normally so overburdened with facts, with names and numbers, it is a particular irony that they should be absent just when they are desperately needed. It is as though the spheres of "fact" and "opinion" have been given restraining orders, forbidding them from mingling with each other. When the floor is open for opinion, as in this case, research data have no place; when, on the other hand, there are facts to cover, moral and existential questions—full of controversy, complexity, and ambiguity—are banished.

I am not suggesting that Ms. Hayes should have had all the relevant facts or sources of data at her disposal at the instant these questions arose. The teaching opportunity here was not to provide the facts, but to help the students see that facts are *relevant* to charged, emotional, moral questions. One might have taken the opportunity to guide the students to formulate precise, relevant questions; to consider what sources of evidence might be brought to bear; to think about where to find that evidence; and to make a plan to do collectively the research that would build a deep understanding of the issues—or at least to take one or two of these steps. Sounding off is fine for a radio call-in show, I suppose. But because a central aim of school is to help students learn to use their minds well, when an issue is important enough to sound off about in school, it is important enough to analyze in a disciplined way. As it is, this discussion stands alone, unconnected with the ongoing work of the course and contributing nothing to the development of disciplined habits of mind.

MEANDERING CONVERSATION. If the above discussion has the feel of an unmoderated talk show, the following one seems like an exercise in free association. Unlike some of the examples I have described so far, where teachers sent students the message that their questions were somehow out of place, in this case Ms. Andrews demonstrates admirable, tireless readiness to listen and respond. The result of following student questions wherever they lead, however, is an aimless discussion in which no question is pursued in any depth.

As its final unit of the school year, Ms. Andrews' ninth- and tenth-grade English class at Frontier High had been reading John Hersey's *Hiroshima* aloud. Amber read to the class from the book: "The Japanese radio broadcast an announcement that 'Hiroshima suffered considerable damage. It is likely that a new type of bomb was used....'" After she finished, Ms. Andrews started the following discussion.

Ms. Andrews: This is going to lead me to one of the questions I'm going to ask you on the final. Has anyone been following what's been happening in China? [referring to a recent diplomatic crisis, set off by China's plan to test nuclear weapons.] ... We dropped the bomb on Hiroshima, but now we are resisting other countries that want to develop nuclear weapons.

Renee: What's the most powerful country in the world now?

Ms. Andrews: In what terms? Financially? Militarily?

Renee: Just the most powerful—

Ms. Andrews: I think most people would say that Japan or the U.S. is the most powerful.

Renee: Because from the point of view of education, we're not good—because I saw a commercial that says we're really low on everything.

Ms. Andrews: What are the criticisms of education in the U.S.?

Renee: Well, what are we doing in here [in this class]?

Other students: Yeah, what are we doing?

Inis: What's this class for?

Ms. Andrews: Well, my bias is that it's about teaching you to learn.

Renee: But we're not really learning in here; it's not a regular class.

Ms. Andrews: You're not?

Raphael: Well, we do learn in here, but we do art in here—what's that for?

Ms. Andrews: Okay, I know I'm changing direction, but what do you guys want to do when you grow up?

Latisha: I want to be a psychologist.

Inis: Me, too.

Amber: I want to take care of little kids.

Ms. Andrews: So why do you need to get educated? What's the connection? Do we all need a certain basis in history? What happens if you don't learn history? Why do many Jewish people believe we should learn about the Holocaust?

Amber: So it doesn't happen again.

Renee: What's that? I don't know what that [the Holocaust] is. Why don't you teach us about that?

Ms. Andrews: Well, give me a week, and I will.

This conversation was coherent; each individual comment followed clearly from the preceding one. Furthermore, a review of the path of the discussion reveals that almost all the points involved important moral and existential issues. But the topics flew by, like images on a television whose remote control has gone wild. The topics included:

- An incomplete introduction of what was intended as a key question for the reading of *Hiroshima:* whether America should have dropped the atomic bomb
- A quick mention of countries that are currently trying to improve their nuclear capacity
- A quick estimate of which countries are currently the most powerful in the world
- A move from the idea that there are problems in American education to a question about the purpose of the current class
- A quick exchange about what some of the students want to do when they grow up
- A quick rationale of the importance of education, especially history
- A question about what the Holocaust is, followed by an offer by the teacher to teach about the Holocaust next week (an offer that went unfulfilled).

The discussion ended without further reference to the intended central question about the dropping of the bomb, and thereby without construction of any framework for future reading of the core text, *Hiroshima*. Ms. Andrews, responding to the students' every question and comment, lost her focus, and the opportunity for a meaningful discussion was lost as well.

Throughout this chapter I have raised examples in which questions of moral or existential import are ignored or closed down. It is worth noting, in light of this final example, that entertaining too many morally laden questions at one time has the same effect as entertaining none at all—important questions are not pursued in depth. Powerful discussions of moral issues do not simply follow the stream of consciousness of a teacher or the class as a whole. Just as discussions of moral issues need grounding in evidence, they need focus. It strains the imagination to think of doing justice on the same day to the dropping of the atomic bomb and also to the purposes of education. If core high school courses are redesigned around questions that matter, as I suggest they should be, careful consideration will need to be given to how many and which questions can be addressed.

Especially in light of these last two cases, one might raise an important question regarding the arguments offered in this chapter. One might note that the kind of teaching I looked for—teaching that fosters meaningful, sustained discussion among a class full of students—is rare in any circumstances, not only when moral or existential issues arise. One might ask whether the phenomenon I have described reflects a particular reticence on the part of teachers to discuss moral and existential issues or rather simply reflects the inherent difficulty of discussion-based pedagogy. This question has merit. It could well be that much of the difficulty in addressing moral and existential issues in the classroom is connected to the challenging nature of the pedagogy it requires. Certainly, a school that seeks to treat moral and existential issues seriously must help teachers develop their pedagogical strategies.

Powerful pedagogical strategies, however—like the ability to engage students in discussion—would not in themselves address the problem I have highlighted in this chapter. For the most part, the teachers' choices depicted here seem to reflect a belief—or an unspoken tradition—that the material teachers are responsible to teach is not primarily of a moral or existential nature. Important knowledge about the Civil War is not, for example, how soldiers were treated but the names of generals and battles. Details of plot comprise the necessary knowledge about novels. Knowing the names of organs and hormones constitutes knowing about the human reproductive system.

As long as these conceptions of knowledge and the subject matters are in place, no amount of pedagogical skill or versatility can make the courses more meaningful or intellectually powerful. The stories in this chapter are not those of teachers who cannot, or could not, with training and practice, lead discussions. These are stories of teachers who—because of the various constraints they feel—push the exploration of moral and existential matters to the periphery of their courses. Skill at leading discussions is significant, but it is only one of the factors that limits the frequency and depth of exploration of these matters.

In this chapter we have seen, on one hand, potentially powerful discussions cut off prematurely out of an apparent fear of the controversy they might raise and out of a desire to get back to the facts. We have seen, on the other hand, free-flowing discussions in which tenuously related comments proceed apace, without recourse to facts or to an organizing structure. It seems to be neither pedagogically nor politically easy to dedicate class time to discussions that are controversial yet constructive, flexible yet focused, and grounded in what matters morally and existentially as well as in factual evidence. The next chapter is devoted to class sessions in which two teachers—dedicated to the idea of providing a forum for discussing moral and existential issues and having the freedom to act on that dedication—succeeded more fully in striking these balances.

CHAPTER 5

"It Makes You Think"

*Sustained Discussions of Moral and
Existential Questions*

A S I STATED IN CHAPTER 1, FAIRLY WIDE CONSENSUS EXISTS among policymakers and theoreticians regarding the idea that schools should be—and cannot help but be—involved in moral education. The consensus about the necessity and inevitability of engaging in moral education falls apart, however, when such groups discuss what the nature of explicit moral education in schools should be. The curricular philosophy that I have termed the virtues approach—a particular strand of the much wider "character education" movement—is being implemented in schools around the country.[1] If, as I believe, the virtues approach falls short, it is clear that its critics, like me, need to present viable alternate approaches. By providing examples of real-life teaching regarding moral and existential issues—teaching that in my view avoids the pitfalls of the virtues approach—this chapter aims to provide what Shulman refers to as "visions of the possible."[2]

This chapter includes exceptional discussions from history and biology classes. Unfortunately, I have no example I can hold up as exceptional from an English class. As I review notes and transcripts from my class observations, I see that the English teachers I observed did regularly touch on moral and existential issues, but somehow those discussions were not sustained in depth or did not include students' voices to a significant degree. This is a particularly disappointing finding, for on the surface, at least, the study of literature seems even more open than other disciplines to deliberation of moral and existential issues. Given the small size of my study, I cannot, of course, generalize about the nature of English classes; certainly some English classes do provide forums for meaningful discussions of moral issues. It is worth noting, however, that despite the ostensibly open-ended nature of the study of literature and writing, many English courses emphasize the more tangible, testable elements of the discipline—spelling, vocabulary, grammar, details of plot, and the like.[3]

In my observations of English classes, when moral issues regarding literature arose, one of the teachers I studied tended to ask leading questions with implied "right answers"; another regularly cut off such discussions in the name of covering more course material; a third tended to dominate the discussions, or else to relegate them to small groups or to journals; a fourth happened to be giving the students time to edit and critique one another's writing during nearly the whole time I was there.[4] For whatever combination of reasons, my months of observations yielded no sustained, engaged, whole-group discussions of moral issues in English classes.

Here, then, are four examples—two from history, and two from biology—where teachers and students took the time to examine complicated, even frightening moral and existential issues in some depth. I provide extensive commentary on each of the discussions, attempting to analyze in detail just how they negotiated this difficult terrain. In the context of typical school life, I found these sessions remarkable.

War and Peace Class

When reviewing transcripts to select class sessions for this chapter, I found several exceptional discussions in Larry Carlson's War and Peace class at Frontier High. This is the only history, literature, or biology class—of the ten I visited on a regular basis—where I heard thoughtful, provocative discussions, filled with different student voices, at least a couple of days each week. The peculiarity of the course, I think, is no mere coincidence, and deserves exploration. Larry is an experienced, skilled, creative teacher—but then, so were virtually all of the teachers I observed. War and Peace, however, unique among the courses I observed regularly, is an elective.

Chosen freely by its students and designed by Larry himself, it lacks the constraints of the courses in the required curriculum: there is no comprehensive textbook to race through, no impending achievement tests, no legacy of facts or titles to be included in the curriculum in the name of "cultural literacy."[5]

In War and Peace, Larry feels he has the freedom to spend a whole day or several days on a pregnant question, such as the two that will be explored in the discussions described below. (Like Tom Atlas, Larry invites his students to call him by his first name, and most of them do.) When I asked Larry in an interview about what keeps him fresh and enthusiastic after more than thirty years in the classroom, he spoke of the special pleasure he takes in the War and Peace class: "People don't throw away what you give them in terms of their life views. That always has energized me. That always moves me deeply. It's a very emotional feeling. Talking about it now makes me feel emotional about it. . . . Graduation has always been a difficult time to emotionally disconnect from kids who you've made contact with, you care about as people, and there's been some reciprocal relationship there. That has always been true. I enjoy what I do, particularly in the War and Peace class, where we have intellectual struggles. I enjoy that. I enjoy the repartee that goes on with the challenging of ideas, the exploring of ideas." The War and Peace class, more than other courses, revolves around the exploration of ideas and their connection to students' lives. No matter what course he teaches, Larry remains, of course, skilled and thoughtful. But I did not see him lead discussions of this caliber in his U.S. history class—which has a similar student population (even some of the same individual students) but where the pressure to cover material is greater.[6]

My observations of Larry across two of his courses—one elective and one required—reinforce Linda McNeil's finding that teaching creativity tends to flourish in indirect proportion to the amount of administrative control under which teachers operate.[7] As I have argued, the missed opportunities in the previous chapter are not necessarily a result of teachers' inability to lead such discussions— although certainly leading discussions is a skill that requires much more training and practice than it receives. In core courses, teachers feel compelled to deliver content, even when experience shows specific, factual content is quickly forgotten.[8] Larry, operating under relatively little administrative control in War and Peace, by contrast, has defined his role as the facilitator of group deliberations. I turn now to two discussions from this class.

Existential Considerations of War

At some point several years ago, Larry, who had been teaching War and Peace for nearly twenty years, decided that if he was going to teach a course about war, he needed first to talk about death with his students in a personal way. And so, on August 28—the second day of the school year—he opened his War and Peace class by telling his students that he had some very special information in his possession: he had, he told them, a list of the dates on which each of the individual students would die. The students were to decide whether they wanted the information or not. In a rare hour in the life of a public school, eleventh and twelfth graders shared some of their thoughts and feelings about death.

I pick up the discussion a few minutes after it has begun.[9] The period lasts fifty minutes, and the conversation excerpted here continues to the final seconds of class.

Valerie: First of all, I want to know how you got these dates.

Larry: I knew somebody would ask. Well, I'm a little reluctant to say this, but I have a special pipeline. The Almighty has given me these dates because He—She knows that I want to have this conversation in class. So, you know, Valerie, that I don't have the dates.

Valerie: I know, but still.

Larry: For intellectual purposes, we'll say that She has given me the dates. Now. Do you want to know [your date]?

Valerie: No.

Larry: Why not?

Valerie: I don't want to know when I'm going to die. If I die, then I die. If I don't, then, I don't.

Though she began in all earnestness, Valerie caught the humor of her last sentence as she uttered it and burst out laughing, as did many of her classmates. Almost immediately, and with much good humor, the conversation has come around to one of the central human responses to death—denial. The topic could hardly be more appropriate for a course that is meant to explore, in part, why nations address conflict through war. The short exchange between Larry and Valerie also exposes some of the hazards of engaging in this kind of discussion in a public school setting. It is not hard to imagine students and parents who would be offended at the way "the Almighty" was referred to here, or at the fact that "the Almighty" was referred to at all.

These possible hazards notwithstanding, Larry pushes Valerie on her "decision" to remain ignorant (hypothetically) of the date of her death.

Larry: Valerie, you know that knowing the date of your death is not going to take that fact away. Right? If you're going to die, then you are going to die when you die.

Valerie: If I know when I'm going to die, I'm going to be frantically saying, "Oh, I have to do this, I have to do that. Before I die, I have to do this, I have to do that." And your whole thing is to do things that maybe you don't even want to but you're just doing [because] you're going to die and so you can say that before you die—do you understand what I'm saying?

Larry: I heard you—let me see if I've got this: if you knew the day of your death and it was in the near future, you might do things that you really don't want to do, but you would do it because you feel that you have to experience that before you die.

Valerie: Yeah, I'd go cliff diving. I would never go cliff diving now.

Larry: Why would you go cliff diving if you knew you were going to die in a year?

Valerie: Because you could say, "I went cliff diving."

Larry: You mean, after you're dead, you're going to walk around and say, "Hey, I went cliff diving." Do you think anybody is going to care?

Valerie: No, but I don't want to know that date of my death, mainly because I'm scared to death of death. It would scare me out of my mind. I'm so scared about death. I'm afraid of dying. So that's why I don't want to know.

Much of school is filled with students striving to give right answers about things that they do not necessarily care much about. Here, a young woman seems to be talking genuinely about her deep motivations and fears. Larry, not the purveyor of wisdom, but a fellow discussant of issues that matter to human beings, takes the opportunity to share his feelings, too.

Larry: Valerie, I'll be real honest with you. I'm scared of death, too. And in those moments, usually late at night when I'm awake, and thinking about death scares the bejabbers out of me—so what I do is I conjure up some kind of grandiose, heroic death for myself. It somehow makes it meaningful.

When the class is discussing a political issue or historical event, Larry takes great care not to disclose his own opinion. As we will see in the following discussion, regarding America's use of the atomic bomb during World War II, Larry goes out of his way to argue from every possible angle. In this discussion, though, about a more personal, intimate matter, Larry takes several opportunities to share his feelings. His willingness to share his own fears in this context reinforces the idea that the matter at hand—death, in this case—is a universal human concern, not just "school knowledge" or an opportunity to please the teacher. The essential equality of death—and other human existential concerns—outweighs the usual status differences between teacher and student. Larry's willingness to share, furthermore, sets the stage for the students to do so as well.

After Susan reveals her answer—that she would not look at the date of her death—she addresses the question to Larry.

Susan: I wouldn't want to know. Think about it—suppose that you knew that you were going to die. [Inaudible] Would you look?

Larry: I'm going to give you a straight answer. I would look. And I would look because there are certain things I'd like to do. There are certain people I'd like to say good-bye to. I'm married, I've got children, so there are things that I'd want to make sure were in order—a will, finances. I'd like to be able to know that all of that was okay. I don't want to all of the sudden die, bang, like that. I'd like to know that I'm dying. And I'd like to be able to prepare for it. I'm going to throw the question back to you. Isn't there some benefit to knowing that you are going to die on a particular day?

Susan: Yeah, practical benefits—

Larry: But there are also—I don't think some of them are practical. Loved ones—the ability to say good-bye. I mean, I treasure—my mom died a year and a half ago, and I treasure that on her last day, I was able to go in there and tell her that I love her and have her tell me that she loved me. In fact, right now, I just feel it inside myself, just even saying the words. I treasure that. Those were the last things we said to each other.

As Larry speaks about his mother's death, he chokes up. The students listen, rapt, and when he finishes speaking, five hands shoot up to participate. The conversation has arrived at a core issue: what can make a death meaningful? Susan argues that a death doesn't have to include intentional good-byes.

Susan: But you should already know that [she loves you], before she even dies. The people that I love right now, know it, you know? So if I were to die, there wouldn't be any questions in my mind about it.

Tiffany: There's just something—I would die happier if I could say good-bye to the people I love, if I had a chance to express it, even though they know it already. I know that the people I love love me too, and we say that to each other all our lives, but still—

Students now have taken up two different points of view, and other students have been listening well, as is demonstrated by the mixed feelings that several of them are about to express. Having heard "both sides" of what would make dying easier or more meaningful, Charlie is torn. He wonders whether knowing the date of his death would affect the choices he makes about how to live. Pursuing this thought, Charlie brings the conversation to the question of what makes for a meaningful life.

Charlie: I think, if I was given that choice, I'd really be in a dilemma, because I see the reason for choosing not to look at it *and* for looking at the date. If you decide to look at it, and they tell you you are going to die in five years—In my position, personally, I would quit school, because I'd like to take as much time with myself and what I would like to do—like take up my hobbies, maybe go see the world a little bit more. Live, you know, the day. But—

Larry: But why go to school—because it's a future thing?

Charlie: It's [for] the future. It builds you up—if you get good grades in this school, you go to college and then you get a good job, and then your future, your well-being when you're adult, and when you're older, like in retirement, and benefits like that are better. But, you know, it would really be wasted if I have five years [left to live]. I'd finish high school and I'd die before college ended and it's all wasted, and I could have had all this time to explore the world, and it would just be wasted, it'd be gone.

Charlie's reflection on school here is a particularly sad commentary, and worth attending to—it sums up, to a degree, one of the key themes of this book: as it stands, many students see school as having no intrinsic value, as merely a means to an end. My sense is that if there were more investigation in school of things that matter, the years in school would feel more valuable in themselves.

Jerry and Edna, meanwhile, pick up on the idea of how knowing the date of one's death would affect the nature and the quality of life. As they speak, several other hands hang in the air; lots of students seem to want to get involved in this discussion, as do I. Jerry makes the point that one of the things that characterizes life as we know it is that we do not know, for the most part, how long we will live. It would alarm Jerry to alter his consciousness so fundamentally. Jerry expresses this sentiment using a baseball metaphor.

Jerry: I mean, one of the nice things about life is that it is unknown. I mean there's all these curve balls that life throws, and death just happens to be one of them. And so if you know when you are going to die, I think you'll start—like Valerie said—you'll start doing a lot of things that normally you wouldn't do, that aren't really part of your personality.

Edna: I agree with Alissa [who had spoken earlier].... [If you knew the date] you would be living for the day of your death. Why should we spend the time preparing for that one day?

After a few more exchanges, Carrie brings the topic back to the question of good-byes. She seems on the verge of tears as she speaks.

Carrie: I think that good-byes are very important. [Inaudible.] I had a person very close to me die and I'd give anything to let him know how close he was to us. I know it would be more fulfilling to know that he knew. [Inaudible.]

Larry: I know this might be a little hard to talk about, but let's give it a shot. Why would it have been important for him to know that you loved him? Why would it have been important for him to know that?

Carrie: Because, it's like [inaudible].

Carrie starts to cry. Larry goes to her, briefly puts his hand on her shoulder, pauses, then continues the conversation with another student. Shortly thereafter, Carrie excuses herself and leaves the room. She returns a few moments later.

For some, Carrie's tears might be an indication that this discussion has gone too far, that it is too personal for an academic setting. When talking about issues that matter deeply to students, there is a risk of treading on territory more appropriate to a therapeutic setting. In fact, several teachers articulated to me their determination not to cross that line. Ms. Hayes told me that when she taught in public school, she tried to resist "the pressure to be a kind of social worker." Her goal, rather, was "to try to be a good teacher, and give them the best education I could." Larry himself told me of the experience he had had on the Student Assistance Team, where he had gotten to know about the personal problems of many students. After three years of that work, he had left it, finding that he was "too consumed by the personal pain of some of the kids." Larry sees his primary responsibility as helping the students academically:

Ultimately I have to say to them, "I see your pain; I hear your pain; I feel it as best I can; I know life has not dealt you a very good hand. But having said all that, what we're doing here in this class is trying to give you some intellectual, educational values and skills and tools to deal with that world. And you've got to produce for me academically.... I'm incredibly sad for you, but you've got some power to determine the future and the way you've got to do that is to compartmentalize your life and set that aside and say, 'I've got some other responsibilities.'"

Whether or not it is an important line to protect, I do not think the line into social work was crossed here. I found the moment that Carrie started to cry unique and powerful; it was the only time I witnessed a discussion that engaged the heart enough to evoke tears in a student.[10] I am not advocating that class discussions be focused particularly on topics that will make students cry; but when this occurs, it is at least a sign that something important to them is being discussed. As I learned from Larry later, Carrie's sister's fiancé had died suddenly in a hiking accident several months before, so questions regarding death's timing and death's meaning were especially poignant to her. Without getting into the particulars of her story, and without becoming a counseling session, this discussion provided an opportunity for Carrie to be a little less alone in her ruminations about death and perhaps even in her grief.

After Carrie, a few more students speak about whether or not they would want to know the date of their deaths, and why. With several students still eager to get a word in, Larry raises a slightly different question.

Larry: I know there are a lot of hands [waiting to be called upon]. Let me shift the question and you'll get a shot at this. This might be a tough one, but let's try it: At what point, and you can think about it specifically, at what age, what time, what event did you come to the awareness that all living things die? When do you think you actually came to a clear understanding that living things die? Is there a time, a place?

Rebecca: I think when the first person who you're really close to dies.

Larry: Has that happened to you?

Rebecca: Yes. [Inaudible.] You wake the next morning and you know they are not going to be there.... When I was in eighth grade, there was a girl, and her mother had cancer, and she died. I went to the viewing, saw her body there. I think that that's what really hit me.

Larry: How did you feel?

Rebecca: I felt, obviously, sad. But I don't know, it may sound cruel in a way, but I was really glad that I was alive, that it wasn't me.

Larry: You made a connection between her death and your death.

This last exchange typifies one of the remarkable aspects of this class discussion. Usually, classroom talk revolves around distant details of a text or around generalizable rules. Rebecca had come up with an answer that would be acceptable in most classes; she had provided a general rule regarding when one begins to understand death ("when the first person you're really close to dies"). Reclaiming "you" to refer to Rebecca herself, Larry pushed the discussion away from generalities and toward the more personal. Rebecca, following Larry's lead, succeeded in shifting from the distanced "you" to a concrete memory of her own. Her remark, in turn, paved the way for Charlie.

Charlie: I haven't had a point in time, really, when anything happened to me, that I realized that people eventually die. But I get that feeling every time I think that my father won't be there for me— so many times—because he's probably the closest person to me in the world—and just recently he was in a really bad car accident. I saw the car. He only had bruises from the seat belt, but when I saw the car, I got really afraid because the whole front end was smashed in. That was really a tough time for me. I went into a—what do they call it—rejection of it—I was laughing like crazy and everything and I was really surprised. My dad could have died. But the day I found out I was all, "Ha ha ha, we're going to get a new car." You know, just kind of a rejection of it. Weirdest kind of feeling.

Larry: I think the word would be "denial."

Charlie: Denial, yeah, that's it. Denying what happened.

Larry: Because it's so frightening.

Charlie: Yeah—he's the closest person to me in the world and he really knows me and he's helped me out a lot when I needed it. I just—really, every time I think about it I get really depressed because he's not going to be there one day.

It is particularly rare to hear an adolescent boy talk about his feelings of dependence and love for his father, especially in a classroom setting. I am not sure how consciously he planned it, but Larry's decision to share his own feelings about his mother's recent death, early in this conversation, seems to have created an atmosphere of safety for the students.

Larry's and Charlie's self-revelations opened the door for Sandra to speak very personally, too.

Sandra: I found out about death when I almost died once.

Larry: Do you want to talk about that?

Sandra: I'll just say it was something I did myself—I almost died by my own hand.

Larry: And at some later point, did that frighten you, that you could have done that?

Sandra: Oh yeah, oh yeah. [Inaudible.] When I woke up and they told me what I had gone through, what had happened, it really scared me.

I was surprised by this turn in the conversation. I had not realized how much the students would have to say about their own confrontations with death; I certainly had not anticipated how open they would be. But of course students of high school age have confronted death, some many times, some at very close range. As Sandra admits, some have come close to taking their own lives, either accidentally or intentionally. Though Sandra's revelation was hard to hear, I had a feeling of relief, hearing this discussion, that topics that generally are shrouded in silence in school had come to the surface. Imagine what it must feel like to sit in school after one has nearly killed oneself or after having lost or almost lost a loved one, and then to continue blithely studying cell structures, plot details, and nineteenth-century troop movements. Here, at least, there is acknowledgment that larger concerns occupy students' hearts and minds, and a hope that some of the material of this course might link to those larger concerns.

After a few more students talk about their first encounters with death, Larry again changes the question: he asks students how they would like to die, if they could choose the manner of their death. Tiffany wants to die painlessly; Andrea wants to die doing something active that she loves, like skiing. Wilson mentions—for the first time in this discussion—the belief that there is life after death.

Wilson: I'd love to say I don't think about dying, but what makes me feel better is I personally feel that dying—the death of our bodies is just one step, there are a lot of spiritual levels beyond [inaudible]. It doesn't scare me as much when I think about it, that this is only one place.

It seems almost inevitable that during a conversation about death someone would refer directly to religious beliefs. I would guess that this near inevitability serves to deter many public school teachers from bringing up the topic. But religious beliefs are such an important part of many students' lives, and religion is such a powerful force in human history, it cannot be educative simply to ignore any subject that might touch on religion. Here, Wilson is able to share his belief, and his perspective contributes to the feeling of authenticity and openness of the conversation as a whole.

David follows Wilson, considering another, more earthly way of living on after death.

David: If I had to choose my death I think I'd agree with you that I'd like to do some sort of heroic something—because I think the biggest thing that worries me about the whole death thing is that I'll be gone and I'm not going to leave a mark on anybody....
Somebody's going to pass a grave with "David K." and it's going to be, "Who's he? What was he good for?" That's why it's kind of nice to think you can go out and you know you can die, but somebody's going to definitely remember you and you leave a final mark on life.

In these remarks, both Wilson and David demonstrated something students rarely have the opportunity to confess at school: that existential questions matter to them and that they are deeply engaged with the question of what gives life meaning.

Larry brings closure to the lesson by asking the students to think about what their discussion today had to do with the topic of the class—War and Peace. Larry and some students begin to make these connections.

Larry: I'm trying to resist connecting to a lot of things in the class, but I want you to remember what David just said when we get to the [unit on the] Middle East and we talk about terrorists—suicide terrorists—and why do they do it. I only have got two minutes, so let me bring it to a close. Why do you think, on the second day of the class, that Larry, who has some reputation among some people of sort of playing around, why do you think I talked about death? It's a real kind of a bummer subject. Why would I do that?

Mabel: It's one of the things that happens in war.

Larry: Right. In war, a lot of people die, right? So why should you and I talk about it before we get to talking about war?

Anna: So we question, like, what the point of war is [and we think about] why do we start war.

Larry: Do you suppose that the young men and women who have died in war have many of the same feelings, fears, anxieties that you and I have? What is going to happen in class is that you are going to see some films, we're going to talk a lot about some numbers, and they are going to be abstract, impersonal.

I would hope that at some point at some time in some of our discussions, you'll remember back to this day and to tomorrow when you think about what does it mean for an individual to die. What does it mean for me to die? What does it mean for somebody else to die? And realize that the millions and millions of people who have died in war share much in common with you in this room.

When I first started teaching this class, we never talked about death. We did, but it was all numbers, statistics. It was very impersonal, very abstract. And I realized after some time that we had to bring up very early in class what does death mean, what does it mean to you, what does it mean to me. So it's a very real thing. I've enjoyed the conversation with you guys today. I look forward to many more days.

This discussion stands out for the authenticity of feelings

engaged and for the importance of the topics discussed; in one class period, it delved in some depth into such things as denial of death, aspects of a meaningful death, aspects of a meaningful life, the mystery of what happens after death, and personal confrontations with death. Though I cannot document the ways in which this discussion in fact was connected—collectively or privately—to the later study of particular wars, one can see that there is great potential for such connections. As Larry alluded here in his closing comments, the ideas about what would make for a good or glorious death certainly connect to the phenomenon of suicide bombings in the Middle East, to be studied later. The thoughts about the pain of not having a chance to say good-bye will likely resonate during upcoming discussions of the Nazi treatment of the Jews and of the atomic bombing of Hiroshima. When one considers how often wars are studied in school, and when one considers how much human beings—teenagers included—confront the pain of death, it is a wonder that the two are not more often explicitly connected. Larry points toward how they can be connected for mutual illumination of the subject matter and of the students' (and teachers') lives.

The Morality of Historical Actions

The War and Peace unit from which the following discussion is taken revolves around the central question, "Should there be limits placed on war?" Together the class studies the Nuremberg trials, the use of the atomic bomb by the United States on Hiroshima, and the trial of Lieutenant Calley following the My Lai massacre in Vietnam. Before this discussion, the class had spent approximately four weeks studying each of these historic events through lectures, films, videotapes, and the reading of primary and secondary sources. What follows is excerpted from a discussion that took the whole class period, about fifty minutes, on the day before the students were to take an essay test on "the limits of war." The timing of this discussion is worth noting. It probably would have been impossible earlier in the unit, for it clearly builds on the readings and other material that have gone before. A discussion of this sort could not be held every day. In this discussion, the class focuses on the question of what constitutes a war crime, and specifically whether it was a war crime to drop the atomic bomb on Hiroshima. Larry begins in a tone of "trying to get to the bottom of this."

Larry: Was it a war crime to drop the atomic bomb on Hiroshima?

Several students shake their heads in dissent; others say, "Nah." I do not hear any responses in the affirmative.

Larry: Why not? Hal?

Hal: No—it wasn't a war crime, because it was a reasonable action that the U.S. felt it had to take in order to save lives, and to not prolong the war—just to end it.

Already we see something fairly unusual: the teacher asks a question with profound moral implications in a wide-open manner—and a student answers with a well-reasoned response. Now Larry makes a move that I saw quite often in his teaching and quite rarely in classrooms in general. Although Hal has already given a coherent response to the question at hand, Larry refrains from commenting on the response in the normal teacher-initiation, student-response, teacher-evaluation format.[11] Rather, he pushes Hal further by rephrasing and drawing a principle out of Hal's words.

Larry: Any weapon—you know what's coming—any weapon that's used to end a war quickly is a fair thing to do, and is not a war crime. If the object is to end the war quickly, then it is okay to end the war quickly, and the use of that weapon is not a war crime. Right, Hal?

Hal: No. You're making a rule—

Larry: Okay—I want to hear why you don't agree with yourself.

Larry, Hal, and many of the students laugh here. Larry sets up the fun—and his serious expectations—by rubbing his hands together, as if plotting his strategy, when he tells Hal to explain himself. There is plenty of good humor, but one can see that the students recognize the request: they are going to be expected to take responsibility for the implications of their answers; in short, no glib or easy answers will be accepted here. Hal takes the challenge and refines his opening remark.

Hal: Okay, using the A bomb was not a war crime because—okay—by ending the war we were saving American troops' lives. Because the estimations were that by prolonging the war there would be lots of American casualties, especially if we invaded Japan. So you can say, any weapon used to end the war and to save your own troops' lives—like by a drastic amount—is not a war crime.

In another move that I saw him make repeatedly, Larry here takes a principle a student has articulated with regard to one situation and asks the student to apply it to another.

Larry: Would it have been a war crime for the United States to have dropped an atomic bomb on Baghdad during the Persian Gulf War?

I was particularly struck by the next couple of exchanges. This time, instead of the standard teacher-asks, student-responds routine, the student turns the tables; Hal goes on a fact-finding mission himself. He knows that in order to apply his principle to a new context, he has to understand that new context better. And so he asks, "Were there lots of casualties?"

Larry: Well, we know that there were a hundred and some odd—

Hal: Were we directly involved?

Larry: We were involved in fighting the Iraqi army. Rather than attack the Iraqi army, why didn't we just go in there and drop a nuke on Baghdad?

Hal: I think it's different because it wasn't a direct threat to U.S. troops.

Again, Hal has arrived at a tentative conclusion; again, Larry pushes him to clarify and refine his stand.

Larry: What was not a direct threat?

Hal: I mean, like the Iraqi army.

Larry: Well, we were fighting them.

Hal: I realize that, but it's like—see, there—like in this case [of Japan], they estimated how many deaths there would be if we didn't use the bomb. And I don't think in Iraq there were any big numbers or anything.

Larry: Right. So the fact that in Iraq we were talking about numbers of hundreds rather than in Japan where we were talking about hundreds of thousands, that makes the bomb at Hiroshima not a war crime. But the bomb, if we had dropped a bomb on Baghdad—probably a war crime?

Hal: Probably—

Larry: So you can use the atomic bomb to save hundreds of thousands, but you can't use an atomic bomb to save hundreds. And all you and I have to do—which we aren't going to do—but all you and I have to do is to continue to argue this until we find out where the break point is between one hundred and one hundred thousand.

Hal: I'll go with that, sure.

Larry: Okay, Hal.

We have arrived at the end of a certain line of logic: using a terribly destructive weapon can be justified if its intent is to save a large number of lives from "our" side. This might be a stopping point for the discussion. But obviously unsatisfied by the arbitrary nature of drawing a line somewhere between one hundred and one hundred thousand—and aware that in this classroom time will be allowed for some in-depth inquiry—Jeff, another student, jumps into the discussion, unprompted. He agrees with Hal that dropping the atomic bomb was not a war crime, but that "because we know what it can do, we should just never do it again." He is trying for some distinction, in other words, between what is a "war crime" and what is a "bad thing to do." After several exchanges, in which Larry presses Jeff for clarification in his characteristic Socratic way, Larry gives the floor to Jennifer.

Jennifer: I was just going to say that we didn't know what it [the atomic bomb] was going to do—for all we knew it could just do what a normal bomb did.

Larry: Aw, now, Jennifer. Jennifer. Wait—

One of the great strengths of this conversation is the assumption, brought into the open quite frequently, that the remarks must correspond to facts: there is to be no opinion throwing that loses sight of what has been documented regarding each of the historical periods. And so, in this case, Larry stops Jennifer—not for giving the wrong answer—but for playing fast and loose with well-documented history. What is even more striking here is that Jennifer knows the rules, and she supports her remark with recourse to evidence—films she had seen (in another class, apparently) where American soldiers were stationed near the sites of atomic tests.

Jennifer: If you've ever watched those films, they have the soldiers sitting out in the field right next to the bomb. Like, you know, we thought that we could run in and tell everybody that was left. I mean we thought that there were actually going to be people left under the bomb.

Larry: It is true that we did not understand radiation well. But we knew it was going to kill a lot of people.

Jennifer: Yeah, but I—I think it wasn't a war crime.

Jennifer here has fallen back into opinion, unsupported by a solid rationale. Larry questions her closely, to help her articulate a rationale—or to expose that she does not have one.

One might be uncomfortable with the approach Larry takes in the section that follows; indeed, he conducts what might sound like a cross-examination whose intent is to discredit the witness. The question, hard to answer without knowing the students well, and impossible to judge from a transcript, is whether students in the hot seat find the experience humiliating. My sense is that Larry knows his students well enough to know how hard to push whom. In this case, in any event, after a few moments of such questioning of Jennifer, Susie takes the floor, hurling a well-placed question at Larry. Again, the teacher is not the only one who gets to ask questions here.

Larry: Oh! [It's not a war crime] because? [Because] we didn't know exactly what it [the bomb] was going to do?

Jennifer: Well, no.

Larry: Then why wasn't it a war crime? Did it kill people?

Jennifer: Yes.

Larry: Did it maim people?

Jennifer: Yes.

Larry: Did it hurt people badly? Torture people?

Susie: What's the difference between conventional bombing and the atomic bomb? You put enough conventional bombs on a city like Dresden, you blow it up.

Mack: People a mile away don't get leukemia for the next thirty years—that's a difference!

This conversation manages to tread a very difficult line between pure intellectual scrutiny and more emotional recognition of the horrors that are being discussed. Both Susie's and Mack's comments, above, articulate pain and disgust along with the attempt to reason cogently.

In the following passage, I find Larry's teasing response to Mack's passionate comment about leukemia misplaced. Larry goes on, however, to validate the gravity of Mack's point by rephrasing it, and then, in typical fashion, to push Mack to give reasons for his passionately held position.

Larry: Mack, I haven't heard such passion from you. [Teasing:] Are you finding this discussion upsetting? [After a pause, seriously:] Was it a war crime, Mack?

Mack: I think it was, because they dropped it before they knew what it was, really. I mean—[they thought you could] put your jacket over your head to protect yourself from radiation—

Larry: So we were experimenting on people.

Mack: Yeah.

Larry: So experimenting weapons on people is wrong. It was a war crime.

Mack: Yeah.

Larry: I want to understand why it was wrong, Mack. It was wrong because we experimented on people and tortured people?

Mack: Yes.

Larry: Was it wrong to kill them?

Just a few moments earlier, with Jennifer, Larry had taken the point of view of the prosecution, intimating with his questions that dropping the atomic bomb *should* be considered a war crime. Here, with Mack, who has articulated his disgust at the bomb, Larry asks questions from the point of view of one who thinks that it is *not* a war crime. By taking all sides, rendering his true position next to impossible to discern, Larry sends a strong message that the students may take any stand, as long as they can support it well. Even while discussing a *moral* issue, fairly strict rules of *intellectual* argumentation will be in force. Larry explained this strategy to me in an interview:

> In general, my philosophy as a teacher [says] my role is not to give them the answers, but [to] help them search for the truth, and to be a searcher with them. My most normal role in discussions is sort of the devil's advocate of challenging their thought processes, of posing questions, . . . of taking their statements and restating them into general principles and seeing what they like about it. Kids feel frustrated sometimes by it. Some of the kids think that my entire role is to confuse them. To some degree, it is. Because I think that rather than having all the pat answers of our world or of the world they've been given, I like them to think about some of these things.

In the face of Larry's questioning, Mack seems less sure that dropping the atomic bomb is a war crime. Like Hal before him, Mack, too, seeks information from Larry to help him formulate his argument. Though this information had been covered in readings and in previous class sessions, Larry does not chide Mack for asking. It is smart, apparently, to review the facts when deliberating over moral questions.

Mack: I don't know—I mean, I guess—were there targets of military importance near Hiroshima?

Larry: Yeah, there were.

Mack: Factories, and stuff like that, right?

Larry: There were chemical factories, there were major military bases there. But a lot more [civilian] people were killed than military personnel.

Mack: I don't know—the dropping of it seems less to destroy those factories than as a demonstration of what we could do—so maybe a demonstration would have been better.

Larry: You seem to be getting a little fuzzy here, a little soft. Does that mean that it maybe wasn't quite as bad of a war crime as we initially heard?

Mack: I don't know, I think they could have demonstrated it somewhere else.

Mack started with outrage; now he has moved to the wavering thought that perhaps the bomb could have been demonstrated elsewhere. Mack's current uncertainty seems less comfortable for him than his original sense of indignation. Larry's purpose seems to be to help the students see shades of gray with regard to complex moral issues. Far from the dismissive sense that arguing is futile because "we could argue about that all day," here we get the sense that thoughtful arguing can lead to a more refined understanding of the issues at hand, and ultimately to a more grounded moral stance.

In what follows, Larry displays another fine bit of discussion leading, a skill that looks simple but that can be difficult in a highly charged discussion. He keeps returning to the central question—in this case, that of what constitutes a war crime, and whether dropping the bomb on Hiroshima falls into that category. After a few minutes of having dabbled in analogies and gray areas, Larry refocuses the discussion.

Larry: Leo, would you be willing to be on the hot seat for a minute?

Leo: Okay.

Larry: Would you tell me what your definition of a war crime is, Leo, as you understand it, as you are going to apply it tomorrow on the test?

Leo: The killing of people who have nothing to do with, you know, what you are fighting over—innocent people.

Larry: Now, does anybody have any trouble with this definition? Hal, what's the problem you have with it?

Hal: What if you are fighting in guerrilla warfare and you don't know who's who and what's what?

Larry: So what is innocent, Leo?

Leo: People who are not involved.

Larry: Not involved. Okay—let's just leave it there for a second. Leo, with the Nazis—in their treatment of the Jews—did they commit war crimes?

Leo: Yes.

Larry: Was there a war crime at My Lai?

Leo: Yes.

Larry: Was there a war crime at Hiroshima?

Leo: Yes.

As he and Leo talk, Larry draws a chart on the board, filling it in with a "yes" in the appropriate space as Leo replies.

DEFINITION OF WAR CRIME	NAZIS	MY LAI	HIROSHIMA
Killing of innocents	Yes	Yes	Yes

Having elicited a quick response—and filled in the chart—with regard to all three cases, Larry questions Leo about each case individually.

Larry: How come? How come the Nazis [should be considered war criminals]?

Leo: Because the Jews weren't even fighting back. I mean, they just rounded them up.

Larry: How come My Lai?

Leo: Same thing—they [the Vietnamese] had no weapons, no guns, they were just, you know, going about their business.

Larry: So maybe this is "unarmed" [adding the word to the chart, next to "innocents"]. If somebody is unarmed you can't kill them.

Leo: They weren't resisting. I mean—it's a mixture of all of them, Larry, not just one.

Larry: Oh, nonresisting, and unarmed, and uninvolved. Right?

Leo: Right.

Larry: Now, what about Hiroshima? Why was that a war crime?

Leo: We could just have bombed a military site, instead of bombing a whole city.

Larry: And by bombing a whole city, we committed a war crime? Why?

Leo: Because innocent people were killed.

Here, again, an answer has come too easy. A war crime has been committed, argues Leo, when innocent people are killed. But what does it mean to be innocent when one's country is at war? Or, as the question might be put—is it possible to conduct a war without killing innocent people? Larry pursues the question with Leo.

Larry: Were the Japanese people unresisting, unarmed, and not involved?

Leo: Yeah.

Larry: Wasn't the Japanese nation fighting against us?

Leo: The army was.

Larry: The military.

Leo: Yeah.

Larry: Is the military supported by the civilians? Do the civilians pay taxes to pay for the military and the military goods? And were the civilians cheering on the military?

Larry uses a powerful kind of rhetoric here, in his role as devil's advocate. Each question must obviously be answered by a "yes," implying that the Japanese nation as a whole, and not just the military, was a legitimate target. Before Larry finishes the inexorable string of questions, Zeke cuts in with a question of his own. It is particularly exciting, for Zeke has taken on Larry's rhetorical style. This time, however, the question obviously begs for a response of "No!"

Zeke: Were children participating?

Larry congratulates Zeke in a backhanded way, offering a variation on "touché."

Larry: Zeke says, "Oh, I got you now, Larry." Were children doing it? Well, at some age. Six months old? No.

Zeke: We killed them, too.

Larry: So let me see if I've got Zeke here now. Killing six-month-old people is a war crime.

Zeke: Six months and twelve months and three years and five years, and—

Larry: Eighteen?

Zeke: Yeah.

Larry: Why? They are the enemy, aren't they?

Zeke: No, the army is the enemy.

As can already be anticipated, Larry will find a way to problematize Zeke's fairly straightforward conclusion that the only appropriate target in a war is the opposing army. "What if, as in Vietnam, the soldiers do not wear uniforms? What if you cannot tell who might attack you?"

After a couple of students respond to these problems, Hal makes a move very much like one of Larry's. He seeks to apply the conclusions drawn with regard to Hiroshima—that attacking unarmed people constitutes a war crime—to another situation, Pearl Harbor. We will see in the following segment, too, that several of the students start questioning one another. No longer is Larry the sole mediator, the sole purveyor of questions to students.

Hal: Was there a war crime at Pearl Harbor? Unarmed people with no intentions to attack—

Leo: But it was a military site.

Debbie: Well, what do you think, Hal? I mean, do you think Pearl Harbor was a war crime?

Hal: No—because it's a military site.

Debbie: But it still killed innocent—

Leo: It killed innocent, unarmed, nonthreatening people.

Larry: Leo—munitions plant; workers making weapons; civilians. Can we bomb that plant?

Leo: It depends on your definition.

Larry: They are unarmed, they are just making the stuff. They aren't sitting there with the guns while they are making the guns. But are they involved?

Leo: Yeah.

Larry: They are involved because—?

Richard: They are directly supporting the war effort. They are making weapons for the army.

Larry: Were the Japanese civilians directly supporting the war effort in Japan?

Richard: Not everybody was making weapons—

Angie: But most of them were. Look at America when we went to war—80–90 percent of our work force was making stuff for the war—making food, making whatever. Same thing with Japan. Everyone was involved.

Richard: But in this case I'm talking about people making, like, I don't know, military weapons. It's different.

Angie: But what about people making like rations for the war? Is that wrong?

Larry: You can't kill somebody who's making food that's going to feed the soldiers. But you can kill somebody who's making the guns that the soldiers use. What's the distinction?

Richard: Because they can't beat you with their food; they're going to beat you with their guns.

Angie: Yes, you can. Look at what we were going to do to Japan! We were going to squeeze them until they ran out of food.

Richard: Well, I'm just saying that it's a worse wrong to kill people in their houses and so forth, you know, women and children, than people who are working in a factory building bombs and guns and all that stuff.

Richard's final comment introduces a new idea to the discussion, the concept of what he calls a "worse wrong." For the first time, some kind of continuum of "wrongness," something more complicated than "yes, a war crime," "no, not a war crime" is suggested. If I were scripting this discussion, I would have had Larry note the idea of the continuum and press it further. But class discussions, where students are given room to speak, will take unexpected turns. Here, something even more powerful than my hypothetical script for Larry happens: Liz, who has not said a word all period, recalls a much earlier piece of the conversation (edited out of this recounting), and asks one of her classmates to extend his logic. Liz's question demonstrates the way a conversation like this one can build on itself. It is not just a chance to "hear both sides of the issue"; rather, it is a chance to think more deeply about the issues. She sounds sincere here, not so much challenging as trying to make sense of Jeff's position.

Liz: I just wanted to ask Jeff—since you thought dropping the atomic on Hiroshima was okay because we didn't know what the effects would be, then do you think Nagasaki is a war crime? Because we already saw what happened—

Larry: Good question, Liz.

Liz: We didn't see the effects of the radiation, but we definitely saw the immediate effects of the bomb going off.

Jeff hesitates briefly. As he thinks, there is some whispering among other students as they consider the question with their neighbors.

Jeff: I go back to what I said. Morally, we shouldn't drop it.

Larry: Essentially, if you're saying morally we shouldn't drop it, you're saying it's a war crime.

Jeff: I don't think we should do it at all.

Larry booms out an analogy, much closer to home, and draws a big laugh from the class.

Larry: Well, then, is it a war crime if you do? Jeff, I want to tell you, I think it's morally wrong for you to kill Natalie—but if you kill her, it's not a crime. What have you said?

Jeff: Are we in war and is she the enemy?

Larry: Oh! Is that the key?

Jeff: Yeah.

Larry: What about Zeke's question about the six-month-old baby? Would they be the enemy?

There is a long pause as Jeff thinks this over. The class waits in silence. Larry sees Jeff's struggle, and says, "I appreciate your agony."

Larry does appreciate Jeff's agony—in fact, he sees it as his role to put Jeff into this kind of agony. It is from this place of "agony"—confusion, really—that Jeff makes one of the most poignant remarks of the day, drawing loud hoots, hisses, and boos from many students in the class.

Jeff: They were the same race as the enemy.

Larry: The peanut gallery doesn't like that answer, Jeff. Diana?

Diana: I understand why he's saying that. You can't say, "Oh, that's a nice little baby." You don't want to have to kill those people, but when you go into war, you can't stop that. You go into war knowing that people are going to die, people are going to—you just can't get out of that when you go into a war.

Larry presses Diana for clarification, asking her in turn about the treatment of the Jews and others in the concentration camps, about the My Lai massacre, and about Hiroshima. It is clear to Diana that the Nazis' treatment of the Jews is a war crime; My Lai is not; and Hiroshima is definitely not a war crime. Larry pushes her to compare the situations; Debby steps in to argue that the Americans should not have killed the civilians of My Lai—they should have looked for evidence of participation in the war and should have killed only people actually involved in fighting. Diana responds with some impatience and with considerable sympathy for the people who found themselves trying to fight amid danger and confusion.

Diana: I don't think you do that in war—you are not trained to do that. You are trained to kill people you think are the enemy—you really can't tell. And if you are in that situation—I think that—people, obviously, seeing what they were going through, would do the same thing that they did.

Debbie: It doesn't make it right.

Hal: I agree with you—but the way they killed the people. The way they started doing the mutilations, shooting all the little babies, okay—are those war crimes? The mutilations. Mutilations.

Larry: Hal, we know you set yourself up for a fall, but you can't say that to Diana and then five minutes later say that Hiroshima was not a war crime. People threw up their stomach lining, their intestines. Isn't that just as bad as cutting somebody's tongue off? Their guts come out? That's what happens in war, right?

Hal: So *all* bombs are crimes. Is that what *you* are saying?

Hal's remark generates lots of laughter—he is demanding that Larry be consistent, putting him in the hot seat normally reserved for students.

Larry: That's good, Hal; I like that. My role in this, as you know, is to be a gadfly, to just run around all over the place just poking holes at you and arguing with you. I'm not taking any particular stand. I mean if you want me to, I could.

Richard: If you were to take that stand, you would say that all—

Larry: Yeah, I'd say that Hal had me there. Either I'd have to say, at that point, that all bombs are war crimes. If you argued to Diana that mutilation is wrong—then mutilation happens with all of these things. So I wonder if the question is really mutilation or the question is really killing.

Larry now turns the floor over to Natalie, who has a comment of a different order, triggered at least partly, I believe, by Jeff's earlier remark about the race of the enemy.

Larry: Natalie has been patient, and we know that Natalie has strong feelings on this one.

Natalie: I think that a lot of us suffer from a point of view/perspective problem.

Larry: Point of view/perspective problem? What is a "point of view/perspective problem"?

Natalie: My point is—the thing is that what we're dealing with here is the U.S.'s actions and so we say, "Well, we've got the atomic bomb, and so we drop that and kill one hundred thousand, and then we have My Lai, where we kill a bunch of civilians that obviously weren't resisting," and then we say, "Well, those aren't crimes."

But say that the Japanese come over and drop a bomb on San Francisco. Everyone dies; they've got skin peeling off; it's pretty horrible, and then we're not going to say, "Well, it probably wasn't a war crime because that's just what happens in war." It's just totally what you see.... We're in a war with another country, and then all of the sudden we are discriminating against people in our country that have the same race, you know, because we have to identify them with the enemy. We're fighting army against army, but what ends up happening is it's people against people.

Larry: People against people is wrong, but army against army is right?

Natalie: It's war.

Larry: So I can kill the armed enemy.

Natalie: That's right. I mean, that's what war is—I'm not saying that war is right.

Larry: So, to you, the problem we are having in the classroom is that the last two examples are essentially American examples.

Natalie: Yeah, exactly.

Natalie has done something extremely important here. Whereas other students have said something to the effect that "war involves doing some unsavory things," Natalie goes further, implying that war itself might be wrong. I heard her brief remark, "That's what war is— I'm not saying that war is right," as hinting that given war, given a general context of evil, it is hard to judge what is criminal and what is permissible. And certainly, she asserts, our judgment about that question is clouded by our standpoint. Implicitly, Natalie has set the class to looking at a set of larger questions. It is no longer "Are Hiroshima and My Lai and the concentration camps war crimes?" but rather, "Does the concept of 'war' itself imply crime?" And "How is one's judgment of what is good or bad influenced by one's own allegiances?" Larry puts this point of Natalie's into more concrete terms.

Larry: If I said that it was the Koreans that went in (because there were Koreans involved in Vietnam), if I said it was the Koreans that went in and did that, do you think it would be easier for us to say, "Oh, yeah, they committed a war crime?"

Ensemble: Yeah.

Larry: Tougher to judge ourselves?

Natalie: Of course.

The same issue that arose in the previous chapter in the episode from Ms. Gilman's class arises here: Larry refers to the American military in World War II and during the Vietnam War as "ourselves." Given a diverse group of American teenagers in the 1990s, some of whom likely are immigrants from Southeast Asian countries or are of Japanese descent, how much sense does it make to use the word "we" in discussions of recent American history? This issue goes unexamined here, as Larry pursues the question of the difficulty of judging one's own country. Diana, who previously seemed quite convinced that American actions were justified by the context of war, seems to have taken Natalie's words to heart.

Larry: Well, if we know that it's tougher, then why—I mean, if you guys were all saying, "Oh, no, it's not tougher," that's one thing—but if you guys are saying, "Yeah, it is tougher to judge ourselves"—if you know it's tougher, why aren't you more introspective as to what we do?

Diana: I think it's proven that it's harder. Because in My Lai we only tried one person. Or we tried more people, but only one person was found guilty of that crime. And he was let out in thirty days. And so it's obvious that we can't try ourselves. We think that everything that someone else does is wrong, but when we do something that's wrong, we think it's okay.

Larry: What if the Japanese had had the capacity to try us for Hiroshima, do you think they would have found us guilty?

Students: Yeah.

Debbie: They did find us guilty, but they couldn't like—

Larry: Yes, they did, you are absolutely right. In the Shimane lawsuit, in that decision, they found us guilty, but found that they could not in fact enforce the lawsuit, the penalty, because the Japanese government signed away—

The school bell rings, announcing the end of class.

Larry: I've enjoyed today. Good luck on tomorrow's test.

To my taste, the discussion ends too abruptly; I would rather see more conscious closure of the discussion, rather than simply letting the school bell announce the end. But this is a small quibble, as the students will have an opportunity to put closure of their own on the discussion in the essays they will write the following day. I might have preferred it, too, if there had been even more unmediated exchanges directly between students, because learning to listen and respond to one another seems to be such a crucial part of carrying on this kind of discussion. Finally, without timing speeches or counting words exactly, my observation is that boys had more speaking time than girls.[12]

These concerns aside, this discussion displayed unusual and enviable qualities. First, the students were interested, moved, provoked. Even those who did not speak sat up during class with attentive and responsive faces. Several students continued the conversation as they walked out of the classroom; others told me that because of these kinds of discussions, the War and Peace class as a whole meant something to them that other courses had not. Commenting on the class's uniqueness, Aida said: "I really enjoy War and Peace just because...it makes you think. It makes you look into yourself, look around at society, look around at what's going on in the world, and how other people think." After the first week of class (during which the discussion about death recounted above took place), David told me excitedly, "Wow. This is going to be a good class." He was "really struck," he told me, by the way the class discussed "these big philosophical type questions." In a general context where boredom and passivity is rampant, this is high praise.

Second, there is much to learn from Larry's example here of techniques that engage and push students intellectually. I have no particular preference for the Socratic style that Larry uses over other possible styles.[13] Even so, Larry's ability to argue all sides of an issue, to balance seriousness with mirth, to focus on a hard question and stick with it, to draw refined thoughts out of students' off-the-cuff responses, to push past the glib toward bumpier truths, to lead students to see analogies between different cases, to encourage student questions, to step off the stage long enough for students to speak to one another—all these deserve study and emulation for any style of discussion leading.

Most important, the students' learning-through-talking is palpable. They run into areas where they need more facts to support their ideas, and, like Hal and Mack, they seek them; they listen to one another, recalling which classmates made particular comments; and they shift their views, as we saw Diana do, based on more evidence and the arguments of others. This lesson implicitly reinforces the idea, so crucial in a democracy, that students can and should be thinkers about the good. Most history classes present history as a list of inevitabilities. The question is overwhelmingly, "What happened?"[14] Here, instead, Larry asks, "Did the people involved do the right thing?" In so doing, he conveys the notion that human beings have power over the course of history; human beings make decisions upon which moral scrutiny ought to be focused. For now, at least, we cannot find consensus in our country about the question Larry asked, about whether it was right to drop the atomic bomb on Japan.[15] I think we should be able to agree, however, on the idea that moral scrutiny ought to be brought to bear on the decisions made by historical players. As I argued in the previous chapter with regard to Ms. Hayes' lesson on Frederick Taylor, students ought to be able both to see the difficulties and ambiguities involved in historical decisions and to make informed judgments about the mixtures of harm and good they engendered.

Critics of recent revisions in the teaching of American history may argue that by opening the actions of historical figures to negative scrutiny, we are making villains of those who should be our national heroes.[16] But teachers and students need not engage in moral scrutiny for the purpose of condemning or lauding historical figures. Rather, we deliberate upon past actions and apply those deliberations to contemporary situations in order to give meaning both to the past and to the present. The discussion presented here cannot, of course, stand alone; to be really effective, it would need to be part of an ongoing discussion of similar issues (which the War and Peace class provides). But having looked in some depth at the question of the American use of force during World War II, the students in War and Peace have become more prepared to consider urgent, contemporary questions about where and when the United States should use military force. They have done more than "learn history"; they have begun to learn *from* history. It is ironic and sad that this discussion took place—perhaps had to take place—outside of a regular history class.

Biology Class—The Existential Implications of Science

The distinction between the acquisition and the evaluation of historical content—between "learning history" and "learning *from* history"—is not unique to that discipline. In science, similarly, one can acquire scientific knowledge of various kinds, or one can seek to make moral or existential sense of scientific knowledge previously gained.[17] Going even further into the mode of moral evaluation, one can stop and consider what kind of scientific (or historical) knowledge is worth having. For example, a meta-scientific inquiry that could be explored as a corollary to the historical question pursued in Larry Carlson's class about whether the United States should have dropped the atomic bomb would be the question of whether scientists—aware of its potential destructive effects—should have uncovered the secret of atomic energy.

Narrowly speaking, of course, grappling with a question like this is no longer "doing science"—it is engaging in the history, philosophy, or sociology of science. I argue, however, that questions linking scientific findings to the social realm do have a role in high school science classes, partly because students continually seek to attach the knowledge they acquire to their worlds of meaning.[18] Students sought such understanding in the examples from the previous chapter on skin cells and on human reproduction. In both those cases, there was an opportunity to relate the scientific data at hand to immediate existential concerns of the students—how to keep one's skin healthy and good looking, or how to prevent unwanted pregnancy—and thereby to answer the omnipresent questions, "*Why* are we learning this?" "Why does this stuff matter?" Students who ask these questions are, in deceptively simple language, expressing their desire to engage in the "meta" questions, to consider the value of the study demanded of them. If only to satisfy this desire on the part of students for relevance, it would make sense to take a step back in science classes and consider the moral and existential implications of the pursuit of scientific knowledge.

But there is even more at stake here than satisfying students' desire for relevance. As I argued in Chapter 1, our twentieth-century scientific and technological achievements have outstripped our understanding of how to use those achievements for good. Where better to consider the connections between our scientific achievements and our moral and existential needs than in the classes that prepare students to extend even farther our scientific knowledge? In the previous chapter, the skin and reproduction discussions dealt with areas of immediate concern to the students; but we also saw the potential for discussion of more ultimate concerns having to do with science, like the questions that might have ensued from the report on *Diet for a New America*. In what ways are the world's scientific resources being directed toward sustaining the well-being of the earth and its inhabitants? This kind of meta-scientific discussion seeks to understand science as a social enterprise and to analyze the effect of scientific achievements on our quality of life. Both these kinds of inquiry—the connection of science to students' immediate concerns and the connection of science to humanity's ultimate concerns—have a place in science classes.

The following two classroom excerpts, taken from Angela Rivers' biology class at Saint Paul, are much less extensive than those from Larry Carlson's class described above. This is due in part to constraints of my fieldwork. The biology classroom, with its lab desks, was shaped in such a way that audiotaping class discussion was extremely difficult, so the dialogues that follow are excerpted from field notes rather than taped transcripts. But, more important, the brevity of the examples may be an artifact of the nature of biology classes more generally. Although Ms. Rivers went out of her way to integrate important moral and existential issues into her biology teaching, I did not observe entire class sessions devoted to such issues, as there were in War and Peace. Rather, on a regular basis, Ms. Rivers set aside small blocks of time to discuss moral questions arising from the study of biological phenomena.

The Miracle of Life (The Video)

There are very few topics that have the potential to evoke more wonder and amazement than the birth of a human being, and few more directly connected to the existential concerns of adolescents than sex and sexuality. Lessons about the human reproductive system therefore have great potential for engaging student interest and students' sense of wonder. The excerpt cited in the previous chapter, however, makes clear that units on the human reproductive system do not necessarily address existential concerns. Even units on reproduction can focus almost entirely on mechanics and terminology and completely neglect questions of immediate or ultimate concern.

Here, I present a discussion whose starting place is the wonder, amazement, and curiosity of the students, not the teacher's goal of reviewing a certain list of terms or concepts. As part of a unit on the human reproductive system, Ms. Rivers showed her students a video called The Miracle of Life.[19] The video uses advanced photographic techniques to show the internal workings of the reproductive system of both sexes. Magnifying the tiny cells thousands of times, it tracks individual sperm and eggs on their respective journeys. After showing about fifteen minutes of the video, Ms. Rivers asked her students to react to what they had seen so far. Several hands shot up at once; the students wanted to share what had impressed them. Their contributions were delivered with both humor and a sense of wonder.

Sylvia: It's amazing that all of the genetic information from the male is in the tip of the sperm!

Andy: The sperms sound like a swarm of bees.

Katie: I didn't know that the sperm coagulated in the woman's uterus.

Peter: I like seeing the little spermies swimming up toward the ovaries!

What is most striking to me about the conversation that follows is that, on one hand, it has room for students to express their genuine wonder. On the other hand, the conversation neither rambles nor flits incoherently from idea to idea. Peter has just said that he is impressed with the sperm cells' swimming abilities; Ms. Rivers takes this interest and uses it as an opportunity to teach. Responding to Peter, "Yes, their swim is quite interesting!" Ms. Rivers then draws on the board a picture of a sperm cell, with its long tail, and asks the students to help her label the parts—enzymes, mitochondria, flagella, DNA—and to recall what processes give the sperm the ability to swim in their fascinating way.

The order of events here is all-important. Rather than beginning with her own desire to have the students memorize the names of the cell parts, Ms. Rivers links the learning of those pieces of terminology to already-expressed student interest in the topic. Peter seems intrigued (if also amused and maybe a little embarrassed) by the "spermies" swimming; chances are he is ready to attend to its workings. "Coverage" has not been abandoned here, but the students lead the way toward what will be covered, and when. Then the conversation continues.

Tonia: I thought it was neat that a sperm could have two tails.

Ms. Rivers: Yes, anyone remember what percent of the sperm in a normal, healthy male is defective?

Several: Almost half!

Again, the pattern here is striking. The student notices something surprising, or, as Tonia puts it, "neat," and Ms. Rivers uses the student interest as an opportunity to review one of the facts that she wants the students to know. In a follow-up question, Adrianne asks whether a deformed sperm could ever succeed in fertilizing an egg. I do not think that Ms. Rivers had particularly intended to go over this point with the students. Nevertheless, she takes time with the answer, explaining carefully why that would be unlikely to happen and adding that "there could be a case where the sperm swims fine but there's a problem with the DNA."

There is nothing particularly remarkable in her answer, except that Ms. Rivers is obviously willing to spend time to address Adrianne's question, rather than keeping to a strict agenda of her own. Ms. Rivers sends the message that there is not a great divide between the official, important, intellectual things one is supposed to learn in biology class and the moving or embarrassing or personally pertinent things students are curious about. Part of her biology curriculum, in other words, is quite simply to respond to students' questions. Student curiosity, as we saw in the previous chapter, is sometimes seen as an impediment to the important work of class. By contrast, Ms. Rivers' openness to questions of all sorts and her earnest responses communicate that curiosity is an intellectual virtue. She seems to recognize that there is a connection between her students' curiosity and the biology curriculum, which is itself born of human beings' desire to understand ourselves.

Giving students a chance to ask questions has a wonderful pedagogical side effect, aside from the intrinsic value of addressing their interests: the students' questions reveal their areas of confusion. As a result, making time to explore such questions strengthens the intellectual power—as well as the existential interest—of the course. Here is Peter, seeking to clarify a point that had already been explained, but which he now seems ready to absorb:

Peter: What's the case with twins? Is that two sperms fertilizing one egg?

Ms. Rivers: There is always a ratio of exactly one sperm to one egg—otherwise it messes up the number of DNA.

Ms. Rivers draws a diagram showing the relationship of sperm and egg for identical and for fraternal twins—in each case there is a 1:1 ratio between the number of sperm and eggs involved. The topic of twins seems to fascinate the students, and there is a short discussion of whether or not twins have some kind of special psychic connection. Katie has a more concrete question.

Katie: Have there ever been fraternal eggs that then have identical twins?

Ms. Rivers: So they become quadruplets? Maybe... 1 in a million...

In response to this question and the mention of quadruplets, Ms. Rivers talks about the effect of a current social trend on the incidence of multiple births. She explains that more women are trying to have children at an older age, when they tend to be less fertile, so more women are taking fertility drugs. The fertility drugs cause multiple eggs to be released, so the incidence of multiple births is going up.

One might argue that this discussion, led by student questions, is not so different from the one about *Hiroshima* in the previous chapter. Like that discussion, this one probably meanders too much for some tastes. When a teacher organizes a discussion around student questions, she will always have to balance addressing those questions with building a coherent discussion. What I admire in Ms. Rivers' discussion here, though, and what I think renders it productive rather than meandering, is the way she communicates intellectual seriousness along with openness and fun. There will be a moment to laugh at how the "spermies" look, but there will also be thorough examination of their workings. No student question seems too hot to handle; no student question garners the reprimand heard often in other classes, "we have gone over that already." Moreover, there is easy acknowledgment that the realms of the intellectual, the moral, and the social overlap. The workings of the human body, for example, are not just matters of pure science. Social trends, individual human decisions, and advances in biotechnology all affect such basic, seemingly immutable scientific facts as what percentage of human births involve twins, triplets, and quadruplets.

After a few more questions and answers, Ms. Rivers turns on the remainder of the video, which ends by showing a live birth. When it is over, many, many students' hands pop up with questions: "Why was the baby all white?" "What do they dope the woman up with?" "If you take a [painkilling] drug, can it affect the baby?" "How long do the woman's genitals stay stretched out?" "If you don't want to breast-feed, don't you have to pump the breasts?" Ms. Rivers takes each question in turn, sometimes turning to the board to draw a quick sketch or write down the name of a body part or hormone, sometimes eliciting answers from other students, sometimes pushing the questioner to deduce an answer through a series of other questions.

Most of the students' questions following the video ask for clarifications of factual matters. But as in the case in the previous chapter where Marjorie asked about a woman's period of fertility, these questions have moral and existential implications. In my observations, the time Ms. Rivers gave her students to ask such questions differed markedly from the norm. I saw the very same video, for example, shown in another biology class. There it was used primarily as a way to review a certain set of facts that the teacher had decided beforehand were important: how and where fertilization occurs; the names of the cells, hormones, and organs involved in reproduction; the number of chromosomes carried by each germ cell. These are important pieces of information, all of them. But in a context where the chief concern is covering a certain set of data, the question about how long a woman's vagina stays stretched out, for example, would certainly have been ruled out of bounds, material for the endlessly tarrying "later." Here, without denigrating the importance of getting the facts straight, the study of science was linked to students' curiosity and to their questions about their own bodies and lives.

A Debate About Huntington's Disease

In the classroom excerpt that follows, Ms. Rivers had her class explore a meta-scientific question that touches on both a matter of immediate (though hypothetical) and ultimate concern. Though brief, it illustrates the powerful possibilities for such discussions in the science curriculum. It also illustrates that Larry Carlson's highly interactive Socratic style is not the only possible format for intelligent discussion of morally charged issues: during this class discussion, the teacher remains silent.[20]

In the context of a unit on genes, chromosomes, and heredity, Ms. Rivers taught her students that, because of the incredible advances of the Human Genome Project, doctors now have the capacity to test individuals for the gene that causes Huntington's disease—a devastating, always fatal illness that usually kills the gene's carriers in their mid-thirties. After reviewing this information, Ms. Rivers set up a debate in which two groups of students argued opposite sides of the following question: Should people who have a family history of Huntington's disease be tested for the gene that causes it? Taken narrowly, the question asks what would give more meaning or cause more pain and suffering in an individual life. Taken broadly, the question asks about the proper limits of scientific knowledge. Students in the audience were invited to jump in with questions and comments after each side had given its argument and rebuttal, and several members of the class spoke passionately and articulately on each side of the issue.

Arguing that one should not be tested for the gene, Sylvia said with much feeling, "A person knowing that they are going to die at age thirty-five would be devastated. It would ruin their life." Another member of her team agreed, warning of other dire possibilities: "You should not find out, because if you told people that you had the disease, they might abandon you." And another added: "Since there is no cure, you can't really do anything with the information. It would just upset you. If you knew, you might not want to apply for a job or get involved in anything, because then people would be counting on you, but you would know you were going to die."

Vince, on the opposite team, argued that testing for the gene would not make such a big difference in a person's life: "Everybody is going to die. So whether you know you have the gene or not— you still know you are going to die." His teammate, sounding both philosophical and optimistic, added: "There are always obstacles in life, and Huntington's is like that. You could get yourself ready. And with modern technology, maybe there will be a cure soon." Replying directly to a key claim of the opposite team, another member of the group added, "People would not leave you if they found out about the disease, because it is not contagious."

Often, debates in class hold the danger of polarizing the two sides, rather than moving students toward common ground or exploring gray areas. Ms. Rivers countered that tendency by giving students a chance to speak in their own voices after they had debated the issue from their assigned point of view. After the debate, one of the girls on the pro-testing side jumped in to say: "I can see why somebody would want to get the test. But I still think it's better off not knowing—then you could start a career and a relationship. Also, you said that Huntington's wasn't contagious, so people wouldn't leave you. But I think they would leave you out of fear and not wanting to face the disease."

Though the debate took less than fifteen minutes, it stands out for several reasons. First, quite simply, the debate is centered on an important, complex question. It is one of the few times that I saw a science teacher dedicate class time to wonder about "one of those things that matters most to human beings," in this case, death. If one were going to die young, would it be good to know in advance? Though one can imagine an even fuller exploration, there was significant room here for students to think about the role death plays in bequeathing or stealing meaning from life. Second, biology classes normally have a fair amount of discussion of diseases— their causes and cures. But never have I seen so much overt recognition of the social, financial, and personal implications of disease. Being sick, several students noted, is not only a medical problem but can have severe social and emotional ramifications, for sick people are often shunned or abandoned. One sees threads in this conversation that could be woven together to form a sophisticated understanding of the interplay of basic scientific research, medicine, and social policy. Third, without being at all anti-science, the debate on Huntington's disease implies a larger concern central to post-twentieth-century existence: do we know more science than is good for us?[21]

These questions connect to ethical ones that certainly should be addressed in any science class: What is the social responsibility of acquiring scientific knowledge? What limits should be placed on the quest for knowledge? Under what circumstances is it right for human beings, for example, to experiment with other species to advance our scientific understanding? As students learn and grapple with the morality of the goals and methods of science, they might also consider the epistemological questions at the roots of science: What does it mean to claim knowledge? How is scientific knowledge different from other ways of knowing?

The list of potential expansions of this discussion might seem to overwhelm the debate that actually occurred, for Ms. Rivers chose to integrate discussions of moral and existential questions into class periods that also contained lectures, group work, films, and labs. But Ms. Rivers explicitly opened these questions, seeing the curriculum as an avenue to engage students in high-level thinking: "My major goal is not really so much curriculum, not that they learn photosynthesis or electron transfer, but that they learn how to think in a plastic manner. When I say that here at school, when I say plastic, everyone thinks I'm talking about Tupperware. What I mean is that I want them to problem-solve, to reason something out. I want them to think logically, because the body and biology are very logical systems. Ideally that's what I would like from that. I like them to develop better reading skills, writing skills, problem-solving skills, all through biology, under the guise of biology."

Although the excerpts here are considerably scantier than those from War and Peace, where a whole period was devoted to discussion, they do allow a glimpse into the way biology classes could examine pressing moral and existential issues directly related to topics of scientific inquiry—as Ms. Rivers puts it, biology as a guise for bigger questions. From discussions of human disease and health to the human impact on ecosystems, from evolution to cloning, from photosynthesis to bioengineering—all connect to issues of vital social, economic, political, moral, existential concern to human beings. Science classes have the potential to bring deeper insight into these vital concerns, and in turn to be revitalized by them.

Meaningful Talk About Meaningful Matters

I chose the sessions highlighted in this chapter for their power to show enthusiastic participation by students in conversations that fused solid intellectual inquiry with the exploration of moral and existential issues. I chose these discussions, in short, because they were both conceptually rich and personally intriguing to many students. I also chose them because of the ways the cases contrast with one another either in content or in structure. The first discussion from War and Peace relied on no prior study, and elicited personal responses from both students and the teacher regarding the inevitability of death; the second was based on considerable previous study, and asked students to employ what they had learned to assess the morality of historical events while the teacher played devil's advocate to all positions. The first biology discussion featured Ms. Rivers in a central role, as she fielded any and all student questions, and tied them together into a steadily growing knowledge base; the second allowed Ms. Rivers to slip out of the spotlight, as she turned the floor over to students in a highly structured debate.

Despite their structural differences, these discussions clearly contain common themes, and that is probably not mere coincidence. The first discussion in the chapter inquires into the conditions necessary for a meaningful death, as a means of gaining insight into the human propensity for war. The second, about the dropping of the atomic bomb, focuses on the rules of war and thus touches on how technology has enhanced our powers for cruelty. The third, on *The Miracle of Life*, employs the findings of science to answer practical questions about sustaining and reproducing life on the individual level. And the fourth, about Huntington's disease, picks up the theme of the hazards of scientific knowledge, extends it into the private sphere, and touches, too, on how illness might interact with finding love and meaningful work. Life, death, happiness, cruelty, survival, reproduction, love, sickness, meaningful work—of course these will be recurring themes in conversations selected on the basis of their depth and capacity to engage students. These are matters that human beings care deeply about; students and teachers both seem to come to life during class sessions that focus on these moral and existential issues.

The links between these discussions, taken from the very different disciplines of history and biology, hint at the potential for interdisciplinary inquiry into "the things that matter most." In school days marked by fragmentation and incoherence, the relatedness of the studies that make up the curriculum—based on the moral and existential questions they share—is worth much attention. I will return to this point in the Afterword. In the next chapter, however, I investigate the playing out of moral and existential issues in classes specifically devoted to this work: the religion classes in two religious high schools. From them, I attempt to glean insight into whether corresponding classes have a place in public schools. Then, in Chapter 7, I consider a major stumbling block to widespread acceptance of incorporating the sorts of discussions portrayed in this chapter and the next into the regular public school curriculum: the question of whose values will be taught. If discussions of life, death, cruelty, and meaning are to be discussed in school, whose view of these things shall be promoted? Can and should a teacher simply remain neutral regarding emotionally, morally charged issues? Whose ideas about "the things that matter most" will be promoted? The issues are complicated, and the stakes are high.

CHAPTER 6

From the Sublime to the Mundane

Religion Courses in Religious Schools

HOPING TO GLEAN INSIGHTS FOR PUBLIC SCHOOLS from the religious schools I studied, I chose my religious school sites largely on the basis of their apparent openness in approaching moral issues. I looked for religious schools that, like public schools, serve diverse populations of students, and I looked for teachers within those schools who saw their role as facilitating exploration of moral and existential issues in an intellectually rigorous way rather than to promote a given doctrine. The religion classes I observed at Agnon and Saint Paul fulfilled these criteria well.

It will perhaps seem odd that in a chapter that largely praises the work of classes explicitly focusing on morality in the religious schools, I will argue that they are not a good model for the public schools and that public schools should *not* try to integrate moral issues into the curriculum by initiating new courses in morality. This argument is based not so much on particular negative aspects of the religion classes I observed, but rather on my sense that— given the already highly fragmented nature of public high school education—public schools should attempt to integrate into the regular curriculum the moral and existential issues addressed in religion courses in religious schools.[1] Public high schools should avoid adding another class in another subject area to students' already packed schedules, especially in light of the innumerable opportunities, highlighted in Chapters 4 and 5, for enriching the regular curriculum through the exploration of moral and existential issues. Additionally, for reasons to be elaborated below, some of my findings in religion classes suggest that the study of morality as a discipline in itself—especially outside the context of a particular religious tradition—could be lacking in coherence and substance. So although I hesitate to urge public schools to follow the religious schools in mandating separate courses focused on morality, many of the assignments and techniques used in these courses deserve emulation in the regular curriculum of the public schools.

At Agnon, I visited courses called "Foundations of Jewish Law: Ethics and Practice" and "Introduction to Jewish Thought." The courses at Saint Paul that I studied were "Morality" and "Social Justice and Spirituality."[2] In general, these four courses shared four considerable strengths:

- Addressing important issues: the classes put moral and existential concerns at center stage.
- Providing intellectual tools and student-centered assignments: class assignments were structured around questions that mattered to students and in ways that gave them opportunities to learn actively.
- Fostering open dialogue: students felt free to speak about matters close to the heart and to express opinions differing from those of the teacher.
- Modeling moral behavior: the teachers demonstrated compassion and thoughtfulness along with active intellectual engagement in the questions at hand.[3]

Unfortunately, for each of these very positive attributes, many of the classes demonstrated parallel weaknesses. Although classes almost always focused on moral and existential questions, sometimes the questions were asked without adequate context, and so lacked relevance. Course assignments often demanded the active intellectual engagement of students, but sometimes *assessment* techniques reduced complex conceptual thinking to the memorization of vocabulary and decontextualized facts. Whereas students felt free to express their opinions, teachers often lapsed into a fair amount of sermonizing. And while the teachers often served as moral role models, students sometimes found them—and school administrators—hypocritical in their moral teachings.

I do not intend in this chapter to compare the moral education program at Agnon with that at Saint Paul nor to comment generally on Jewish versus Catholic moral education. Having observed just three religion teachers at Agnon and two at Saint Paul, I have vastly insufficient basis for such comparisons. Further, because Agnon's schedule included eight class periods a day, compared with six at Saint Paul, I was able to sit in on three to four religion classes daily at Agnon, versus two at Saint Paul. As a result, I gathered much more data from the Jewish school. Therefore the chapter is organized not as a comparison between the schools but according to the four areas listed above. For each area, I offer several examples that demonstrate strengths of one or more of the religion classes, and then an example or two demonstrating a parallel weakness. Throughout, I look for ways in which the lessons from Saint Paul and Agnon might be applicable to the public schools.

Moral and Existential Questions at Center Stage

Valuing the Big Questions

An impressive feature of the religion classes—and one that stands most starkly in contrast with the other subject areas—is the explicit value the teachers placed on exploration of difficult existential and moral questions. While teachers in the other fields might see such topics as too hot to handle or as tangential distractions from the subject matter at hand, the religion teachers, from both Agnon and Saint Paul, regularly sought to raise these sorts of questions. It might seem obvious that this should be so, that in religion classes, moral questions would be taken seriously. But surely—as many of us might attest based on our Sunday-school days—a course in religion does not necessarily welcome moral questioning; it might simply intend to impart religious moral truths. All the religion teachers at both schools, instead, regularly gave the impression that a meaningful and moral existence required of them as well as of their students an ongoing search, rather than an easy acceptance of given truths.

Rabbi Arnie Katz, for example, stressed to his students the importance of considering existential questions and sometimes even warned that too much emphasis on "school knowledge" can make one forget the important questions. He told a story to get at just this point while introducing some readings of the twentieth-century German-Jewish theologian Franz Rosenzweig to his twelfth-grade Introduction to Jewish Thought class. Rabbi Katz paraphrased what he said were the words of Jacob Neusner, a widely published contemporary scholar of rabbinic texts, talking to a group of young adults who consulted him on their paths of study.

> [Neusner told the young people] when you went to the seminary, you had burning questions about life. You wanted to know, why is there suffering? Why is there evil? What is love? What about relationships? What is the meaning of life? And you went to the seminary, and your teachers said, "Don't worry about these questions, just study."
>
> You study for five years. Then you go to your teachers and ask those same questions, and the teachers say, "You need a Ph.D.— go study some more." And by the time you've studied that much, you've forgotten all of the burning questions.
>
> Neusner [said Katz] told them to do it the other way—begin with the things that compel you. Then you might study, but always in the service of your burning questions.

"Rosenzweig," Katz concluded, "is like this"—he is interested in the big, burning questions about life. With this introduction, Katz had his students turn to Rosenzweig's writings.

It is worth noting that this class had begun with sustained applause for Rabbi Katz; it was his first day back at school after having missed a week for the birth of his first child. The rabbi walked in, grinning broadly, and the students spent the first fifteen minutes of class asking questions about the baby, the birth, and Rabbi Katz's feelings about it all. Katz talked about the wonder he felt at the birth and about what he and his wife were learning from their *doula* (birth and labor coach) about caring for a newborn. Finally, he made the transition quoted above to studying Rosenzweig. In the course of opening his Rosenzweig text, the rabbi found a picture of his new baby lodged in the pages. When the students saw the book open to a picture of the baby, they asked to see it, oohed and ahhed, and embarked on a few more minutes of questions about the birth and the baby.

The talk about the baby—including some "science" questions about how the birth went and totaling perhaps twenty minutes of class—may in some eyes be seen as a departure from the real work of the course. But it seems to me that Rabbi Katz quite intentionally took the time to answer the students' questions. Doing so fit in wonderfully with the point Katz, Neusner, and Rosenzweig were all making: sometimes the emotions and wonders of daily life— around such marvels as new babies—are more important than any planned course of study. Or one might say that there's some synergy between curriculum and life; if they are not one and the same, at least discussion of one enriches the other.

It may also be noted that a central part of Rabbi Katz's strategy of moral education here involved telling stories—first about his baby, then about Neusner. In my analysis of classroom events I have focused on *discussion* of moral issues, but productive discussions are often initiated, punctuated with, or summarized by a powerful narrative. For me, though, the value of a particular episode of storytelling in school must be sought in the discussion, analysis, and future exploration it engenders. It is because his stories generate questions and discussion that Katz's pedagogy here seems compelling.

Consideration of key existential concerns was also spurred among the seniors at Agnon in their study of Martin Buber's work *I and Thou*.[4] Students in both Rabbi Katz's and Rabbi Singer's class seemed to take a great interest in Buber's formulation of "I–Thou" relationships (in which there is a full connection and recognition of the other's holiness) versus "I–It" relationships (in which the other is seen primarily as an instrument). Phil, a student, told me that the conversation about Buber's theory had helped give him tools to consider when an interpersonal relationship might be purely instrumental, or, as he puts it, "using": "I think it was interesting when we first started talking about Buber and I–It stuff in Rabbi Singer's class. We…were going into like the specific instances of it. It became really interesting, actually…. There were examples like relationships: when you ask someone to get you a Coke, or something like that. Is that an 'I–You' or just an 'I–It'?…Talking about relationships, and how, in relationships, when that relationship becomes an 'I–It' as opposed to an 'I–You' with a mutual perspective, and it becomes using."

The power of the concept for the students was brought home to me in a brief but intense conversation that I heard just before class during the time the students were studying Buber. Some students in the class had heard through the grapevine that Rabbi Singer—for whom the students clearly had much affection—had been upset about their having taken a "senior skip day" (a collective decision to absent themselves from school) without consulting the teachers. I saw students cluster around Rabbi Singer anxiously, clearly wanting to connect with him personally and to apologize. He must have found gratifying the terminology of their appeal, an active application of Buber's concepts: "We feel very close to you; we didn't mean to upset you. Did it make you feel like an 'It'?" The students had started to view their own experiences and actions in light of Buber's theory; it seems to have given them new ways of conceptualizing their own emotional and spiritual lives.

Although only the seniors at Agnon are asked to read Rosenzweig and Buber, the idea that moral and spiritual pursuits are of utmost importance is regular fare for the younger students as well. In just one example of many, Rabbi Singer opened his ninth-grade Foundations of Jewish Law class one early May afternoon with the following quotation from Pinchas Peli, a contemporary theologian, on the board: "The real purpose of life is not to conquer nature but to conquer the self; not to fashion a city out of a forest, but to fashion a soul out of a human being; not to build bridges, but to build human kindness; not to learn to fly like a bird or to swim like a fish but to walk on the earth like a human being; not to erect skyscrapers, but to establish mercy and justice."

The passage from Peli strikes me as fairly closed; it does not particularly invite debate. But the discussion of the passage in class was not nearly so closed. The rabbi had the class copy the quotation into their notebooks—and then he asked them what they thought of it: what is the "real purpose of life"? The students engaged in a brief but lively discussion, some arguing that Peli is right, others claiming that Peli's sentiment, as they read it, is out of touch with the needs of humanity and the way the world works. They claimed that it is both a necessary and even a desirable part of being human to do things like erecting skyscrapers, and that erecting skyscrapers and establishing justice do not necessarily contradict each other. The class soon turned to another matter. But the example underscores the point, made frequently in these classes, that it is important to deliberate regularly about "the real purpose of life."

Similarly, questions of moral and existential importance dominated the curriculum in the Morality courses at Saint Paul. Mr. Yearly demonstrated particular skill in doing what I had hoped to see Ms. Putnam do in the vignette in Chapter 4 regarding *The Good Earth*. There, I suggested how powerful the lesson might have been had Ms. Putnam been able to share with her students her own struggle to understand the tragic choices faced by some poor Chinese families. In the classes I observed, Mr. Yearly regularly took care to reveal his own grappling with difficult moral questions.

In one such example, Mr. Yearly introduced his eleventh-grade class to what he called, with obvious feeling, "one of my least favorite passages from the New Testament." He read aloud from Jesus' sermon, recounted in Matthew 5:38–44: "You have heard that it was said, 'An eye for an eye and a tooth for a tooth.' But I say to you, Do not resist an evildoer. But if anyone strikes you on the right cheek, turn the other also; and if anyone wants to sue you and take your coat, give your cloak as well; and if anyone forces you to go one mile, go also the second mile. Give to everyone who begs from you, and do not refuse anyone who wants to borrow from you. You have heard that it was said, 'You shall love your neighbor and hate your enemy.' But I say to you, Love your enemies and pray for those who persecute you."[5]

Having discussed with the students the topic of revenge the previous week, Mr. Yearly asked them to interpret the idea of turning the other cheek in this passage. Jeb suggested that Jesus is using hyperbole here, speaking "in an extreme so that people will go part of the way." Danny ventured that Jesus might be using reverse psychology. "If someone wants to attack," reasoned Danny, "and you invite them to, then maybe they will stop." Danny, Jeb, and a couple of other students thus interpreted against the grain of the text, not believing that Jesus really intended that people should submit passively to violence.

Mr. Yearly turned the tide of interpretation slightly by asking for evidence from the stories of Jesus' life to support the idea that Jesus really did intend for people to turn the other cheek.[6] After several students helped him make a case from Jesus' life for a nonviolent response to violence, Mr. Yearly again told them: "I don't like the teaching. I like the idea that I can defend myself and my family, my home." When students jumped in to express *their* dislike of the teaching, arguing that showing such restraint is not in human nature, Mr. Yearly argued in defense of the passage: "You know what the message of the cross is. Physical survival is only a secondary consideration when it comes to your own humanity. If he [Jesus] is a real person, not just a divine being parading as a human, then he shows us we could do it."

Finding powerful meaning in a passage he claims not to like, Mr. Yearly may seem to be contradicting himself. He clearly did work to ensure that several different readings—some positive, some negative—of the passage were put on the table. But as I read it, Mr. Yearly's contradictory statements are not discussion-spurring attempts to play devil's advocate in the manner of Larry Carlson. Rather, he demonstrates a different, rare, and impressive pedagogical strategy: he shares with his students his own ambivalence. He does not like the teaching to turn the other cheek, for he knows the impulse to defend himself; yet he, as the students know, is a practicing Catholic who takes "the message of the cross" quite seriously. As such, he is drawn to the teaching by his faith in Jesus and by the appeal of nonviolence. Mr. Yearly does not have this passage all figured out. Yet he teaches it, sharing his own struggle with its meaning, and thereby inviting his students to grapple with the complexity of moral theory and practice.

Perhaps Matthew would not be the text of choice in American public schools, but one can see how they might address these same important issues of the theory and complexity of nonviolence by beginning, for example, with a discussion of the pacifism of such figures such as Mohandas Gandhi and Martin Luther King, Jr. The issues raised by such religious texts as Buber, Rosenzweig, Peli, and Matthew, if not the texts themselves, belong in everyone's education. Texts that include these subjects—"burning questions about life," the meaning of genuine relationships, love, hate, revenge, non-violence—already are assigned in public schools, of course. The task is to engage in the meaningful conversations the texts were written to inspire, and in which students long to participate.

Big Questions Out of Context

The discussions of Buber, the baby, and turning the other cheek provide excellent examples of the sort of conversation I think belongs in schools. And yet, despite my affinity for big issues and my desire to see more of them integrated into all courses on a regular basis, I must also admit that they are not always interesting or relevant. Quite understandably, not everyone always wants to talk about such enormous concerns as the meaning of "one's own humanity" (in Mr. Yearly's words).

The point is illustrated by the following lesson, which, on the face of it, seems like it could have resulted in a fascinating discussion. Rabbi Sally Ross had been teaching her twelfth-grade class the Genesis text in which it is written that human beings were created in the image of God. She had asked her students to read a few other texts that speak about the essence of being human, including one from the Talmud and one by Nietzsche. On the basis of these readings and their own reflections, the students were to write their answers to the question, "What is the essence of being human if we are made in the image of God?" (a question that remarkably is also at the center of the Matthew text cited above). Rather than delving with enthusiasm into one of the perennial questions of Western theology, the students exhibited classic signs of boredom and lack of interest. After hearing the assignment, Gabe launched what was clearly a complaint: "Do we have to use all of the texts?" When Rabbi Ross replied that they could use the texts they found meaningful, Gabe and several other students continued their assault on the assignment.

Gabe: I mean, what if these texts didn't change your opinion at all?

Ben: What if you don't have much of a view on what's the essence of being human?

Daniella: I don't get the question.

At this point, Rabbi Ross tried to clarify the question and to initiate a discussion about it: "What distinguishes you as a human being? What makes you different from an animal, a table?" Daniella brushed off the idea that there was anything interesting to talk about here, delivering her answer as if the case were closed: "We're just smarter." Meanwhile, a group of boys near me ignored Rabbi Ross altogether, talking about a great musical jam session they had had the previous day. Other students passed notes; several rested their heads on their desks.

In another, similar episode, Rabbi Katz, who so ably led the discussion a day earlier, tried to focus students' attention on how existential needs like the yearning for connection to community and to God might send one to the Torah for insight. As he carried on a discussion on the connections of Torah to real human needs with a few students, several girls busily wrote and exchanged notes in the back of the class; two boys spoke to each other across the room in a language of facial expressions and hand gestures; another girl carefully examined her appointment book. Out of twenty students, it seemed that not more than five or six were engaged in the discussion.

It is clear, in short, that "big questions" about the meaning of life or the essence of humanity do not *automatically* make students perk up their ears and launch into animated conversation. It is my sense, in fact, that these questions make sense and evoke interest only *in context*—in Larry Carlson's class, for example, they came in the context of studying about particular historical periods; in Angela Rivers' class, they came in the context of learning scientific concepts and discoveries; in Mr. Yearly's class, they came in the context of Jesus' provocative sermon and the stories about Jesus' life. Big questions, as much as small, detailed questions—like those on a biology quiz (recall, for example, "What does phagocytosis mean?")—need an intellectual context in order to be meaningful. Just like those small questions, big questions should be addressed when class activities arouse students' curiosity about them. Classes focusing exclusively on moral and existential issues do not always provide that intellectual or personal context. I will say more in the Afterword about practical steps one might take to provide an intellectual context that can motivate both grappling with big questions and digesting small details.

Intellectual Tools, Assignments, and Assessments

The Powerful and Engaging

One of the areas in which the religion courses can speak to public schools is in their example of providing tools that facilitate exploration of moral and existential issues. The Jewish law and Jewish thought classes, for example, provided strategies for ongoing interpretation of sacred texts. It was clear that there was to be no easy literalism with regard to the Bible or the Talmud. Students at Agnon were regularly praised for coming up with interpretations of their own, and much class time was devoted to understanding different interpreters' readings of the same texts. Lesson after lesson stressed that human beings have the authority and the imperative to decide what the sacred texts mean and how they apply to contemporary life. Nowhere in any other context—including history and literature courses, where the necessity of interpretation would seem to be a central tenet of the disciplines—did I see so much emphasis on or practice of interpretation as a key component of expanding knowledge and building meaning.

One of the specific tools used most impressively in the religion classes at Agnon were the concepts of *p'shat* (meaning "literal" or "simple reading") and *d'rash* (meaning "interpretive reading"). Whenever scripture was read in class, there would be an attempt to ferret out, with the help of commentators, a wide variety of possible interpretations of the text; often, these interpretations would be given more weight than the apparent "simple" meaning of the text. Drawing on the root of the word, which means "demand," Rabbi Katz translated *d'rash* for his students as "demanding personal meaning from the text"—and suggested that it was a hugely important part of all reading, especially the reading of sacred texts.

Using techniques of interpretation studied in religion classes, different twelfth graders regularly delivered to the whole school a "Senior D'rash," a brief, homiletic interpretation of the week's Torah portion, during the Thursday morning assembly.[7] At one such assembly, Rabbi Cohen introduced the second of two seniors who were to speak on the section from Genesis 12–17, where God commands Abraham to go to Canaan, and promises, despite Abraham's current childlessness, that his offspring will be as plentiful as the stars. Rabbi Cohen said: "We've been taught that you can turn and turn the Torah and find many things in it. That is what our two senior sermonizers are doing for us here today. Margalit used the events of this week's Torah portion to talk about Abraham as a model of faith; Parvin will now discuss Abraham as a model of doubt."

In spite of their different conclusions, each of the sermons had intellectual integrity. Both Margalit and Parvin had prepared their sermons with the consultation of their Judaism teachers; both used passages from the text to support their interpretations. And despite their differences—one lauding Abraham as an exemplar of faith and obedience, the other as a model of questioning and doubt— both received warm applause from the audience of students and teachers, and both won public words of praise from the principal. Listeners got the message that, however contradictory, both readings contained valid teachings about Abraham and the virtues of both faith and doubt.

The concepts of "literal meaning" and "personal or interpretive meaning" seem to me to have promising applications for the necessarily pluralistic teaching of moral issues in public schools, where "teaching morality" will have to mean creating contexts for thoughtful discussion of morally charged issues rather than marketing any particular set of moral doctrines.[8] They are also wonderful examples of the kinds of conceptual terminology that help students build their capacity to engage in intelligent discourse on moral issues.[9]

Along with providing useful intellectual tools, such as the concepts of *p'shat* and *d'rash*, the Foundations of Jewish Law courses at Agnon were particularly strong in grappling with the philosophical underpinnings and the practical implications of certain moral concepts. Rather than teach "a virtue a week," as some of the current character education curricula recommend, the teachers took the time to help students turn over and over a single idea, with the help of original sources, looking at it from as many angles as possible.[10] One such ongoing discussion in Rabbi Katz's class involved the concept of *tzedakah*, usually translated as "charity" but based on the Hebrew root word for "justice."

I came in on the discussion in early April, when the class was reviewing some of these complexities, in the form of a disagreement in the Talmud and later commentaries about whether or not a community can compel a person to give tzedakah.[11] Analyzing the dispute, students struggled with the idea of whether tzedakah is more for the benefit of the donor or the recipient. In so doing, the students also displayed exemplary discussion skills, tying their own comments to those of the previous speakers.

Avital: One side of the argument is that you should only give tzedakah if it makes you feel good, if it comes from your own free will.

Gabe: You want me to enhance that side of the argument? Giving tzedakah should be about feeling the divine presence. Forcing people to give may lead to animosity.

Ilana: I want to add to that if you force somebody to give, there's also a problem deciding how much is enough.

After Rabbi Katz reviewed this side of the argument, other students articulated the opposing view.

Ivan: The other side is that you are commanded to give tzedakah, and if you don't you will be forced. This is more for the poor person rather than for the giver. It doesn't have to be a spiritual experience for the giver.

Monica: The point is to think about the needy person, not the giver all of the time.

Gabe, troubled by this view, objected, "If you are forced to give, you cannot call it giving."

Using these competing visions of tzedakah as background, the students embarked on planning a tzedakah campaign for the school that, as another student commented, would have "the end result that we get money for the poor, but we should make the atmosphere so that the giver will feel good about it." During the several weeks that the students planned the campaign, they continued to study classical Jewish texts regarding tzedakah, confronting both on paper and in their own project complex questions: To whom is it best to give? Should one care for those in need locally before those in need at a distance? Should one help people to whom one feels most connected, or those who are most in need? Must everyone give money, even those who feel they don't have enough to give? When is one poor enough to receive? When is one too poor to give? What are the mechanics of fund-raising and how can one ensure the trustworthiness of fund-raisers? What "counts" as tzedakah besides giving money? The class even considered such practical questions as whether, if one is going to give away 10 percent of one's income, the percentage should be calculated before or after taxes.

"Charity" and "generosity" are two of those words that usually appear on lists of values that children should be taught as part of the program in a virtues approach to character education. Rarely, though, does one see in such programs attention to the problematics of such desirable traits. Rarely do they get beyond ideas like "it's good to give charity." Here was a unit that focused in a sustained way on the complexities of charitability.

One might wonder why I so value complexity. Maybe some things in life should just be simple. Giving is good—why complicate it? To the extent that a person can just accept and incorporate simple truths into their lives, I am all for it. But for me, at least, while I can happily agree to the generality that giving is good, if I take it seriously as an obligation, knowing when and how to give is genuinely vexing. Should I give money to people on the street? To everyone who asks? How much? Which charities of the endless solicitations I receive in the mail deserve my support? How much do I genuinely need to live on and to save and how much should I give away? The point of recognizing the complexities of any virtue is not to encourage moral relativism, but to make it possible to act thoughtfully in the real world. There was nothing sentimental or abstract about the students' deliberations; they resonated with the complexities of real life. Even better, the students had a vehicle to put their deliberations to the test by designing the schoolwide tzedakah campaign. One can easily imagine parallels to the tzedakah project being enacted to good effect in the public schools as well.

This assignment embodies the major strengths of the religion classes in general: addressing important moral issues, they allowed for a diversity of opinions while providing students with the intellectual tools necessary both to understand those various opinions and to take meaningful real-world action. Certainly similar sorts of ongoing, action-oriented conversations have a place in the public schools. Shulman, in fact, argues that performing community service is a necessary and logical practical application of studying the liberal arts and sciences. He speaks in the context of undergraduate education, but his point is equally relevant in the high school setting: "One of the real deficiencies of the undergraduate liberal arts education has been that it lacks what we in education for the professions call a clinical component. Let me also suggest that public service activity can be thought of as the *missing* clinical component of the liberal arts and sciences.... What is the value of the public service activity? My hypothesis is that the value lies in being a crucible for learning, a test for the learning that has gone on, and a unique setting or opportunity for the moral development of the learner in relation to the academic learning that has preceded it." The best examples of "service learning" currently in place in the public high schools exhibit what we have seen in the religious school tzedakah project—a powerful combination of intellectually demanding deliberation about moral issues accompanied by moral action.[12]

The teachers at Saint Paul similarly designed activities that seemed well calculated to evoke careful thinking about moral and existential issues. A full two weeks of class time in the eleventh-grade Morality classes, for example, were devoted to the presentation of student reports on contemporary social issues, usually controversial in nature. The students were asked to pick a topic they cared about and to research it, using written and also, if possible, human resources. Students picked such topics as the legalization of marijuana, capital punishment, elder abuse, police brutality, date rape, abortion, teenagers and alcohol, and custody battles, among others.

In most cases, the students followed a "pro" and "con" format in their reports, striving to give a balance of arguments regarding their issue before outlining their own opinions. In cases where the issue was not controversial—for example, the problem of elder abuse— the students' reports centered more on informing the class of the existence and extent of the problem. Several students delivered their reports with obvious passion, evoking questions and even lively challenge by other students. The teachers, meanwhile, strove to let the students reason out the various arguments for or against a particular position, usually without betraying their own opinions. Dick, a student, told me that this is one of the characteristics of Ms. Castle that he most appreciated: "She can go through the whole year talking about everything and you'll never know where she stands, so she's not pushing her opinion on you. I like that."

When I asked students at Saint Paul which school assignments they had found most meaningful over the years, more than any other single assignment they recalled their controversial-issue report for Morality class, even when it had been given many months before. I asked Delaine, a twelfth grader, "Is there any particular paper or project or lesson or discussion or anything connected to school that you think you'll keep with you?" She recalled her report from the previous school year: "Yeah. Last year in Morality, we had to do... individual projects—write an essay, do research and all that. There were different topics concerning moral problems or whatever. And I had child molestation. I learned so much from that, and I will always remember it. Like I can still remember things that I wrote down. I will always, you know, love the fact that I had the opportunity to talk about that and share it with others, because there was a [question and answer] part of it too, which got—it was like [we had] the whole class period to talk about this and I just, I remember that as one of the greatest things I had ever done."

Delaine's words—"I will always love the fact that I had the opportunity to talk about that"—highlight how rare it is for students to share intelligent talk in school about issues that really matter to them. And as Delaine's words suggest, conversations such as these go beyond mere talk. Delaine remembers her report as "one of the greatest things" she had "ever *done*"—more than just speaking publicly, she has taken an active role in her own learning and in the learning of the class as a whole. The controversial-issue reports provided Saint Paul students with excellent opportunities to engage in a morally important act—teaching—about moral and existential issues that mattered deeply to them. The combination of the content of the discussions and the role students played as teachers was often powerful indeed. Applications of this sort of assignment in the public schools would not be difficult to design.[13]

The Reductive

Unfortunately, the controversial-issue reports were not *always* interesting. Some of the reports were delivered in nearly unintelligible monotones, lulling classmates into heavy-headed slouches on their desks, and evoking no questions or comments. As I argued regarding episodes in Rabbi Ross's and Rabbi Katz's class, provocative topics alone do not necessarily ensure engagement. In this case, it seems to me that the students needed more support in public speaking. The excitement inherent in even the most controversial of issues can get lost in the rapid reading of a written report or in inaudible mumbles. This finding suggests that any program of moral education must pay considerable attention to instructional issues. No program of moral education can rest on content alone. Given the importance of the subject matter, teaching strategies designed to promote active participation and deliberation—important in all contexts—are crucial here.

Perhaps even more striking than the problems of instructional design were those connected with assessing the students' learning from the controversial-issue unit. The test Ms. Castle gave following the reports, indeed, reveals the ever present danger of reducing important issues to memorizable soundbites: the test required that the students learn one "fact" from each of the reports. After all the reports were finished, Ms. Castle dictated to the students particular "facts" taken from the oral reports to help them prepare for the test. Here is a sampling of the statements that students busily copied into their notebooks:

Pornography in movies: Studies have shown a direct link between rape and pornography.

White supremacy: The ideals of most white supremacist groups are genocidal.

Capital punishment: Capital punishment is a racially, socially, and economically biased practice in the United States.

Teen pregnancy: Most teenage girls who get pregnant end up dropping out of school.

Subliminal advertising: Subliminal advertising is one of the most highly effective forms of advertising.

Gangs: Many teens turn to gangs to feel loved and respected by peers.

Animal rights: Three main issues: (1) factory farming, (2) use in clothing, (3) animal experimentation.

War: According to some, war is a "necessary evil."

Abortion: Since abortion has been legalized, the number of deaths related to abortion has decreased.

Given the power of the original assignment, in which students explored various sides of complex issues that they themselves had chosen to investigate, there was potential for students to come away understanding the value differences that cause intelligent people of good will to differ on many such issues. I was particularly surprised, therefore, that the unit's summative exercise required memorization of these decontextualized statements, which seemed only remotely related to the understandings the students had gained.

The trivialization of the issues involved becomes even more stark in light of the inherent problems of a "true/false" test. Ms. Castle warned the students before the test that some of the questions were tricky, that a statement had to be 100 percent true to be counted as true. Of course, careful readers could be tripped up by such instructions. Take the statement concerning gangs, for example. The student giving the report on gangs did say that most teenagers who join gangs join them "for love and respect from peers." But the statement to be learned for the test said that "*many* teens turn to gangs to feel loved and respected by peers." What "many" means, in this context, is hard to say. If one reasoned that only relatively few teenagers actually do join gangs (for any reason), then the above statement on the test would be false. In a similar kind of problem, the statement on the test regarding abortion refers to a decrease in deaths of pregnant women because of access to safe abortions. If one considers the death of the fetuses as "deaths," the "fact" as stated in the test may indeed be untrue. As one would expect, the post-test class discussion was full of tension over such matters as these—not constructive reconsideration of the substantive issues, but anxious haggling over points regarding the minutia or the semantics of the "facts."

Given the context—which most teachers face in schools as they are currently structured—Ms. Castle's decision to test the students in this way can be understood. She had just spent what must have been dozens of hours supporting students in their research and then reading and grading each individual report (which had a written as well as an oral component). She wanted to hold the students accountable in some way for the information contained in other students' reports. She needed something that would evenly cover all the reports given and that could be graded quickly. Asking the students to respond in essay form to the complex issues involved in the various subjects would have demanded too much extra time from her. But because of this sort of assessment, I fear that students were encouraged to think deeply only about the issue that they themselves had researched—and to think reductively about the rest.

It is imperative, therefore, as part of an advocacy for deep discussion of moral issues in school, that attention be paid to structural features of schools, such as how students are given credit for their effort, their knowledge, and the complexity of their thinking. If we expect students to think deeply about vexing issues, we have to create systems that allow them to be evaluated on their best thinking and also provide teachers time to respond thoughtfully to student work. The Coalition of Essential Schools, making use of such things as portfolios and exhibitions, has done promising work in this arena.[14] Meanwhile, the true/false test and the haggling over points in Ms. Castle's class serve as a reminder of the insidious way the norms of grading discourage thoughtful exploration of complicated issues.

I have discussed above how new terminology like *p'shat* and *d'rash* and "I–Thou" and "I–It" can give students access to flexible and subtle ways of thinking that might otherwise be beyond their reach. Yet clearly a balance must be found between too much and too little terminology, between overwhelming students with so many new words that a lesson becomes memorization alone and neglecting vocabulary that would actually enrich students' imaginative and intellectual capacities. My sense is that in some cases, perhaps again because of the exigencies of grading, the balance in the Morality classes tipped toward the "overwhelming" end of the continuum.

The final exam in Ms. Castle's class was to be based on five chapters from the Morality textbook, "Justice," "Wholeness," "Honesty," "Respect for Creation," and "Peacemaking."[15] To review for the test, which would involve short answers and matching, the students were asked to remember (or learn) definitions for the following: parables, justice, "love's minimum requirement," survival rights, "thrival rights," ecological justice, individual justice, social justice, distributive justice, the common good, wholeness, temperance, freedom, short-term pleasure, long-term pleasure, self-deception, addiction, "the long view," bulimia, anorexia, anabolic steroids, honesty, "the web of deceit," integrity, white lies, Chief Seattle, stewardship, human creation, nonhuman creation, Saint Francis of Assisi, peacemaking, pacifist, just-war theory, "love for the enemy," Martin Luther King, Jr., nonviolent protest, passivity, I–you statements, forgiveness, conscientious objector, selective conscientious objector, communication.[16]

These concepts all seem important. I would have a hard time deciding which ones to eliminate from the list. But like the example in Chapter 4 from a biology class, where students were asked to know the meaning of "estradiol," "testosterone," "vasopressin," and "progesterone" before understanding the duration of fertility during a woman's menstrual cycle, here it seems that students' knowledge of the definitions of the morally related words took on more importance than their ability to think about the issues.

Aside from their content, quizzes and tests frequently seemed to bring out the worst in relations between students and teachers. For example, when giving quizzes, Ms. Castle—I assume with good cause—took all the regular provisions against cheating, separating students sitting close together and asking them to keep their arms over their quiz papers so others would not be able to copy. She frequently repeated admonitions for the students to keep their eyes on their own papers. Toward the end of the quiz, she told students, "We are still taking the quiz; keep your mouth shut until they are all collected."

There is something ironic about it all, taking a quiz on moral concepts—including such things as "honesty" and alternative strategies for resolving conflicts—and being reminded frequently not to cheat. On another occasion, in the course of urging her students to review for their upcoming exam, Ms. Castle told them, "If I see any yearbooks, they're mine, and I won't give them back." Teaching morality as a subject in itself, in other words, does not automatically change the norms or necessities of classroom management behavior, and these often promote distance and antagonism rather than caring between teachers and students.[17]

Part of the work of successfully incorporating the study of moral issues into the curriculum is the work of individual teachers. But the phenomena I have described here underscore the point that a large part of the work, as I have argued, is changing the norms of schooling—rethinking the whole enterprise, from how we design curriculum to how many minutes we allot to a class period to how we assess students' progress.[18]

Who Is Talking?

Room for Students' Selves

One aspect of the religion classes at Saint Paul was quite different from "business as usual" at school: the opportunities provided in class for prayer. Along with its other potential benefits, prayer time served as a vehicle to provide space for students' voices and concerns.[19] Usually, Mr. Yearly or Ms. Castle would begin class by saying, "Let us remember we are in the holy presence of God." Then the teacher would ask the students for any special intentions for the day. On any given day, perhaps four to eight students would volunteer prayers, varying greatly in levels of specificity and gravity, including such things as: "I'd like to pray for a friend who is going through a lot of trouble," "I'd like to pray for my neighbor who has cancer," "I would like to thank God because my dad's brother woke up out of his coma," "I had a fight with a friend and I hope we make up soon," as well as, "Let's pray for the guys on the baseball team, who have a really big game today."

Usually, too, the teacher would offer some kind of intention, and often these intentions had a fairly didactic tone, more or less subtly conveying a value held by the teacher. Following a couple of days when students had given reports in class on child abuse and elder abuse, and on a day when new student officers were announced, Mr. Yearly expressed his prayer: "We offer a special intention today that has to do with a theme that's come up in many of our reports— abuse and violence, the victims, and the perpetrators, who are sometimes in a strange way victims themselves. So let us pray for anyone you know who might be caught up in that kind of cycle. Second, for all of our new student leaders for next year, that they'll lead with commitment and energy, and that you will support them and work with them."

Toward the end of the school year, Ms. Castle took the forum of the intention period to note the special stresses faced by her students: "We need to pray real hard today for students who are worried about their grades, and especially for students with D's and F's, that they may have the energy and the endurance to hang in there, and for all of us...for all who are under a lot of pressure, for students who have a lot riding on their exams."

Following the intentions, which usually took just a couple of minutes, the teacher or a student would lead the class in a recitation of the Lord's Prayer or "Hail Mary." The recitation would be punctuated at the end with a responsive calling.

Teacher: Saint Francis of Assisi

Students: Pray for us.

Teacher: Saint Bernadette of Lourdes

Students: Pray for us.

Teacher: Live Jesus in our hearts—

Students: Forever.

Teacher: Amen.[20]

At this point, the teacher would turn to the lesson plan for the day.

The time allocated to speaking "intentions" seemed quite valuable to me. Hearing heartfelt wishes and fears at the beginning of each class added a kind of grounding in the reality of students' lives that is quite rare in most classrooms. In the context of analyzing one of the discussions in Larry Carlson's War and Peace class in the previous chapter, I noted how remarkable it was to hear students name genuine feelings regarding loved ones—the boy who realized, after a car accident, how much his father meant to him; the girl who wished she had had a chance to say good-bye to a friend who died suddenly. While most classes, across the curriculum, begin with some equivalent of "Please turn to page 214 in your textbook," without reference to the emotional states or preoccupations of the students, here in Morality class, every day, there was a moment to acknowledge that page 214 will be studied in the context of many other concerns—some of which, in fact, are much, much more pressing.

To put it differently, these intentions gave a moment for students to bring their whole selves and consciousnesses into the classroom—the self that was worrying about a cousin, about a test; the self that was excited about a game, or thankful for a loved one's recovery. They also served to alert the teacher to any special circumstances a student might be facing. Teachers of other courses rarely receive such signals, for the whole of the students' selves are rarely allowed, let alone invited, into classrooms or the school more generally.[21] It seems to me that the time set aside for intentions may well have made it possible for students to be more emotionally present for the rest of what transpired in class. It would be worthwhile, thus, to consider how students' "selves" might be welcomed into public school classrooms in a much more secular idiom.

At Agnon, there were also mechanisms in place to help make the classroom hospitable to students' thoughts and feelings. Rabbi Katz, for example, established certain explicit norms of discussion to help ensure that students' voices would be heard. One such practice involved the possibility of making comments "on" and "off the table." A student might choose to say something and put it "on the table"—opening it to question, analysis, and discussion. Alternatively, a student could make a comment that was "off the table"—perhaps relating a personal experience or belief, not a matter of opinion to be questioned or argued with. Although I did not see students in Rabbi Katz's class make comments "off the table" in the time I was there, there were occasions when students checked about a comment's status before launching into a refutation of what another had said. When one thinks of Sandra's mention in Larry Carlson's class of nearly taking her own life, one can see the value of protecting some comments from immediate cross-examination or rebuttal.

Talking about things that matter requires a degree of safety, and the norms built into discussions in the religion classes seemed to work. Students at both Agnon and Saint Paul described to me the sense of openness in the religion classes, and their pleasure at being able to express themselves. Art, a student commenting on Rabbi Katz's class, implies that the norms in the Judaica classes are quite different from those found in most classes: "You can talk about anything with that guy.... When I come out of that class sometimes, you just have got a feeling of like 'nothing could ever top this.' You know, there's—you can say anything. You can talk about anything: Philosophy, this, that. 'I feel this way; I feel that way.'"

Phil, another student, elaborated on the idea that there is plenty of room for student ideas and beliefs in the religion classes—along with a demand for reasoned thinking: "I think in Judaica [classes] there is the idea of catering to those who aren't sure about what their beliefs are—[the teachers] do that well. [You can] even say 'That's a crock!' or whatever. [And then we] talk about it. You discuss why you feel that way, or what your reasons are for that. As long as your opinion was backed up by something. I mean, you have to supply it with some sort of reasoning. As long as you're not rude, I think, you're respectful to the religion, the rabbi, and the rest of the students, you can pretty much say anything, as long as it's well thought out." Students' thoughts, Phil seems to be saying, are part of what goes into constructing knowledge in the religion classes.

Maria, from Ms. Castle's class at Saint Paul, refers to a similar kind of openness to and integration of student views in the course: "I was glad to have Ms. Castle cause she's, she's—I don't know about her views, but she seems pretty open with other people's views. She'll let us have our own thing. She won't, like, press on to us, you know, she won't say 'Well, I don't agree with that.' You know? I mean, because there are certain teachers I know who will say things like that." June, also from Ms. Castle's class, put her sense of the course this way: "[Morality] is a good class because it keeps everyone awake, and everyone going, because everyone participates. And, usually what you say sticks with you during the day. And sometimes you get really good ideas."

I read in these remarks the students' sense that the teachers' openness fosters the safety students need to speak and also leads to considerable intellectual rewards: when you get a chance to speak, as June puts it, "sometimes you get really good ideas." With very little translation, it seems to me, some of these norms for creating safety and valuing student speech could be incorporated into public school classes.

Teacher Sermons

Despite the impressive norms in place at both Saint Paul and Agnon for encouraging students to speak, several of the teachers in the religion classes tended to talk at greater length than seemed to me conducive to facilitating meaningful discussion on the part of the students. The problem of teachers talking more than students seem interested in listening exists, of course, across the curriculum and across schools. But because discussion is such a crucial element of moral deliberation, this flaw seemed even more egregious than it might be in other contexts.

Paradoxically, the temptation for a teacher to talk instead of allowing students to learn through their own talking may be even greater in a religion class. When one is working on important issues, on existential questions about life, the urge to make sure that students "get it right" can sometimes be overwhelming, as some of the teachers confessed to me. Teachers tend to have a more sophisticated vocabulary than their students; they can weave words together with greater flair; they have the authority and may feel a moral imperative to speak; they are not being evaluated for a grade on what they say; and they simply talk louder. Given all these things, there seems to be a strong pull—on the part of both students and teachers—to let teachers do the talking.

One classic demonstration of this tendency occurred one morning in Rabbi Katz's class. The rabbi had set up what he said would be a role play in which one student, Todd, was supposed to play the "seeker" of Buber's "Eternal You" and another student, Phil, was to play the "master," a wise one who can help the seeker find his way, based on what he knows of Buber. The seeker seemed unclear about what to ask and the master uncertain about what guidance to give, so the rabbi kept stepping in, giving lines to the players, saying things like, "Well, the seeker might ask, 'How could I prepare myself to get to the Eternal You?'"

At one point it became so obvious and amusing that the rabbi was going back and forth playing both parts, questioning and answering himself, while both of the students were almost silent, that the rabbi said, "Now what would the master answer? Here, Phil is speaking; I'm just throwing my voice." Rabbi Katz proceeded to "throw his voice," speaking in the manner he thought appropriate to the master role he had originally assigned to Phil, then taking up Todd's voice to ask another question. In this episode, the teacher displays self-awareness and perhaps even some regret at doing most of the talking. Other times, teachers seemed less aware that they were dominating what apparently was meant to be a conversation.

Rabbi Singer, for example, began class one day by saying, "I want to get a sense of where you are as far as understanding where we have gone in our discussion of Buber." But after eliciting no more than a few words from four students, the rabbi launched into a kind of a sermon on how to relate to other people, based on Buber's understanding of the "Eternal You." Here is part of his talk.

Rabbi Singer: It's a great statement of faith when we talk about the Eternal You. The implication is that God is always there. Something that Buber would say is that what gives our life fulfillment is the relationship that we have with others and the relationships that come through how we express our entire being in relating to another person. And vice versa, hopefully that other person is relating to you with their entire being. What Buber's saying by calling it the "Eternal You" and referring to God that way, he's saying—"This is the ultimate." If your hope is that when you relate to another person with your entire being that someone's going to relate to you with their entire being—can you guarantee that?

Several: No.

Rabbi Singer: You can't guarantee that. I have no—I may begin to relate to you that way, but I have no idea if you are going to respond that way. But as far as Buber is concerned, God is the Eternal You. And there is the sense that you can always count on God—

Josh: —to relate to you.

Rabbi Singer: And we can't perceive it, we can't necessarily know it, that we have to take it as a statement of faith that God is constantly there for us as the Eternal You in our relationships. We may not always relate to God with our entire being, although we may want to, the perception is that God is there as a constant, relating to us with God's entire being.... In looking at other people—we see a glimpse of that holiness, a glimpse of the divine of God. Buber's saying that there's no question that people are created in the image of God. We come to know God better, when we encounter another being, when we have glimpsed their holiness.

Holly: Are you saying that about every single person?

Rabbi Singer: It's a given in Judaism that every single one of us was created in God's image. No question that there is something that is holy about every single one of us.... There are times when we have the sense of that holiness and times when we can't see it at all. I've seen it in people when I've seen people do incredible things that I never would have thought that they would do—I can think of people in our school who give of themselves in such an incredible way that I am in awe—when I see that, that's a glimpse of God, and when I see that I feel that I am much closer to knowing the Eternal You. Because I have known you, I am that much closer to knowing the Eternal You, and I am that much closer to understanding what it means to be in relationship with God.

The conversation continued with roughly this same ratio of teacher talk to student talk.

In this same class the following day, when Rabbi Singer asked for an explanation of Buber's distinction between "religion" and "religiosity," Ken volunteered the idea that "religion" had to do with "culture." Rabbi Singer tried to get him to say more: "Okay, how is culture—if you just want to explain a little bit—how is culture a characteristic of religion?" Ken declined the offer to expand on this thought, saying, "I think we have the same ideas, but I think you can articulate it a little better." Surprisingly to me, given his stated desire to hear from the students, Rabbi Singer took Ken's bait—and proceeded to elaborate at length on the meaning and the importance of Buber's distinction between religion and religiosity.

In both cases, I found Rabbi Singer interesting and his message appealing, and I think his students did as well. There is nothing objectionable about a teacher using his powers of articulation to explain difficult concepts or to tell wonderful stories. But there is no reason to assume that an idea powerfully stated will be absorbed by students. There is a reason, on the other hand, that the controversial-issue reports and the discussions in War and Peace, for example, were memorable for so many students: in those instances, the students had a chance to struggle to articulate their own ideas. Here, though, there seemed to be a kind of tacit agreement that the students would be let off the hook in articulating anything complicated.

Believing, as I do, that students need to practice big ideas by trying them out in their own mouths, these discussions seem not to live up to their potential. Furthermore, to the extent that teacher talk on moral issues can easily slip into a kind of sermonizing— think of not only Rabbi Singer but also Ms. Gilman talking about "what history texts of the future should look like"—it would seem especially important that the dominant mode of instruction in classes focused on moral questions *not* be teacher lecture.

If one is looking for models applicable to the public school, especially, the image of a teacher who takes over most of the talk time and advocates particular moral messages, though commonplace, is unappealing. Whether or not Rabbi Singer's teaching works at Agnon, we need a different model of teaching about moral and existential issues for the pluralistic public schools, where teacher-aspreacher seems particularly inappropriate. Again, the instructional practices connected to moral education would seem to be almost as important as the content. I will suggest some useful instructional strategies for these kinds of contexts in the Afterword.

Modeling Morality

Grace and a True Heart

I found that the teachers in the religion courses took very seriously their role as models of moral behavior for their students. Their care in this regard expressed itself mostly in subtle ways, hard to capture in print: an avoidance of sarcasm, a slowness to anger, a quickness to appreciate a student comment or deed. I cannot argue that the teachers of religion classes attended to these things more than teachers of other subjects—indeed, serving as a role model was a concern of all the teachers I interviewed. But because of the subject matter in the religion courses, any mismatch between virtues discussed and the teacher's example would seem particularly grating. For the most part, the teachers impressed me (and their students) with a seemingly endless supply of graciousness and good humor. I shall illustrate with just one brief example from class and a student testimonial.

Mr. Yearly showed his students a videotape called *The Heart Has Its Reasons*, about L'Arche, a remarkable home in France for the severely disabled. Introducing the film, Mr. Yearly said that it was "about handicapped children whose families have abandoned them in an institution." Jill raised her hand to correct Mr. Yearly: "Sometimes, when handicapped peoples' parents put them into an institution, it's not that they don't want them, it's that they couldn't take care of them properly—my cousins go to visit my cousin all of the time; it's a really nice facility, it's not that they don't love him."

Jill no doubt raised this point knowing from experience that it would be accepted warmly, and Mr. Yearly responded with characteristic gracious acceptance of the correction and validation of Jill's point: "Thanks for balancing my statement. This video doesn't emphasize that point, so it's especially important that Jill did." Quick to acknowledge the validity of Jill's comment, Mr. Yearly sends the message that students' comments matter, that they are an integral part of the learning in the course.

Most of the other teachers of the religion classes regularly demonstrated similar open, nondefensive stances toward students. Rabbi Singer, exemplary in this regard, won these high, unsolicited praises from Elisheva: "I love Rabbi Singer. He is the greatest man in the world. I've been here for three years and all three years all I could do was dream about having him. Now that I have him, I feel sorry for everyone who does not get to have him.... Everyone respects him. Students who have no respect, respect him. I think— he's just so nice and true-hearted—like he's honest, and everything."

In the world of school, where students often feel distant from and ambivalent about their teachers, the comment that one is "true-hearted" is especially powerful. My sense is that talking regularly about things that matter to both students and teacher—talking about moral and existential issues—helps give students the sense that they actually know the heart of their teacher.

Perceived Hypocrisy

Although the teachers of the religion classes generally won praise from students for their openness and decency, having required courses dedicated to teaching morality seemed to encourage students to cast a particularly critical eye—quite legitimately—on the moral standards of the school as a whole. At both Agnon and Saint Paul (and never at Frontier), I heard repeated complaints on the part of students that the schools' administrators were in some way hypocritical: they did not "walk their talk" with regard to moral teachings. Without regard to the fairness or accuracy of the student accusations of hypocrisy on the part of the administration, their prevalence does suggest the possibility that taking on the business of moral education opens a school to special scrutiny. If student expectations for moral behavior on the part of adults is particularly high in the religious schools, their disappointment when those expectations are not fulfilled also seemed particularly sharp.

During the time I was at Saint Paul, there was a fire down the block from the school that destroyed several homes of low-income people; the inhabitants were rendered homeless in a matter of minutes. Although school administrators asked students, via the public address system, to bring blankets and toiletries to school to donate to the neighbors who had lost their homes, the school did not offer any of its facilities to the newly homeless. Marcia expressed what several other students said to me that week:

> Brother Nicholas came on to the p.a. and said we should pray for people who lost their homes in the fire. But the school did not do anything, and they refused to open the gymnasium doors the night of the fire for them, for those people. I think that's part of one of the things that bother me about this school is that they preach, "Be nice" and everything, but then they don't take that step. It just shocked me yesterday, when I heard them wanting us to pray for the people. I think it's a pattern. I think this school does a lot of stuff, organized in a real nice way, just certain activities, but that's it. In my experience, it seems that that's the Catholic way. You preach being, loving your neighbor, but you never really do.

It seemed to Marcia that the school administration exhorted the students to do good deeds, but did not put the resources or energy of the school as an institution into helping people in need. Marcia's sense of disappointment and disillusionment was palpable.

Students at Saint Paul also suggested that students of color were given a harder time by the administration when they got in trouble than white students. May told me, "Two people I knew were going to be kicked out of the school. And, one person, he just was not in dress code all the time. He didn't do his work. The other person, she was going to be kicked out because of drug possession—selling and I think usage also. And they just kicked out the guy immediately. And he was, he was Latino. And, and the girl, they let her stay on until the end of the year, and she was white. And like, I seem to notice there's a pattern of things."

Similarly, several students at Agnon assured me that "money talks" at the school, citing incidents in which students who were to have been expelled were allowed back into the school after their parents made contributions to the school. And students at Agnon expressed disgust over small hypocrisies they saw in their principal, Dr. Robinson. Moussah and Jack's remarks were typical.

Moussah: He always tells us never to make a left turn [out of the parking lot]. And every day I see him make a left turn on that street.

Jack: And there's a double yellow line....

Moussah: I think he's a phony.

Jack: I think he's a hypocrite....

Moussah: I have no respect for him when I see him. I don't take him seriously at all. I mean, if he said something to me like "You know, if you do this again, you're going to be expelled." You laugh. But he'd never say that to me. But if—

Jack: You practice what you preach. And Dr. Robinson is always telling us, "You got to do this, you can't do this." Then we see him doing it. And if he's doing something hypocritical, we're going to think he's full of shit. And we're not going to believe him, not do what he says when it's right.

Moussah: Kind of like crying wolf.

Again, without my speculating on the validity of such remarks, the extra moral scrutiny students bring to bear on those who hold themselves up as moral role models is as it should be; it can be taken as a sign that the students take their moral lessons seriously.[22] The claims of hypocrisy on the part of the students can even be seen as a tribute to the standards set by the religious schools. But this natural reaction on the part of students must be taken into account when planning a program of moral education for a school. The heightened moral scrutiny faced by a school with a moral mission suggests the importance of adopting "moral education" not just as the purview of a few courses but as a schoolwide, ongoing effort to build a moral culture.

What Public Schools Can Do

I studied the religion classes at Agnon and Saint Paul hoping that I might glean insights from them for public schools. I expected that thoughtful and experienced teachers of a curriculum about morality—working inside an institution with explicitly stated moral aims and without fear of violating the separation of church and state—would have wrestled with the difficulties inherent in teaching the subject and thereby would have gained wisdom useful for other teachers wishing to incorporate moral issues into their curriculum. I wanted to learn from these teachers how to address diversity of opinions and backgrounds in the context of discussions of moral issues; I wanted to learn from them how they advocated certain moral positions without "moralizing" in the negative sense; and I wanted to witness what the teachers did to try to bridge for the students the gap between moral talk and moral action.

The teachers and courses I observed displayed some great strengths: they provided structures for including students' voices, welcomed students' "private selves" into the classroom, fostered openness to multiple interpretations and points of view, and created engaging assignments that sometimes even linked moral deliberation to moral action. These features deserve attention from anyone seeking to incorporate moral education into a school program. The norms of discussion cited from Rabbi Katz's class, in which students could choose to put comments "on" or "off the table" and where they used such phrases as "I want to enhance that side of the argument" to connect their comments to one another, were particularly striking. Perhaps most memorable was Delaine's comment on her controversial-issue report in Ms. Castle's Morality class: "I learned so much from that, and I will always remember it." In interviews with more than sixty students, I never heard a similarly enthusiastic comment about an assignment from a U.S. history, English, or biology course (except War and Peace).

Despite these strengths, I must sound a cautionary note about trying to adopt these religion courses as a model for morality courses in the public school. I suggested in Chapters 4 and 5 that facts and experiences derive meaning from the shape they take within a moral or existential frame. It seems to me that the reverse is true as well: moral or existential questions derive meaning from a particular context of facts and experiences. The religious schools differ from the public schools in having the history of thought and practice of a particular religious group in which to frame their investigations of moral and existential questions. One grapples with what it means to be a good human being and with the meaning of life, in a Jewish or Catholic school, within the context of a particular set of practices—perhaps engaged in at home as well as at school—and a particular set of texts all focused on those questions. Even then, the context is not always strong enough to bring life to such discussions.

In add-on courses on morality in public schools, on the other hand, where using the Talmud or the Gospels, for example, to frame a course would probably be untenable, the framework for moral and existential questions is far too likely to be a decontextualized list of "big questions" or "important values." We see this, indeed, in moral education curricula that are already being adopted around the country. Kilpatrick describes such a curriculum being implemented in a school district in Oregon.

> Teachers there have developed a four-year cycle designed to emphasize a particular set of character traits each year. Year one concentrates on patriotism, integrity and honesty, and courtesy; year two focuses on respect for authority, respect for others, for property, and for environment, and self-esteem; year three, on compassion, self-discipline and responsibility, work ethic, and appreciation for education; year four, on patience, courage, and cooperation. After the first four years of school, the cycle begins again with the difference that the students are now expected to understand these traits on a deeper level. The curriculum includes definitions, the study of people from the past and the present who have demonstrated a particular virtue, concrete ways of putting the virtue into practice, and activities such as poster, essay, or photo contests. Here are examples of definitions:
> Patience is a calm endurance of a trying or difficult situation.
> Patience reflects a proper appreciation and understanding of other people's beliefs, perceptions or conditions.
> Patience helps one to wait for certain responsibilities, privileges or events until a future maturity or a scheduled time.
> Patience is waiting one's turn....
> After learning these definitions, students are encouraged to discuss the concepts.[23]

Kilpatrick speaks of this program approvingly, but there is very little reason to expect that students would be any more interested in or affected by such decontextualized moral concepts than they are by knowledge-out-of-context in any of the other subject areas.[24] This chapter, moreover, has provided glimpses of how such overemphasis on moral terminology and "facts" can trivialize the subject matter.

There is no inherent reason, of course, that morality courses in public schools would *have* to emphasize memorization of terms or otherwise trivialize the subject matter. One can imagine inspired, thought-provoking courses in morality in the public schools. Certainly they exist.[25] As a matter of policy, however, there is no reason to think that public schools—which have not yet addressed problems across the curriculum such as too much teacher talk, the endless rush to cover material, and the overemphasis on facts—would suddenly be able to institute courses in morality that would avoid these pitfalls. And as I have suggested, morality classes poorly taught are even more disturbing and undesirable than other subject areas poorly taught.

Rather than squeezing a potentially uninspiring new course into an already tight schedule, it seems to me that the challenge is to embrace these issues and questions in their natural contexts in the core subject areas.[26] As I argued in Chapters 4 and 5, the various academic disciplines have abundant potential to provide context-rich and content-rich opportunities for examination of a wide variety of moral and existential issues. Big questions like "what is the meaning of human life?" as well as consideration of such virtues as honesty and charity—which we saw investigated in the religious schools in religion classes—have a natural place in public school studies of science, literature, and social studies. Integrating big questions into current fact-rich curricula would likely have the simultaneous effect of breathing life into the questions themselves and into the disciplines in which they are embedded. The theoretical and practical challenge—not sufficiently solved by the religion classes in the religious schools—is to meld moral and existential inquiry with the other realms of human inquiry and knowledge.

Taking on this challenge in public schools will require much courage and hard work. It will require redefinition of the teacher's role, re-creation of the curriculum, redesign of assessment tools, and, for teachers, ongoing development of specific skills in discussion leading and the nurturing of habits of inquiry. This list is daunting, and might be dismissed as simply too much. The good news is that this list of reforms is precisely the list of reforms that are the target of all thoughtful "comprehensive school reform designs," as they are currently called; it is precisely the list that demands attention even when we think in much narrower terms about improving "student achievement." How much more exciting to take on these changes when they also hold the promise of helping schools become places of meaning.

A very difficult obstacle to the work is finding a way to incorporate serious exploration of moral and existential issues in the context of what Gerald Graff and others have called the "culture wars."[27] In communities of people with diverse political, religious, and moral orientations, how shall teachers and schools develop a program that will not erupt into endless conflict and strife? As the question is often put in short, "Whose values should be taught?" The next chapter addresses this question.

Whose Values Will Get Taught?

The Challenge of Pluralism

W HEN I MENTION IN ANY CONTEXT THAT I AM WRITING about how public schools might thoughtfully engage in moral education, the following question almost invariably arises: "If public schools engage in moral education, whose values will they teach?" In a society as diverse as ours, the question is both inevitable and confoundingly difficult. In this chapter, I briefly examine four existing answers to this challenge: (1) the status quo, (2) "universal values," (3) "values clarification," and (4) "pedagogical neutrality." I then provide a fifth answer, "schoolwide inquiry," that, though extremely demanding, holds more promise than the other approaches.

Answer #1: Avoid Teaching Anyone's Values

One way of answering the question of whose values to teach is to try to avoid discussing moral and existential issues altogether. This approach is most similar to the status quo in schools today. It is not that moral and existential issues never arise—they arise unavoidably. It is that when they do arise, the questions are most often closed down in one of the several ways documented in Chapter 4: the teacher rushes on to another topic, the teacher answers the question definitively herself, the teacher refers the question to an outside expert, or the teacher focuses on the technical and informational rather than the moral aspects of the topic.

In a purely theoretical universe, this avoidance approach—a more intentional version of current practice—might have some merit. It is tempting to think that we could distinguish between the intellectual, the moral, and the existential, and could allocate development of each realm to separate educational spheres. One can understand the sentiment behind Robert Maynard Hutchins' declaration that schools should leave the business of moral and spiritual education to families and churches, lest the schools fail at the role that is properly theirs, the development of the intellect.

Parents from either the left or the right may be concerned about values being introduced from an opposing political viewpoint. As Nel Noddings writes, when the idea of teaching values is introduced, "each faction in the community fears that the values of some other group will dominate."[1] I understand these fears. I shudder to think of the remarks relating to gender roles, religion, sexuality, and war, to name a few, that children hear from teachers speaking in all good conscience. Given the remarks my imagination and my memory can conjure up, part of me prefers that these and other topics about which any particular teacher and I might disagree would be actively avoided in school. But this silencing of moral issues is unfeasible. There is simply no way to divorce the moral from the intellectual content of school subjects without radically impoverishing those subjects.

The point deserves elaboration. The moral and the intellectual are inescapably intertwined. Understanding this, various religious groups have worked hard over the years to ban from schools books that they feel contain objectionable values. In addition to protesting science textbooks for their treatment of evolution and history books for including material seen as "anti-religious, anti-creationist, anti-authoritarian, and anti-family," various groups have objected to a wide variety of fictional and dramatic literature as well. Included among the scores of books targeted for removal from schools are *Oedipus Rex, The Canterbury Tales, Macbeth, Twelfth Night, King Lear, Hamlet, Huckleberry Finn, The Prince and the Pauper, Great Expectations, The Red Badge of Courage, Wuthering Heights, The Mayor of Casterbridge, Of Mice and Men, The Grapes of Wrath, The Great Gatsby, The Old Man and the Sea, The Glass Menagerie, As I Lay Dying, Death of a Salesman,* and *The Crucible.*[2] Although I disagree with attempts to ban books, these advocates have an important insight: one cannot teach or learn any of these great works in any depth without confronting controversial moral issues.

Shall we just keep banning until everything objectionable is gone? Clearly, if we did, we would rob the shelves of every text upon which one might build a rich intellectual life. Shall we keep the books but ignore their moral aspects? There is simply no way to eradicate moral content while reading well. I managed to "teach" *Macbeth* without fostering any deep thought about the "Tomorrow and tomorrow" speech, but this cannot be what we hope for in school. As David Purpel argues: "We cannot in good educational conscience avoid the serious and volatile disputes on religious and moral matters because they are controversial, complex, and outrageously perplexing. Quite the contrary: *because* they are so important and *since* they beg for awareness, understanding, clarification, and insight, they are central to significant educational inquiry."[3]

As calming as it would be for all of us, on the left and the right, if we could somehow ensure that objectionable moral material would be sifted out of school—and as much as some public schools and public school teachers may currently be striving to enforce this separation—it is neither possible nor ultimately desirable. We need a different answer to the question of whose values should be taught.

Answer #2: Teach Values Held by All

Some advocates of moral education answer the question of whose values should be taught by saying simply, "we should teach values we can all agree on." As I mentioned in Chapter 2, advocates of the virtues approach to character education argue that basic morality does not engender controversy among people of good will. While there are certainly disputes regarding morality at fairly abstract or advanced levels, the theory argues that the basics are indisputable. These character educators draw on the Aristotelian idea that moral education requires first teaching students how to behave, then getting them to understand the right reasons for good behavior. Only after students have achieved both these steps should they explore *why* the right reasons are correct. Habitual good behavior—the precepts of which are universal—must precede moral inquiry.[4]

Advocates of this approach, like William Bennett, posit that children and teenagers should learn such common values as "honesty, fairness, self-discipline, fidelity to task, friends, and family, personal responsibility, love of country, and belief in the principles of liberty, equality, and the freedom to practice one's faith." Controversial issues can wait for later.

> We need not get into issues like nuclear war, abortion, creationism, or euthanasia. This may come as a disappointment to some people, but the fact is that the formation of character in young people is educationally a task different from, and prior to, the discussion of the great, difficult controversies of the day. First things first. We should teach values the same way we teach other things: one step at a time. We should not use the fact that there are many difficult and controversial moral questions as an argument against basic instruction in the subject. After all, we do not argue against teaching physics because laser physics is difficult, against teaching biology or chemistry because gene splicing and cloning are complex and controversial.... Every field has its complexities and its controversies. And every field has its basics, its fundamentals.

Bennett does not make clear at what age or what phase of development he thinks students *are* ready to face the "complexities and controversies" of morality, but he seems to include both elementary- and secondary-school children when he advocates sticking to the "fundamentals."[5]

Other theorists, including Lickona, admit the possibility of studying controversial issues like abortion with older students in well-developed programs of moral education. But, Lickona cautions,

> I *don't* recommend that schools plunge into controversial issues when they're trying to get a values education program off the ground. Given our highly pluralistic, contentious society, people are already prone to expect conflict and division when you suggest teaching values in the schools. Fortunately, as we've seen, there are many noncontroversial values (e.g., respect, responsibility, honesty) that schools can and do teach in

noncontroversial ways (modeling, community-building, cooperative learning, and so on).

These commonly accepted ways of teaching commonly accepted values must be kept in the forefront of any values education effort. They represent the common ethical ground that is foundational for both moral education and the building of a moral society.[6]

Bennett and Lickona, in short, share the assumption that it is possible for programs of moral education to avoid engaging in controversy.

The universal values approach has considerable appeal. Given the number of divisive issues in our local and national politics, it is comforting to think that Americans share at least some common ground. And it is true, on the face of it, that hardly anyone would care to launch an argument against honesty, fairness, fidelity, and the like. What the approach fails to acknowledge, though, is that very basic values like honesty and fairness, not to mention ones like love of country and self-discipline, become complicated when they are put to the test. How often in human history, for example, have several of these innocuous-sounding values been embraced for evil ends? During World War II, honest, country-loving Germans told the Gestapo where to find Jews in hiding; currently, in our own country, the values of "fidelity to friends" and "self-discipline" stand at the core of cults, violent gangs, and militia groups. The advocates of universal values do not say nearly enough about the dark side of the values they espouse.

Furthermore, one need not know much about history or current events to discover that the values championed on the above list are more complicated than they seem. Take fairness: more than a few seven-year-olds, upon seeing homeless people in the street, or experiencing homelessness themselves, have turned to their parents or teachers and asked, "How come some people have such big houses and some people don't have any?" Children wonder, even without all the vocabulary, about the fairness of our system of distribution of wealth. How shall we answer them? Is the answer that our economic system is "fair"—a value we supposedly all believe in—and that those who deserve houses get them? If we answer in this way, then what do we do with another value we are told to hold dear, the principle of equality? What does the principle of equality mean in a social system that gives rise to such vast differences in wealth? If the answer is that our economic system is not fair, then should that conclusion have any effect on the virtue of love of country? What does "love of country" mean, anyway? Are we to love our country, right or wrong?[7]

Advocates of the virtues approach would likely argue that it is typical of their critics to muddy the waters unnecessarily by raising such questions. In most cases, the demands of honesty, equality, and the other virtues they name are quite straightforward. In an age when these simple virtues seem to be regularly ignored, certainly we can all agree that they should be promoted in schools.

To this extent, I concur with the virtues approach: in circumstances in which everyone agrees about what constitutes virtue or good behavior, we (by definition) have no disagreement. As I stated earlier, there are rules of conduct that help meet all our needs for safety, order, even kindness, and we can easily make a list of examples.

- Don't throw trash on the ground
- Don't make fun of others
- Do help little children and old people cross the street
- Do share your lunch with someone who doesn't have any
- Resolve conflicts using words, not fists

These "norms of behavior" or "rules for living together peacefully" evoke general agreement. It is completely appropriate to help students of all ages learn to participate in creating a safe, orderly, kind world by following these norms. In these cases, no one would raise the concern this chapter seeks to address, the question of whose values should be taught. If a value is truly universal and noncontroversial, it will, of course, rule the day.

The main problem is that the virtues approach does not help us when there is controversy; it simply denies that important differences regarding basic values exist. Here we can make a second list, this one of moral questions that are both controversial and complex, which is to say that answering them well requires information gathering and rigorous analysis.

- How should society distribute its wealth?
- What, if anything, constitutes a just war?
- Are there scientific discoveries that should not be pursued?
- Is affirmative action a sensible way to address inequities?
- Which of our society's laws or norms contradict its espoused values?

Furthermore, the virtues approach has nothing to say about the existential questions that are so salient to adolescents, questions about life and meaning. Such questions might include:

- What gives rise to cruelty among human beings?
- What constitutes a good life?
- What does it mean to be a good human being?
- Who, if anyone, is an outsider in American society?
- How do the experiences of an outsider differ from those of an insider?

I agree with the virtues approach that rules of conduct need to be agreed upon in any community, including a classroom community, and upheld. But an adequate program of moral education must include work in the other two categories, in areas where there is not consensus and where relying on a list of virtues will not help.

Another serious critique of the "universal values" approach is that, relying on a list of virtues, it leaves unexplored the ways in which schooling may reinforce the *vices* that virtues educators would like to eradicate. As John Goodlad observes: "It is difficult to be sanguine about the moral and ethical learnings accompanying many of the experiences of schooling. My perception is that the emphasis on individual performance and achievement would be more conducive to cheating than to the development of moral integrity."[8]

Rather than being the stuff of advanced courses, moral complexity permeates the day-to-day world of children and teenagers. And though classrooms tend to be removed from students' worlds of meaning, classrooms, too, abound with moral complexity. Getting around the problem of whose values to teach by teaching "universal fundamental values" just will not work. Children—even young children—recognize that there are value differences; they see and live the complexity in the world around them. They deserve something more than a list of terms to hold dear. They deserve to be engaged in thoughtful and honest discussions of the world, discussions that do not presume that we all agree.

Answer #3:
Don't Teach Values—Encourage All Points of View

If teaching a list of commonly held values does not solve the "whose values" question, another tempting option is to have the teacher try to avoid promoting any particular values. The most prominent strategy along these lines is the "values clarification" approach. As I explained at greater length in Chapter 2, according to this approach the teacher must avoid declaring superior or even comparing one set of values to another. Rather, the students are urged to arrive at their own, freely formed opinions. The act of stating one's values, rather than the content of belief, becomes primary.

Although the approach is attractive for its openness to a range of opinions and the value it places on students' voices, its drawbacks are overwhelming. In its effort to acknowledge the diversity of views, it provides no criteria to help students distinguish better from worse moral decisions. Bent on ensuring that everyone can arrive without pressure at his or her own viewpoint, the approach provides neither theoretical basis nor practical strategies for conducting thoughtful discussions among those holding various stances. Like the "unmoderated talk show" discussed in Chapter 4, the goal is to get everyone to express an opinion, not to grow toward a just, compassionate, or well-reasoned one. But for discussions of moral issues to be appropriate for our schools, they must help students do more than just express their opinions.

Answer #4: Teach Everyone's Values

Much more sophisticated and promising, in my view, than any of the approaches discussed above is what I shall call the "pedagogical neutrality" approach, following Noddings. To the question of whose values should be taught, this approach answers, "everyone's." Noddings explains the idea:

In the discussion of controversial moral issues it is the job of teachers to be pedagogically neutral; that is, teachers have an obligation to present all significant sides of an issue in their full passion and best reasoning. This is not to say that teachers should not disclose their own beliefs and commitments (although sometimes they should not), but that they should always help students to see why an issue *is* controversial. If it were settled, if the teacher's belief were necessarily right, there would be no controversy. Clearly, it can be very hard for teachers with strong religious commitments to maintain pedagogical neutrality, but they must be helped to understand that pedagogical neutrality is not the same as ethical neutrality. I may be completely convinced that abortion is usually morally acceptable and often morally obligatory and yet encourage a dialogue that brings forth the strong points in opposing positions and exposes the weaknesses in my own. In doing so, I make a special moral affirmation as a teacher: Students must be allowed, even encouraged, to ask how, why, and on what grounds.[9]

Strengths of the Pedagogical Neutrality Approach

Pedagogical neutrality, like values clarification, may seem to tend toward relativism—everyone's and anyone's views merit a hearing, at least if they are considered "significant." As Noddings argues here, pedagogical neutrality requires that opposing views be treated respectfully and in their best logic. However, it does not promote the idea, as values clarification tends to, that one view is as good as another. In its advocacy for critical inquiry into a wide range of views, pedagogical neutrality goes far beyond values clarification in affirming that all positions are *not* equal. Some opinions stand on more solid intellectual ground than others, and rationality is to be highly prized in arriving at moral positions. Neither does pedagogical neutrality require that the teacher abdicate or refrain from stating his or her own moral positions. One can certainly imagine a teacher who, with her students' knowledge, participated in some sort of political rally—supporting or opposing the death penalty, for example—and yet still took care to encourage the sort of balanced dialogue that Noddings describes. There is no inherent contradiction in a teacher's holding a strong belief and yet promoting honest and thorough exploration of the strengths of opposing positions.

At the same time, the notion of pedagogical neutrality recognizes that, along with reason, what Noddings calls "passion" lies at the core of many moral positions. One of the important potential consequences of discussions of moral issues conducted according to pedagogical neutrality, indeed, is that they would allow participants to uncover and examine the emotions and commitments that shape their fundamental assumptions and values.

This kind of pedagogical approach is ably demonstrated in the war-crime discussion in Larry Carlson's class (Chapter 5). Without betraying his own opinion, Carlson sends the message that it is important for citizens of a country that makes war to come to a thoughtful position on the legitimacy of various acts of war; that intelligent people may differ on this issue; that it is incumbent upon one to rally evidence to support one's view; and that some positions are more well reasoned, more in line with one's values, and will provide a better basis for future action than others. Such a discussion seems to me to be inarguably educative and fully deserving of a place in public schools.

To me, then, pedagogical neutrality is a satisfying approach for addressing controversial issues in public schools. Though tremendously demanding (and more must be said regarding how teachers could adequately prepare themselves to conduct such discussions), it provides a solid vision of how to cope with the problem of whose values to teach when controversial issues arise. It is tempting to think that the "whose values" problem would disappear if teachers adopted the principle of pedagogical neutrality.

But there is a catch. The theory makes sense when discussing things like evolution, abortion, and gun control. Not all morally laden topics that arise in school, however, arise in the context of a recognizably controversial issue. Much more often than teachers arbitrate discussions of controversial moral issues, they make other decisions that have an enormous impact on how moral issues are explored in the classroom. Outside of discussing controversial issues, pedagogical neutrality fails to provide a framework for action.

The following sections spell out two key areas of teacher decision making for which we need a more encompassing theory: deciding on curricular materials and deciding when to engage in or refrain from moral guidance through exhortation and admonition.[10] These are areas that pedagogical neutrality does not address satisfactorily. Expanding on this approach, however, in the way that I call "a schoolwide inquiry into values," does provide an answer to the "whose values" question that includes these aspects of the moral work of teachers.

Shortcomings of Pedagogical Neutrality

TEACHERS OMIT, INCLUDE, AND SHAPE CURRICULAR MATERIALS. Pedagogical neutrality requires balance. And so while discussing *The Grapes of Wrath*, a teacher might, following the precepts of pedagogical neutrality, elicit and present a balanced set of opinions regarding, for example, the economic structure that supports sharecropping.[11] The crucial decision to assign *The Grapes of Wrath* and to leave another novel out of the curriculum, however, has already been made. As many theorists have pointed out, and as the attempts at book banning mentioned above underscore, the inclusion or exclusion of curricular materials is replete with moral implications.[12]

Although one might choose texts according to their similar or contrasting themes, to present a variety of views, one cannot simply line up novels or history or biology units, one against another like opposing sides in a controversy, to create balance. What text would one choose to "balance" Steinbeck's novel? As the next example will attest, literary works might be paired in ways that would highlight contrasting perspectives on society, but such works would not speak to one another as directly as two sides of the abortion or gun-control issue do. Choices of texts and curricular units, thus, are not neutral; they reflect the values of the teachers and the school-district personnel who design the curriculum, as well as those of textbook authors and state school boards that adopt the books.[13]

Another example makes the point in a somewhat different way. When I taught English to eleventh graders, I was required to teach both Fitzgerald's *The Great Gatsby* and Ellison's *Black Boy*. As is common, I integrated the study of *Gatsby* into a broader unit on life in America during the 1920s. As part of the unit, I had each of my students choose a topic to research from a list that included the following: Henry Ford and the assembly line, jazz, flappers, the women's vote, Charles Lindbergh, Al Capone, prohibition, dance crazes, and baseball. Later in the year, I taught *Black Boy*, which is also set in the 1920s, though I do not think that I did more than mention that fact to my students. During this unit, we discussed such things as the Jim Crow laws, prejudice of all sorts, and stereotyping.

Why hadn't I connected the unit on the 1920s to Ellison's autobiography along with Fitzgerald's novel? I realized only after the end of the school year what I had done. I had allowed *The Great Gatsby*—a fictional story about upper-class white people—to symbolize Life in America in the 1920s. Meanwhile, I used *Black Boy*, a true tale from the same time period, as a window into the perspective of "the other."

Why had I "other-ized" the experience of Ellison, certainly as common an experience among Americans as that of Gatsby? Why hadn't I used *Black Boy* as central to the unit on 1920s America? Aptitude in the principles of pedagogical neutrality in themselves would not have helped me avoid the message of marginality I unwittingly sent about African-American experience in this case. I would have needed some other strategy to help me examine the moral messages embedded in the design of my curricular units. Teachers design courses based on what we think is important, on what we value, and on what we know, and neither pedagogical neutrality nor an emphasis on universal values goes far enough to help us explore the implications of the curricular decisions we make.[14] Choice, order, and juxtaposition of curricular materials all have moral ramifications; they all have an impact on whose values ultimately get taught. We need a way to factor those things into our strategy of making schools morally educative.

TEACHERS PROVIDE GUIDANCE REGARDING SPECIFIC BEHAVIOR, POLITICS AND SOCIETY, AND PHILOSOPHIES OF LIFE. Another shortcoming of the approaches examined above is that they do not provide a framework for thinking about how teachers are to serve as moral guides. All the teachers I interviewed see themselves in that role at least to some degree. Of course, a key element of moral guidance is the modeling of positive traits, examples of which I pointed out earlier in Mr. Carlson's regular good humor and respect for ideas and in Mr. Yearly's patient, gracious responses to student questions. But beyond modeling, teachers also comment explicitly on moral matters. The point bears repeating, because it is so inevitable, and also mostly desirable: teachers, like parents, regularly share with students what they see as indisputable wisdom and guidance with regard to moral and existential issues. And when sharing wisdom, they do not typically present the "other side" in a balanced way, any more than I present the other side of "Drive safely!" when bidding a loved one good-bye.

But often teachers' moral messages are more controversial than an admonition to take care on the road. Teachers admonish students regarding a wide range of behaviors inside and outside of class; they comment spontaneously about issues regarding politics and society; and they offer students wisdom from their own life experiences. The challenge is to include these sorts of explicit moral messages from teachers, along with discussions of controversial issues, in a framework for teaching. What kind of explicit moral messages are appropriate in schools? Under what circumstances should they be sent? Who decides?

ADMONITIONS REGARDING SPECIFIC BEHAVIOR. A quick answer to these questions, it seems to me, would be that it is important for a teacher to send messages about appropriate behavior when the immediate health, safety, or even emotional comfort of students is involved—the sort of thing that would be included on the "rules of conduct" list in the section on universal values above. Lickona articulates this idea quite reasonably.

> The teacher is the central moral authority in the classroom.
> That authority is based, first of all, on the fact that the school

has given the teacher the responsibility of creating a good moral and learning environment and of looking after students' safety and general welfare. That responsibility gives the teacher the right to tell students to follow directions, do their work, obey the classroom rules, and stop any behavior the teacher considers contrary to the best interests of an individual or the group.

In the course of managing the classroom, the teacher also functions as a moral mentor—instructing children in why it's not polite to interrupt, not fair to cut in line, not kind to call names, not respectful to "borrow" somebody's property without asking, and so on.[15]

As Lickona suggests, very few of us would question a teacher who said, "Stop fighting!" or "I ask you to refrain from laughing at or heckling your classmates as they make their presentations."

Ms. Davis, the drama teacher at St. Paul, describes starting her class each semester with such an admonition:

Well, the first day of class I do an acting job where I tell them what behaviors are not acceptable. And I know you're not supposed to start off negative, but in a class like drama where someone's going up on the stage—and most people have never stepped foot on a stage—to go on stage and then have someone laugh at you or snort or just be bored or pulling out papers from another class or doing their makeup, that's rude. And I don't tolerate rudeness. I demonstrate. I put someone up on the stage and then I start being [rude], but of course I overexaggerate it, and so they know....

One false move with a shy kid on stage, and they'll never go back. They'll never trust you; they'll never trust the audience; and trust is something you can't get back. You can forgive, but you can't forget. I also tell them on the first day of class how important it is that we all trust each other.

Laying the ground rules regarding disruptive behavior in this way seems entirely acceptable. But what about moral admonitions of a more abstract kind? Here are a few examples of what I mean.

Five times a day on Friday, like every other day, the bell signaling the end of class rings in Larry Carlson's room. Five times a day, as the bell rings and the backpacks hit the thirty-odd backs heading to the door, Larry bellows, "Have a good weekend. Stay sober!" The students expect the ritual. As Larry explains to me, "They laugh, but they also know I'm serious about it, too. Doesn't do any good—they don't go out and think about Larry during the weekend." Whether it "does good" or not, Larry sees it as his duty to express his care for his students—and his disapproval of their drinking—in this way.

Whereas this involves a moral message regarding student behavior out of class, beyond Larry's eyeshot, the following example involves in-class student behavior, where I, the teacher, enacted what some might view as a kind of political agenda. For four years, I taught drama in a large, diversely populated high school south of San Francisco. Often, I had my students perform improvisational skits, taking on the role of a wide variety of characters. Almost as often, one of the students would come up with a stock, stereotypical character, and play it to the hilt: a Chinese-American with extremely broken English and slits for eyes doing dry-cleaning; an African-American, loaded with crack, selling drugs on a street corner; a gay man, limp-wristed and sway-hipped, making unwanted passes at other men. These were by far the favorite characters of a number of students in the class, and their appearance was always greeted with laughter and applause.

Before long I decided I did not want to see these characters anymore. I explained to the students that one of the most important goals in the acting work was to empathize with the characters they were playing, to understand them from the inside, not to make fun of them. The students argued that well-known actors and comedians played these sorts of stereotypical characters on television shows like *Saturday Night Live*. If professionals could do it, why couldn't they? Debating whether or not the skits on television comedy shows represent "good acting" seemed a losing battle, so I simply made a rule: in my classroom, I did not want to see acting that perpetuated negative stereotypes.

I gave some time for discussion of the new rule. Students wanted to know if they could play a "dumb blonde," or a flaky Californian, or a smart Asian. We talked about whether stereotypes contain truths and about the pain they cause. Mostly, students claimed that the stereotypes do not cause pain. An African-American student said, "Hey—I don't mind the crack character"; other students contended, "Nobody in here is gay, anyway, so what does it matter?" They talked about free speech; I talked about its limits. In the end, I enforced the rule; when those characters appeared, I cut off the scene. I chose to allow the value of protecting the feelings of those (including myself) who might be hurt by the stereotypes to outweigh the value of student autonomy and free choice.

Perhaps readers will see both Larry's reminder to stay sober and my moral line-drawing as falling easily into the "rules of conduct" category named above, in which teachers rightfully do what they can to promote the health, safety, and emotional comfort of their students. But whether or not one approves of these particular choices, at some point the line does get fuzzy: teachers do sometimes assert "moral" guidance in questionable ways. One unforgettable example from my high school teaching will suffice to represent the category. As a colleague and I sat in the English department office during our "prep" period, another English teacher, the popular football coach, strode through the office looking for a spray bottle of liquid cleanser. "Those damn kids," he said, reaching for the bottle. "They write on the desks all the time. I told them that writing on the desks is going to turn them into faggots." My other colleague and I were struck speechless, and the coach stormed back to his classroom. As odd and distasteful as that remark was, I am sure that he thought he was teaching a legitimate moral lesson: that it is wrong to deface school property.

The question in all these cases is this: what guidelines help us know when and how it is appropriate for teachers to admonish students? Again, the principle of pedagogical neutrality, focusing on controversial issues, is not designed to address this question. The "universal values" approach, while recognizing that the teacher is the "central moral authority in the classroom," seems to assume, quite mistakenly, that all adults of good character will agree on what constitute appropriate admonishments. This realm, therefore, demands a different approach.

SPONTANEOUS LESSONS ON POLITICS AND SOCIETY. In addition to admonitions regarding student behavior, teachers across the curriculum sometimes convey to their students what they regard as truths involving the social and political world and about life generally. In the fall of 1995, when the residents of Quebec voted on whether to secede from Canada, Ms. Gilman told her American history students that it would be economically disastrous for everyone involved if Quebec seceded. The English-speaking Canadians had probably been wrong to allow the French-speaking Canadians to maintain their language and culture, she claimed, as it had only led to divisiveness and strife. She implied, also, that various ethnic groups in America, striving to retain a group identity and language, are similarly creating unnecessary turmoil. On the day following the vote in Quebec, she explained that when American ethnic groups maintain their language and their ties to their home countries, "it's bad for the United States—it eventually causes less loyalty. It's not good for the country—it could lead to splitting the country apart. The 'salad bowl'... is not ultimately good for the U.S. Canada always emphasized the 'salad bowl' and the multicultural approach. That's why Canada almost split apart."

In this situation, the principles of pedagogical neutrality might have saved the day. It seems likely that if Ms. Gilman had intended to teach about the vote in Quebec as part of a regular lesson plan, she would have taken care to present the various sides in a more evenhanded way, for she generally seemed to value the idea of neutrality regarding political issues, as she explained to me: "I'll tell you one thing they always ask the social studies teacher, 'What political party do you belong to? Who will you vote for?' And I will always tell them, 'I don't see that as my job here. My job here is to give you as much of the information I can on both sides, then you become an informed citizen.'"

The news of the day, the "real world," intrudes on classrooms more or less unexpectedly, however. At best, such intrusions provide opportunities for the discussion of moral and existential issues. But because the issues in the daily news do not necessarily come packaged neatly as "controversial issues"—like abortion and the death penalty clearly do in the current political climate—they are likely to be discussed in much more offhand and poorly balanced ways. It seems inevitable that teachers will betray their own biases regarding the issues that come up from day to day. Otherwise, and equally detrimental to the cause of moral education, teachers may simply avoid talking about the world outside as a way of protecting against revealing such biases. The task at hand is to conceive of moral education in school broadly enough that it would provide a framework for teachers to act as moral educators even in these unplanned moments. But first, there is another kind of moral lesson to consider.

A PLANNED LESSON ABOUT LIFE—SERMON #102. Larry Carlson, as we have seen, masterfully demonstrates the ability to present or elicit many sides of a complex issue. He also carefully avoids letting students know his political beliefs, as he describes here in an interview with me.

> I worry a bit, being a respected authority in the room, giving them "the truth" and having them simply accepting it because they have respect for who I am. I think that's inappropriate. I think they need to challenge authority figures and ask questions for themselves and find their own truth that is consistent with their world view. I think that's particularly appropriate for adolescents who are probably doing that anyway. Rather than simply being given "the truth," I think the question is not what Larry thinks or why he thinks but why student A, B, or C—what they think and why they think that and why they come to that conclusion. [They have to] defend it.[16]

And yet, while Larry works scrupulously to avoid giving students "the truth" regarding historical or political issues, he sometimes quite deliberately takes considerable time to share his wisdom on what he calls a "life issue." The following discussion provides a striking example of how a teacher who otherwise values neutrality might sometimes choose to impart a highly charged moral lesson. Because any approach to teaching morality in high school will have to address a choice such as the one Larry makes here, it is worth quoting it at some length. The full discussion, significantly abbreviated here, took approximately forty minutes of class time.

Larry taught a four-day unit in his War and Peace class on the Milgram experiments. Stanley Milgram, a professor of psychology at Yale, conducted an experiment during the 1960s in which he enlisted naive subjects, who were to become "teachers," and employed informed actors, who were to play "learners." Milgram explained to the subjects that the experiment was about the effect of punishment on learning. In each trial, the "teacher" was told to administer electric shocks to the "learner," sitting in an adjacent room, whenever the learner made a mistake on a random memorization task. For each mistake the learner made, the teacher was to slowly raise the intensity of the shock. As the intensity of shock increased, the learners (who were not actually being shocked) would cry out in signs of ever increasing pain and beg to be let out of the chair to which they were supposedly strapped. Finally, when and if the teacher raised the electricity to lethal levels, the learners would respond no more.

On the third day of the unit in class, Larry reviewed the fact that roughly 60 percent of the experiments' subjects—consistently, across various populations and in various settings—went "all the way," administering a high enough voltage to kill the "learners." He then asked the students to consider why the subjects obeyed the scientist. Students gave a variety of answers about authority and the power of science.

Larry: What did the people who quit—before they got to 450 volts—understand, that the people who went all the way never understood—and therefore caused them to go on?

Tiffany: That everyone has their own free will—

Larry: Good. And if you have free will—what do you have?

Tiffany: You have freedom, it's your choice.

Larry: Wonderful. They thought they had no choice.... Now, do you remember why they thought they had no choice? Why did they think they had no choice? Lena?

Lena: Because the experimenter kept saying, "You must continue. The experiment must continue, and you can't stop now," and all that stuff.

Larry: And then, the next phrase was "you have no choice." They thought they had no choice because the authority figure told them they had no choice, right? Now, let's talk about this, because I think this is a good life lesson for you guys. To be real honest with you, I don't care about War and Peace right now, I just think this is a good life lesson.

Explicitly stating that this is "a good life lesson," more important than any particular set of facts about the Milgram experiments, Larry pushes the students to consider the question of free will. He has not, at this point, revealed his own opinion on the issue, and the students seem to have mixed feelings. Larry pursues the line of inquiry, firing one question after another.

Larry: When do you have choices? When do you have free will?

Several: Always.

Larry: Always?

Several: Yes. [And simultaneously] No.

Larry: Always? No? [More "yeses" and "nos" from the students.] Always? We have a quiz Monday. Do you have a choice?

Several: Yes.

Larry: Do you have to take the quiz?

Several: No.

Larry: What do you mean you don't have to take the quiz? What do you mean? [Laughter from class] You do, too.

Several: Do not.

Larry: You'll get a zero.

Mica: You can live with a zero.

Larry: If you choose not to take that quiz, what do you think I'm going to do?

Several: Give a zero...

Larry: I'm going to give you a zero. Did I take away the choice?

Several: No.

Larry: Do consequences take away a choice? You still have a

choice? You really believe that? I've got some people saying no, though.

Until this point, Larry has proceeded in the style we have become used to, doing his best to elicit all sides of the question. But here he jumps into a long story to illustrate his stand on the question.

Larry: Let's talk about the classroom for just a second. I had a group of kids in one class, and they were really upset with me—they thought that I was pretty unfair. And there was a group of about five or six guys—and it was a test day. And they decided that they weren't going to take the test—my tests were too hard, too unfair. So they had their arms crossed like this, and they were going, "Hurumph, rumph, rumph, rumph. Larry, you're too hard, hurumph, rumph, rumph, rumph. Your tests are too hard, hurumph, rumph, rumph. We're not going to take your tests." So they started to organize the class not to take the test—to protest. And I said, "Okay, you don't have to take the test." "We don't?" "No—you've got a choice." "We really don't have to take it?" "No, you don't want to take it you don't have to take it." "Okay, we're not taking it." I said, "Okay, you have choice, you don't want to take it, don't take it."

Larry tells the story to the great interest and amusement of the class. He explains that about half the students chose not to take the test. After some time sitting in silence as others took the test, Larry says, one of the students could contain himself no longer.

Student: "Well, what are you going to do about the grade?" I said, "Oh!! The grade?! You want to know what I'm going to do about the grade?! I'm going to give you a zero." He said, "No, you aren't." I said, "Yes, I am." He said, "You said we have a choice." "Yeah, you have a choice, but you get a zero, because you made the choice not to take the test." He said, "No, you aren't." I said, "Yeah, I am." He said, "Oh, you're fooling." I said no. I showed him the gradebook. There were zeros. He said, "You can't do that. You said we had a choice."

By this time, Larry has made his position—at least with regard to taking tests in school—quite clear. Students have a choice about what to do. He now asks the students to respond to the story. Joe points out that the students' choice over their actions does not mean that they can choose the teacher's actions—they may have choice, but the consequences are out of their control. After a few other responses, Larry introduces another example, that of being intimidated into doing something by someone bigger or stronger, and concludes that even in a situation where someone is holding a gun to one's head, one still has choices about how to respond. He continues, now connecting the idea of "choice" to responsibility.

Larry: If I have choices, am I then responsible for the choices I make?

Jacquie: Yes.

Larry: So if I'm choosing to give that shock, even though the experimenter says "I'm responsible"—isn't it the truth that the responsibility is mine, because I'm choosing this course of action? ... If you have choices, are you responsible? ... I think the answer is yes. We're always responsible. Because the choices are ours—we make the choices....

Ultimately, if you have to admit to yourself that it is my choice to do this or not to do this, then you have to also take on "it's my responsibility." So, "The reason I'm failing the class is not because Larry's an S.O.B. The reason I'm failing the class is because I haven't done what I need to do to get the grade that I want." Right? "I haven't done the reading. I haven't done the studying. That's my choice. I make that choice."

And incidentally, just as a side note to you, I think this really is a good life lesson for you, and ultimately you have to think about your life—nobody ultimately can make you do anything that you don't want to do. You can choose not to do that. And if somebody overpowers you because they're stronger, then you can choose how you want to respond.

Larry, who scrupulously avoids giving his opinion on most curricular material, who believes that students should arrive at their own well-reasoned decisions, here takes great care to draw a "life lesson" from the Milgram experiments. In this case, Larry makes no attempt to present alternate points of view, nor to suggest that although he feels strongly about this point he may be mistaken. And yet, at least on some level, Larry seems to know that one could differ with him; if the point were obvious or accepted by all, he would not need to deliver such an impassioned message.

The lesson might have ended here, but Molly bravely challenges Larry's conclusion.

Molly: Okay, I have a question. You say, like, we always have a choice and stuff? What if in a hypothetical situation, say I've grown up a little, and I'm in my house that I now rent, because I'm going to school and stuff, and I'm at home watching TV. Now I have a choice to be out someplace doing something. But I'm at home because I choose to be at home watching TV, getting ready for bed, and some stranger walks into my house, throws me down on the floor, and rapes me. Where's my choice? I had no choice for him to come into the house.

Larry: Right.

Molly: I mean, he's taken my choice away.

Larry: No. No.

Molly: Then what's my choice?

Larry works to show where the element of choice exists even in this situation of physical coercion.

Larry: Look—you do not have the choice to be raped or not raped, if the person is stronger than you, just as you do not have the choice about whether the person is going to come into your house. What you have the choice is—how you are going to respond.[17]

Molly: But if he's overpowering me so much, he gives me no choice to respond, if he's got me held down on the ground, and tied down and stuff.

Larry: I think it's a real issue, I think it's not sort of, an abstract, intellectual issue. It's a real issue for people. And the question is going to be: what is going to be your response then? There are people who say, "My choice has been taken away, I've been brutalized by the other person, and now, my life is going to be destroyed."

Molly: But many people freeze up in situations like that, where they can't move. I know for a fact, if I was sitting at home watching TV, and some big strange guy, six foot eight, or whatever he is, comes in and throws me down on the ground and rapes me, I'm not going to be able to do anything, because I'm going to be scared out of my mind and I'm just going to break up.

Larry: I would be, too.

Larry has made his comment seriously, but it draws a big laugh. He continues.

Larry: There's not anything funny about this, folks. The problem is a female talks about it, and guys sit here and don't relate. The way to relate is to think of another man raping you, as a man. [Lots of hoots and howls from the students in response to this.] That got you, didn't it, Joe? If some six foot eight guy came in and said, "I'm going to rape you, Larry," I wouldn't know what to do. I have a choice how to respond, and I'll tell you what my choice would be. I would not let my life be destroyed by that event. I would be angry as hell, and I might try to take revenge. But I would not let my life be destroyed by that. I mean, I would not do that. I have a choice to go on living my life and go on to become a person who's still valuable. I would not let that person take that away from me. And that's the problem, I think, with rape. It's not during the act—if the person is larger than you—

Molly : Something like that, sometimes—

Larry: You can't say, "I'm choosing not to be raped. My War and Peace teacher is going to come and get you, because he told me I have a choice." That's not the point. The point is you have a choice about how you respond.

Molly hangs on to her idea that even if one chooses to "go on living life," as Larry has suggested, having lived through an event like a rape will still have ramifications that are not captured by the idea of choice.

Molly: Yeah, but things—but say I choose to go on with my life, and choose to live my life. I'm not going to be able to forget about something like that. I'm not going to sit and dwell on it every day, but things are going to come up in my life, and it's going to remind me of it.

Larry: Every day, Molly, I have to tell you, tiger, every day as a teacher I see kids in class whose lives have been destroyed, they think, because of something. Sally said good-bye to you, or Harry said good-bye to you. Or something awful—your parents abuse you. I think I told you some of the stories—I had a 4.0 student one year who came up to me and told me that her dad was raping her every night, and she was destroyed. And all the response there is— you have some choice. She had some choices in that situation, which was in that case, turn the dad in, turn him in. And she felt so powerless, because her dad was an authority figure, and that's ultimately, that's ultimately the power of this thing [pointing to the board, referring to the Milgram experiments].

Because I sit here and I'm a teacher and I tell you something, you don't have to do what I tell you to do. You know, I tell you to take a test, or I tell you to read a book, you don't have to do that just because I'm the teacher. You should be doing it only because you make the choice that this is somehow worthwhile for you. But, obviously, I have some capacity to punish you because of my power in this position. But you don't have to do these things. And ultimately, some people think I'm really subversive to the school system—and yeah, I am to some degree. If somebody who is malevolent is trying to get you to do something you don't want to do—don't! Don't do it! Just because they're your teacher or your father or a principal, or somebody else—you do what is right, the best you can.

Now again, the caveat here is, if the person's bigger, and he has a gun, you know, obviously, he can force you physically to do some things, but you have some choices even then. You don't have to give in to him. This is the end. Ultimately, you don't have to give in to anybody. Ultimately, you have control of everything that happens inside yourself. And your mind can be someplace else— and you can not give in to this evil. This is sermon #102.

Let's move. I have to tell you, this is really important to me, and that's why I got a little sermon-y. Let me ask you some other questions. I'd like to know whether you'd have liked to have been a part of this [Milgram's] study....

This lesson may evoke a wide range of responses. Two early readers of this transcript, indeed, reacted quite differently to Larry's strategy. Commenting in the margins on a draft of this chapter, one wrote that Larry does not know how he would respond to being raped, that his statement that one is free not to submit to authority or physical coercion is "misleading, even cruel," and that he should have acknowledged that "good thinkers disagree with him" on these issues. Another, meanwhile, wrote regarding Larry's responses to Molly, "This guy is becoming my hero!"

Given the diversity of possible responses, thoughtful discussions of this lesson—of the type I propose should become regular fare for teachers' professional development—might address a number of questions regarding both Larry's conclusions and his mode of argument: Is Larry right to argue that one always has choice regarding one's actions, and that "ultimately, you have control of everything that happens inside yourself"? Are the choices made by the subjects of the Milgram experiment analogous to the choices made by students about whether or not to take a test? Are either of those comparable to situations in which physical coercion or rape is involved? What other responses, besides letting one's mind "be someplace else" might help one survive a trauma or violence? How can we distinguish between the category about which Larry says one has no choice—getting raped—and the category where one perhaps *does* have choice—"getting on with life"? How do other circumstances beyond one's control fit into these categories? What other factors, besides individual human choice, help to explain people's actions and predicaments?

Beyond the content of Larry's message, one might inquire into its pedagogical implications. How might this lesson affect students who do not perceive themselves as having choice in various areas in their life? Would the power or value of this lesson be changed if we assumed that one or more of the students actually had been a victim of rape or severe abuse? Was it valuable, in this case, for Larry to tell it as he sees it, to give "sermon #102," rather than stick to his usual devil's advocate style?

As these sets of questions suggest, I have serious concerns about the message Larry sent here: I think "choice" is a much more complex and nuanced matter than Larry proposes; also, the question of how one might respond to rape, in particular, is inadequately addressed by the concept of choice versus obedience to authority alone.[18] I also recognize and honor, however, the impulse to help adolescents believe that they do have power over the course of their lives. And I respect the desire of a man who has heard many, many horrific stories from teenagers to help them find courage and solace, to help them "choose" to overcome. While the strengths and weaknesses of this lesson are worth analyzing in greater depth, that is not my aim here. My goal is simply to demonstrate that teachers *will*, as Larry puts it, get sermon-y; they *will* send emphatic moral messages regarding their deeply held beliefs, especially if they think those beliefs will help students live safer, better, or happier lives. And when they sermonize, they may be too focused on their own message to remember to present opposing points of view. They may forget—as I think Larry did here—that there *are* valid opposing points of view.

Even given the tendency for "sermons" to be one-sided, not all of them are necessarily bad, as we see here and as we saw earlier with Rabbi Singer. Indeed, it is comforting to think that sensitive, thoughtful teachers will share life wisdom with their students. We shudder, on the other hand, at the idea of a teacher whose value system opposes our own engaging in similar sermonizing. I recognize that for some people my admonition to students not to perpetuate negative stereotypes about gay people, for example, would elicit the very shudder that I felt when I heard Ms. Gilman speak about the dangers of preserving ethnic identity. For different constituencies, different sermons will raise alarm. But if, as I claim, teachers *will* sermonize, we need a way to think through the question of "whose values" in a way that will render schools hospitable to a wide variety of constituencies. I propose another answer to the "whose values" question, one that attempts to speak to the theoretical and practical issues concerning admonitions on behavior, spontaneous lessons on politics and society, and impassioned lessons about life—as well as controversial issues in the curriculum.

Answer #5: A Schoolwide Inquiry into Values

Articulating a Moral Mission for the School

It seems to me that the best answer to the question of whose values should be taught in a public school, given the many ways moral issues arise, would expand on the pedagogical neutrality approach, which tends to focus on the individual teacher. In addition to individual teachers doing their best to teach all significant sides of controversial issues, the school could commit to providing teachers, students, and administrators with regular forums in which to consider the moral implications of the school's curriculum and instruction. There is much to say about what such forums might look like, but first I shall articulate a piece of a "moral mission statement" for a school attempting to integrate moral and existential issues thoughtfully into the curriculum. Such a statement, written in the voice of teachers and administrators and addressing the question of the school's treatment of controversy, might sound something like this.

> Our goal, when discussing controversial issues, is to follow the principles of pedagogical neutrality. We will try to ensure that all sides of controversial issues are explained fully and respectfully and that all sides are critiqued carefully. Beyond this commitment to the balanced discussion of controversial issues, however, our curriculum and pedagogy are unavoidably morally laden, and we cannot in any way guarantee that the moral implications of our work will always be acceptable to everyone. We will teach texts, make comments, and even enforce rules that some people may find objectionable. This is unavoidable, but it is also intentional, for we know that both the moral and the intellectual level of the school would be greatly impoverished if we tried to avoid doing, saying, or teaching anything that might raise controversy. Far from trying to avoid complex questions about morality and life more generally, we aim to integrate them fully into the intellectual life of our school.
>
> What we can promise is that our work, along with its moral implications, will proceed in the full light of day. As a staff, we are committed to the idea that we need to think together about

the moral aspects of our work, and we are developing structures to enable regular, ongoing deliberation of the moral implications of our curricular and pedagogical choices. Further, we shall regularly encourage students to examine the moral aspects of the curriculum. Our classrooms and our curricular materials will be open to parents, researchers, reporters, and other community members, and we will structure opportunities to incorporate their feedback into our ongoing planning. If some of what or how we teach causes controversy, that controversy itself will become important material for study, and as always, we will attempt to teach the controversy fairly.[19]

Creating Forums for Moral Inquiry

What would a school adopting such a philosophy look like? Many schools that are in the process of adopting systemic reform include as one of their principles the idea that teachers need more time to work with other teachers collaboratively and to reflect on their practice.[20] In the past ten years, forums for such discussions have become more common. Teachers are involved in a wide variety of groups organized to focus on various aspects of their professional practice through such means as action research, reciprocal observations and coaching, intra- and interdisciplinary curriculum planning, conferences on the needs of shared students, and mentoring novice teachers.[21] Though only rare schools currently provide adequate amounts of time for teachers to participate in such groups, once such groups are in place and the time is allotted for them, the step I am advocating would be relatively easy. I propose that collaborative teacher groups such as these institute as one of their central purposes the examination of the moral and existential aspects of curriculum and pedagogy.

When one takes into account both the explicit and the implicit features of the curriculum, the whole range of instructional decisions along with everyday interactions among students and between students and teachers, the number of moral and existential issues that one could inquire into would be overwhelming. It will not be possible for people in schools to discuss the moral and existential aspects of every move they make any more than it would be possible for the members of a family or any other organization to do that. But the impossibility of addressing all moral questions is no rationale for ignoring all of them. Collaborative teacher groups may choose to focus on just one or two of the ways that moral and existential issues arise in their classrooms. They might, for example, examine moral questions embedded in texts that are already part of the explicit curriculum, those raised by student questions, those inherent in curricular choices and design, or those implicit in more informal teacher comments and admonitions.

The excerpts from classroom conversations included throughout this book provide specific examples of the kinds of issues teacher groups might address; more are included in the Afterword. Had I, as an English teacher, worked with colleagues in a curriculum-design group, one of whose goals was to attend to the moral and existential issues embedded in the curriculum, we might have considered how to structure a class activity or discussion around the existential content of Macbeth's "sound and fury" speech. Tom Atlas, Mr. Greene, or Ms. Hayes, participating in similar groups, might have found fruitful ways to bring to the fore the moral issues in The Bean Trees, a unit on human reproduction, or the topic of Taylorism. There is no *specific* moral or existential question that must be explored as part of any of these units; indeed, there are many different possibilities for each. But whichever particular questions are chosen, all the units would be greatly enriched if they were taught with attention to some of the underlying moral questions. Teachers, working together, could find ways of incorporating these questions into unit designs and individual lesson plans.[22]

For moral and existential questions that arise spontaneously in class, a "peer coaching" rather than a curriculum-planning group might be appropriate. My teaching would have been greatly enriched had there been one or more colleagues with whom I regularly discussed the unexpected events in my classes. I would have brought them, for example, the question of what to do with the improvisational drama performances that I found offensive. Perhaps one of my colleagues could have observed my class and helped me think through the sticky issues of free artistic expression and the challenge of building a safe classroom. Ms. Putnam might have found support in such an arrangement for considering more deeply Tom's question about the illogic of killing baby girls; Ms. Sherman might have worked with a colleague or two on how to talk about God and faith in the context of reading *Night*. It is extremely hard to address such topics adequately on the spur of the moment when they come up spontaneously in class. But if teachers had "critical friends" with whom they discussed such surprises soon after they occurred, the teachers would find ways to return to class and give student questions—and moral issues—the attention they deserve. Such relationships among teachers do exist, sometimes in the context of a mentoring program.[23] But they are rare, and it is rare that moral issues are explicitly given priority.

These issues could also be explored in the context of an action research group, conducting an investigation of a year's curriculum in any given course. The group might seek to remove lessons heavy in decontextualized fact acquisition and to design ones addressing substantive moral and intellectual issues.[24] Such a group might also inquire into the moral messages implied by curricular choices. I am sure that it would have taken only a couple of well-placed questions from a colleague about the separation of the *Black Boy* unit from the "1920s America" unit to help me see the questionable moral messages embedded there. If the kinds of teacher groups I envision were in place, teachers would not only get help on the issues that arise in class, they would also have vibrant models of the kinds of discussions they might facilitate with their students.

My suggestion to incorporate regular discussions of moral and existential issues into the intellectual life of both teachers and students dovetails quite well with ideas growing out of current research literature and reports from schools undertaking comprehensive reform. They suggest that schools should work to develop a number of "habits of mind." Deborah Meier, for example, names five habits emphasized at Central Park East High that are posted in every classroom and listed in every newsletter: "They are: the question of evidence, or 'How do we know what we know?'; the question of viewpoint in all its multiplicity, or 'Who's speaking?'; the search for connections and patterns, or 'What causes what?'; supposition, or 'How might things have been different?'; and finally, why any of it matters, or 'Who cares?'"[25]

Similarly, students should regularly be asked two basic moral and existential questions about the topics they study: "What are the implications of what I am learning for my own behavior and beliefs?" and "How does this material help me understand my place in the world?" These questions are not far-fetched; they really just elaborate on Meier's habit number 5, which she sums up as the question "Who cares?" Teachers and students are capable of acquiring the habit of asking these questions and integrating them into their work at school. Asking these questions about why what we study matters, I believe, has the potential of helping *school* matter much more deeply to students.

An Example of Teachers Discussing Morality in the Curriculum

After I had completed classroom observations excerpted in this book, I returned to Saint Paul and Frontier with a number of the episodes described in Chapter 4 and asked teachers to react to them. To give an idea of what a group of teachers discussing moral issues arising in the curriculum might sound like, I close this chapter with a passage from one of these discussions. The teacher in the classroom described here was anonymous to the teachers who discussed it—and thus they met more as a favor to me than with an eye to improving their own practice—so the following discussion is significantly different from the teacher groups I envision. Still, it gives a sense of the potential of such discussions.

In this excerpt, a group of teachers at Saint Paul reacts to a written description of the scene described in Chapter 4 from Mr. Manning's class. In it, during a lecture on the Civil War, a student asks about the treatment of black soldiers in the North. This is the scenario the teachers read, repeated here for convenience.

SCENARIO FROM MR. MANNING'S CLASS. Mr. Manning began a review session about the Civil War with his eleventh-grade U.S. history class. He read aloud from an overhead projector until he was interrupted by Bryan. We join Mr. Manning reading, a moment or two before Bryan's question.

Mr. Manning: The North had the economic advantage. They were able to produce war products and the nation's railroad. The Union was able to move troops and supplies at will. The South, however, had excellent military leadership. Most Southern victories resulted from battles of skillful Confederate officers. Among the ablest of southern military leaders was Robert E. Lee.... By the end of 1861, the Union had more than 527,000 soldiers. The Confederacy had more than 258,000 soldiers.... Had the Confederates pursued the Union forces, they might have captured Washington.

Bryan: Was the South using slaves for war?

Mr. Manning: No.

Ian: But the black soldiers in the North weren't treated right—they didn't get shoes or anything.

Mr. Manning: Well, eventually they got it.

Ian: Eventually, but they were basically mistreated.

Mr. Manning: Well, we could argue about that all day—but they were still better off fighting for their freedom in the North than being in slavery in the South. Which would you do?

Ian: But they weren't treated as well as the white soldiers.

Mr. Manning: But they were still better off, that's what I'm saying.

Manning turned back to the overhead, and continued to read.

Mr. Manning: The North had three things in mind: (1) Capture Richmond, (2) Gain control of the Mississippi River, and (3) Naval blockade of the South.

Having completed this section of his lecture, Mr. Manning put the students to work with partners, answering factual review questions for an upcoming test.

THE TEACHERS DISCUSS THE SCENARIO. Ed began the discussion by focusing on the importance of responding to a question raised by a student.[26]

Ed: I think there is a missed opportunity here. There should have been some time spent with this issue, because it is of deep concern to the kid, Ian. Ian is really coming back to this and doesn't want to leave it. His argument, Manning's is, "Well, we could argue about that all day"—that is, whether it is true or not. But rather than say whether it was factually true or not, maybe for a moment suspend that, and say "Okay, let's assume that that was the case. Was that right? Would that have been right?" So, take the issue and examine it, apart from whether it was absolutely historically accurate or not. And then maybe come back to the evidence even later. But examine the idea that "at least they had this" or "at least they were better off.

Already, Ed has thought of an alternate way Mr. Manning might have approached Ian's question; Dan provides another suggestion.

Dan: Well, in a history class I think you could use it as a research thing. "Let's find out, let's do some research on it. Can you do some research and find out exactly what the provisions were for black soldiers, and did it change any?" Things like that. My bias is that in a history class, too often that doesn't happen. Instead, it's "Here are the three main causes, and it doesn't matter what your questions are." To me, that's the waste there. I'm not sure it's even the morality of the situation, but my guess is from reading this that this teacher would do this even if it were a factual question, if he just didn't feel like debating it.

Dan points out that in history class, the "causes" of historical developments are often framed as items to be memorized rather than moral decisions to be scrutinized. This recalls my earlier point, in Chapter 5, that Larry Carlson's teaching in War and Peace derives much of its power from the way he communicates the idea that history is not a list of inevitable causes and effects, but rather is greatly influenced by the morally significant actions of human beings.

Dan's suggestion that Ian's question is an opportunity for research also underscores the conjunction of missed opportunities in the moral and intellectual realms. Ed picks up on the idea that difficult moral-intellectual questions present opportunities for further inquiry.

Ed: I would say, "Oh, gee, that's something I had heard about, too, but I'm not sure about it. Ian, what do you know? Where did you get your information? Or where can you go find out information?" I think that invites—it invites the learning process to open up enough to say that "we're not just spitting back what I'm presenting to you. We're exploring together, a common history. Let's explore it together, not worry about whether we're right or we're wrong."

Playing devil's advocate, I jump in to suggest that one might not want to spend a lot of class time on what seems like a tangential issue.

Laura: I think, though, that if this were an issue that happened then and was no longer alive today, then I may feel more committed to getting through the curriculum. But I think when you look at the treatment of African-Americans in today's society—it's still of concern to many students, if not all of our students, at some level, and for some reason. So, therefore, I think I would want to take some time if I were teaching this, to explore that possibility, what we really know about it. Is it true? If it is true, did it change? Who was in the decision making about that?

Laura's comment helps to uncover the connection—often hidden in history classes—between historical events and students' vital, contemporary concerns.

Dan, changing the focus a bit, raises another morally significant aspect of the exchange between Mr. Manning and Ian. He highlights not the content of Ian's question but rather the nature of Mr. Manning's response.

Dan: Playing devil's advocate, if you're suggesting that that's what this teacher had in mind, then why at one point does he turn the question to the student and say, "Which would you do?" and personalize it.... Why would he do that? It sounds to me like he's just trying to silence the student and take power over him.

Kathy: Spell this out. What's the move, when the teacher turns and says, "Which would you do?"

Dan: He phrases it such a way, "What would you do? Would you be better off fighting for freedom in the North, or being in slavery?"

And I think the implication there is, "You'd be better off fighting for freedom in the North, so be quiet, we don't need to talk about this." That's the implication I read in it—and again, I'm just looking at words on a sheet of paper, again a disclaimer. But... usually, I would personalize something to try to draw students in, but this is personalizing it to try to end the discussion, so I [the teacher] can move back to what I want to do. So I see it as an issue of control.

Kathy: The personalizing is in a negative way that shuts the discussion down.

Dan: Yeah, this is personalizing, because I'm asking a question that could only lead to one answer. And then I can move on.

Sally: Right. Of course I'd rather fight for freedom in the North. And then the kid says, "Well, they weren't treated as well as the white soldiers." So they're still not even free—they are still enslaved to a certain extent.

Ken: Right—to his credit, the kid doesn't answer the question.

Sally: You know, your devil's advocate position, I think as an English teacher, I say that's something that's wrong with so many social studies curriculums is that we're so focused on how much we're going to get through, rather than on skills and issues that are transferable whether we're talking about the Civil War or World War II, or whatever.

Dan: Yeah, they could read those facts in a book, they don't have to get them in a lecture. So I would think the class time would be better spent talking about issues like this that the kids bring up, personally.

Sally notices that the discussion has moved from the specific case to a more general enunciation of the proper goals and methods in a social studies class, and she says, with some humor and a good deal of seriousness, "That's our moral stance on how social studies ought to be taught."

As Sally suggests, pedagogical and curricular philosophies have moral implications. Or, rather, reflecting on the moral implications of a given moment of teaching has forced teachers to examine the design of curriculum and instruction, to investigate whether "less is more," and to consider the proper balance of "facts" with moral issues.

Ed and Sally pursue the idea of integrating the moral and intellectual aspects of studying history.

Ed: I know there are social studies units that specifically deal with the moral implications of history. There's one called "Teaching Tolerance," which I use in my Morality class, which I think is also somewhat used in social studies. So maybe we sometimes see it as something we pursue as a separate learning activity, but we ... [don't know how to] weave it into the fact chase.

Sally: There are all sorts of moral questions involved in this issue of the Civil War. Initially blacks were not allowed to fight, and the moral obligation they felt to be involved in the war—and then as far as the white people who emancipated them, and their moral dilemma about including them in the fight, or their role in society. I mean, there are so many moral questions centering around this issue that you could involve yourself in, and for whatever reason Mr. Manning chose not to.

Laura then jumps to a general fear about the implications of teachers discussing morally charged material in the classroom.

Laura: As we were talking I was thinking, well, maybe—if racism is underlying, an underlying philosophy for this teacher, an underlying issue—maybe it's better not to bring it up. I don't know, I would hope that there wouldn't be racist people teaching history, or teaching, period. But we know that isn't the case—

The discussion continued for some time, but Laura's comment is a good place to conclude, for it brings me full circle to the question at the beginning of the chapter. If moral issues are central to the curriculum, a question of great concern is "Whose values will get taught?" If some teachers hold racist views, for example—and of course, some do—then how can we possibly advocate that they should put moral issues at the center of their curriculum? It is tempting to say, as Laura does, "maybe it is better not to bring it up."

A Community of Moral Educators

In this chapter, however, I have argued that teachers' biases, for better and worse, inevitably assert themselves in the form of curricular choices, admonitions about behavior, and philosophies about life, among other things. Further, one cannot delve very deeply into the core school subjects without running into significant moral and existential questions, and moral and existential questions are among the things that matter most to human beings. The choice to avoid moral and existential issues—even if it were feasible—would exist only at the extreme expense of impoverishing intellectual inquiry and rendering course material tedious and irrelevant. A way must be found to give moral and existential issues their rightful, sizable place in the curriculum, even though the question of whose values will be taught cannot be answered easily.

As they do currently, teachers will continue to teach their own values, explicitly and implicitly. The best hope that a school's moral impact will be both appropriate and beneficial to our highly pluralistic society is, first, to adopt the principles of pedagogical neutrality with regard to controversial issues and, second, to create a culture of dialogue among teachers, other school personnel, and community members in which the moral questions inherent in teaching are regularly divulged and investigated.[27] An atmosphere of open classroom doors and faculty interaction would likely be inhospitable to one who held racist views proudly. Such a culture holds the potential to help teachers to recognize their own biases, to appreciate more deeply the moral import of their work, and—as the discussion excerpted here suggests—to learn from colleagues about the wide variety of instructional and curricular choices open to them. Perhaps most important, such a culture would offer teachers examples of thoughtful discussions of moral issues—of a sort they probably never encountered in their own education—and thus give them some of the tools they need to facilitate similar thoughtful discussions of moral issues among their students.

I have relied heavily on the idea that when teachers share their teaching and their moral dilemmas with their peers, they will be less likely to abuse the power that comes with being a moral educator. I must be clear that the fostering of a culture of discussion of moral issues does not ensure the elimination of objectionable words and actions. It is possible to imagine a culture that validated, rather than critiqued, morally questionable views.[28] I do not mean to suggest that the light of public scrutiny will always promote the good. Yet we must face the dangers of the current situation, in which teachers regularly either ignore moral and existential matters or promote questionable values *without* public scrutiny being brought to bear. Certainly, with all the dangers of community or "group-think," it is a step in the right direction to get teachers talking about what they are doing, about the moral aims and messages of their work.

It is also worth noting that the program I am proposing is highly challenging. The demands of pedagogical neutrality—understanding and being able to communicate the various sides of a wide variety of controversial issues—are huge. Add to that the tasks of examining the curriculum for its implicit moral implications, redesigning curriculum and instruction to center on moral and existential issues, scrutinizing admonitions, political statements, and ad hoc "life lessons" for their moral implications, becoming skilled at fielding unexpected student questions about complex issues, and facilitating discussions on all of this—and the project may seem overwhelming. I am drawn to ask the question Lee Shulman asks regarding the "community of learning" approach to teaching: "Is this conception of teaching... fundamentally impossible?"[29]

Just as I argued in Chapter 4 that missed opportunities in the moral and existential realms did not reflect the shortcomings of individual teachers so much as they reflect the structure of schools more broadly, so I argue here that the program I suggest is not a project for individual teachers. It absolutely depends on groups of teachers working together to support and complement one another, within a context that nurtures this work. The changes of structure and culture I am suggesting work very well with the notions of constructivist learning for teachers that are gaining currency and finding practical expression in collaborative planning time, critical-friends groups, and the like.

Writing about the possibility of teachers developing their craft generally, Shulman argues: "Teachers must be in communities where they can actively and passionately investigate their own teaching, where they can consistently reflect on their own practice and its consequences, where they can engage collaboratively with one another, to investigate, discuss, explore and learn from one another about what happens when chance occurs in their teaching and thereby, where they can, as members of the community, *generate* a base of knowledge that goes beyond what any one of them could learn in the isolation which now characterizes their classrooms."[30]

Even aside from their role as moral educators, Shulman suggests that isolation works against the possibility of teachers improving their practice, period. I would add that when one considers teachers' inevitable role as moral educators, isolating teachers in their classrooms—without structured opportunities to talk about the moral implications of their work—almost ensures teaching that is inadequate to the needs of a pluralistic society.

Teachers and schools adopting the program of schoolwide inquiry that I propose would not avoid controversy, for controversy is inevitable when people talk about things that matter to them. I believe, though, that considerable consensus could be garnered around this simple idea: *schools should place at their center the study of things that human beings wonder about and value the most.* If we agree upon this, we must not let the legitimate concerns surrounding the "whose values" question keep us from creating schools that are alive with all the questioning and grappling and exploration that engage thoughtful people when they seek to understand their lives and the world around them. The answer to the question "Whose values shall we teach?" is that the central value we teach is that of recognizing and learning to think sensitively and intelligently—as both teachers and students—about the moral implications of everything we learn and do. We teach the skills and habits of thinking deeply about how human actions, past, present, and future, affect the well-being of other human beings, animals, and the planet. To teach this value, we strive to build a community that lives this value; a community where we practice exploring together the moral implications of what we learn and do and where we see the purpose of our work together as invigorating our powers of thought and moral understanding.

CHAPTER 8

The Case for Systemic Reform

MY GOAL HAS BEEN BOTH TO SUGGEST CHANGES IN THE
educational system and to inspire individual teachers who
would like to invigorate the intellectual and moral life of their classrooms. I have argued that our schools neglect the issues of most
importance to students and to developing a deep understanding of
the disciplines. Because this neglect riddles the whole system—
from textbooks to standardized tests, from the substance of pre-
service and in-service teacher education programs to the criteria
for teacher evaluations—changing the status quo will require systemic change. On the other hand, there are immediate steps that
teachers, working individually or in teams, can take to improve the
situation for their particular students. In this chapter, I summarize
the main themes that emerged from my classroom observations,
and I note their implications for systemic reforms. In the Afterword, I outline some practical steps that teachers might take now
to infuse their classrooms with meaningful exploration of moral
and existential questions.

Where Schools Stand Today
Moral and Existential Issues Command Little Air Time

Discussions of moral and existential issues in high school classes are
often alarmingly truncated. Although the issues do arise in teachers'
questions, students' questions, class assignments, and textbooks,
many of the teachers I studied seemed reluctant to organize their
courses or class time in ways that would invite students to delve into
these issues on a regular basis or in a sustained way.

The scenarios in this book depict the outcome of that reluctance—
the hurried way in which moral and existential questions tend to be

dropped once they have arisen—more than they reveal its sources. But as a way of beginning to consider how high school courses might more fully encompass such questions it is worth exploring, if briefly, the factors that likely inhibit this pursuit. The classroom episodes described here suggest several such factors: There is pressure, sometimes self-imposed by the teacher, but often imposed by mandatory tests of students or evaluations of teachers, to cover a wide range of material. There is the requirement to give each student a grade for each course—a requirement that necessitates quantifying learning in some way and therefore pushing one to teach what can be readily tested, numerically scored, and ranked. There is the inherent complexity of leading focused discussions of multifaceted, highly charged issues, a challenge made all the greater when one's own education did not include such discussions. There is the reluctance to engage in controversies that might raise ire on the part of students, parents, or administrators. And there is the larger social and political context in which schools are situated, where the complexity of moral issues is often reduced to platitudes or slogans and disputes over moral issues often degenerate into accusations or name calling. In short, there are factors both internal and external to the school that mitigate against this kind of teaching.

The Disciplines Are Defined as "Information to Be Delivered"

If one keeps the focus on the educational world, perhaps the most important element in teachers' reluctance to engage in discussions of moral and existential issues is how the disciplines as school subjects are understood and organized. Many of the teachers I observed seem to conceive their disciplines—or at least the substance that they are called upon to teach—as a set of data to absorb. For Ms. Hayes, teaching the history of the 1920s meant telling the students about a cast of prominent figures and a list of important legislation from that era. For Tom Atlas, teaching American literature implied, in large part, unpacking plot details and figures of speech. For Mr. Greene, teaching about the human reproductive system denoted drilling the students in the names and functions of a list of organs, glands, and hormones.[1]

One might argue that the problem is not how the discipline is defined but that teachers simply lack the skills to lead the kind of in-depth discussions that I am promoting. Leading explorations of complex, controversial issues is very challenging, and teachers need more support and practice in this area. But as things stand, teachers have little impetus to develop the skills to teach complex, controversial issues, for teaching has been defined as imparting information, not as helping students navigate moral questions. And it is not just that teachers have somehow misconceived their work in this way. Dominated by questions that are assumed to have one brief, right answer, textbook writing and discussion activities reinforce this notion, as do standardized tests.[2]

In *Curriculum as Conversation: Transforming Traditions of Teaching and Learning*, Arthur Applebee argues that high school curricula should not be cast "in terms of what students should learn *about*," but rather in terms of "conversations that matter":

> Curriculum planning is usually approached as an exercise in domain specification and task analysis. That is, it begins with an inventory of important skills and concepts, and then moves on to arrange them in logical or psychological order. Taking curriculum as a domain for conversation, however, suggests a different starting point. Rather than beginning with an exhaustive inventory of the structure of the subject matter, we begin with a consideration of the conversations that matter—with traditions and the debates within them that enliven contemporary civilization. The question then becomes, how can we orchestrate these conversations so that students enter into them?[3]

Like Applebee, I have found that curriculum planning and implementation too often focus on teaching inventories of facts rather than on the deep questions that matter to human beings and that animate the disciplines. This finding suggests that, if we want schools to be vibrant places of learning, it is necessary to redefine the school subjects as explorations of perennial moral and existential questions and to redefine the role of schoolteacher as one who engages in and facilitates the engagement of others in such explorations. I believe it is time to redesign textbooks and teacher education programs to reflect this conception of teaching.

The Subject Areas Abound with Important, Engaging Questions

If we achieved the redefinition of teaching that I suggest, we would find that there would be no need to abandon the substantive content of the subject areas that we now teach. The examples cited in this book demonstrate that history, biology, and literature abound with questions that both animate the disciplines and matter to students. Delving deeply into these questions might help alleviate the sense of monotony and purposelessness that plagues so many high school students.

In all the subject areas, I saw classrooms come alive when students asked a question or made a comment that highlighted a morally or existentially important aspect of the subject at hand. "The black soldiers in the North weren't treated right—they didn't get shoes or anything," said Ian, opening a potentially fascinating and potent discussion of the still relevant differences between legally codified and socially condoned racism. "So there's only two to three days when a woman can get pregnant?" asked Marjorie, pushing the teacher to put a long list of hormones-to-be-memorized into practical perspective. "How can Wiesel still believe? How is it possible for anyone to believe in God after the Holocaust?" asked another student, seeking to grapple personally with a core theme of the text being studied. The students I observed continually tried to find ways to connect school subjects to their own interests and worlds of meaning. When students were given the opportunity to pursue moral and existential questions—as they were in the discussions in Larry Carlson's and Angela Rivers' classes—the students were simply riveted.

The finding that fascinating questions regularly arise out of the curriculum is not surprising, for the disciplines are born of human beings' attempts to understand themselves and their place in the world. As Dewey writes: "The various studies, arithmetic, geography, language, botany, etc.... embody the cumulative outcome of the efforts, the strivings, and the successes of the human race generation after generation."[4] That the subject matters are the outcomes of "the strivings and successes" of the human race—that they arise out of the same desire to know that characterizes children—underscores the perplexity and the irony of the fact that so many students find school boring.

This odd combination implies something crucial about the way curriculum should be designed: it suggests that, as Dewey argues, our aim in curriculum design must be to connect the record of humanity's great inquiries to the curiosities of the child. Throughout this book, I have referred to what I believe is the most likely nexus of that connection as "the moral and existential questions implicit in the subject matter." But perhaps a simpler way of putting it is this: For every subject we teach, we must continually search for how it matters, for how it links to the questions that students, like all human beings, perennially ask.

Far from abandoning the subject areas, we need to dig deeper into their vital cores. Students are engaged by the very sorts of questions that occupy those socially aware and self-aware adults who are most deeply engaged in study and reflection: To what extent is violence justified during a war? How shall we cope with the new information and choices made available to us through biotechnology? How shall I spend my time to live a good life, and what must I do to feel prepared for my own death? We must work to locate the important, engaging questions underlying each discipline and then design the curriculum around them.

Moral and Existential Questions
Can Promote Intellectual Accomplishment

I have cited examples from classrooms in which neglecting moral and existential issues robbed students of the chance to practice key intellectual skills. I have also depicted examples, on the other hand, in which discussing moral and existential issues pushed students to levels of sophistication in their thinking that went well beyond the memorization and recitation demanded in classrooms that shied away from such discussions. Depending on one's view of the role of the school, one might find pain or comfort in my claim that moral and existential issues are largely ignored in classrooms. But no one can be comforted by its less obvious corollary: when the moral and existential issues that arise in the curriculum and the day-to-day life of the classroom are ignored, the intellectual vibrancy of the classroom is likely to be sorely damaged as well.

Merely addressing moral and existential issues, however, does not *necessarily* invigorate the intellectual program. Sometimes teachers take a stance (reminiscent of the values clarification model) that says, "Everyone must figure out for him or herself what to believe about this issue," and it is left at that. Sometimes, too, moral issues are simplified in a way that may inhibit intellectual probing. We saw how in-depth investigations of complicated social issues like abortion, pornography, youth gangs, and white supremacists, for example, could be reduced to single sentences for purposes of testing. We saw how a teacher might subtly or implicitly reinforce prejudices without encouraging their exploration, and we saw how teachers might use their position of authority to transmit moral lessons while providing little room for dissent. In such cases, the moral mission of a teacher or a school might in fact work against the development of students' intellectual powers.

Addressing Moral and Existential Issues in a Pluralistic Society Requires Teacher Collaboration

Tales of the reduction of complicated issues and of the reinforcement of prejudices are disturbing enough that they might lead one to believe that schools should steer clear of moral and existential issues. Examples throughout this book, however, suggest that filtering these issues out of school is not viable: all the disciplines are replete with them, and the classroom's intellectual life is impoverished without them. Furthermore, as we have seen, regardless of their subject matter teachers will inevitably admonish students regarding right and wrong and will inevitably share some of their life's wisdom. The question is not how to avoid addressing moral and existential issues, but how to address them in a way that complements the intellectual aims of school and that is compatible with a pluralistic society.

How to address these issues in a pluralistic society is what I label the "whose values?" question. None of the current theories of moral education satisfactorily answer this question. The best way to make sure a wide variety of moral perspectives are examined is for schools to provide structures for teachers to work together regularly, to improve their own capacities for "pedagogical neutrality," and to recognize the moral implications in their choices of subject matter, instructional materials, and pedagogical techniques. This suggestion is within our reach; indeed, it is in line with many current reform initiatives that, in Linda Darling-Hammond's words, attend "more to the capacities of teachers and to the development of schools as inquiring, collaborative organizations than to changes in mandated curricula or management systems."[5]

The idea that teachers planning together, watching one another teach, inviting outsiders to watch them teach, and analyzing their work will ensure balance with regard to moral issues is far from foolproof. Certainly, whole groups of teachers working together could remain unaware of or indifferent to the ways in which their work reinforces prejudice or reifies other forms of injustice. But such a system—by openly emphasizing the importance of addressing complex issues honestly and thoroughly—would be a significant improvement over the status quo, in which teachers either may impoverish the curriculum by trying to avoid all controversy or may simply give students their own, unchallenged version of truth.

Whether it is Mr. Manning's understanding of the Civil War, Ms. Gilman's reflections on the settling of North America by Europeans, or Mr. Carlson's evaluation of the role of choice in an individual's life, all would be enriched by interaction with the alternate views of these issues that certainly exist among their own colleagues. Furthermore, teachers participating in discussions of moral and existential issues with their colleagues would likely be far more able to develop the skills necessary to facilitate such discussions in their classrooms than those who did not themselves share in such discussions in an ongoing way.

We Can Learn from the Religious Schools

Whereas I had originally supposed that being located in a religious school would have a significant effect on the history, English, and biology courses at Agnon and Saint Paul, in actuality these courses differed very little from the same subjects in the public schools. Though the differences between the schools are significant—

including different sources of funding, different mission statements, different student populations, different legal statuses—teachers from all three schools seemed to share the conception of the subject areas described above, in which one's discipline constitutes a particular inventory of facts and skills. This conception of the subject areas seemed so dominant that no more attention to moral and existential issues was apparent in core curriculum classes in the religious schools than in the public school I studied.

The religious schools did, however, set aside whole class periods—religion classes—precisely for the discussion of the moral and existential. Although some of the practices in the religion classes seemed poorly designed to foster deep understanding, others deserve attention from those wishing to address moral and existential issues more systematically in the public schools. The teachers of Morality at Saint Paul, in particular, created a "controversial issues" assignment that explicitly linked contemporary social problems to students' passionate personal concerns and encouraged students to grasp the issues in their complexity. The teachers of Jewish Law and Jewish Thought at Agnon helped devise norms of discussion that made students feel safe to offer personal opinions. Teachers at both schools fostered the use of a vocabulary of moral and existential concepts drawn from their religious traditions, and teachers at both modeled a deep commitment to grappling with the uncertainties and intricacies of moral and existential questions. All these components are crucial to nurturing a school culture where learning centers on the exploration of moral and existential issues. Schools seeking to establish such a culture may benefit from these examples.

Despite my appreciation for many aspects of the religion courses I observed, however, I found nothing to support the notion that "morality," "ethics," or "character education" should be added as a separate course of study in the public schools. The strengths of the religion courses could readily be integrated into any of the subjects where an attempt was being made to include discussion of moral and existential issues. The ubiquity of morally charged questions in *all* the subject areas, indeed, suggests the possibility of conceptualizing the teaching of *each* subject as "moral education."

Further Suggestions for Research and Reform

In the Afterword, I delve into specific suggestions for practical action in schools, ways teachers can work individually and in groups to develop the skills and materials needed to help their students investigate moral and existential issues in a rigorous way. Two other areas for further research and practical work, however, deserve mention.

Revamping Pre-service Teacher Education

We need to define the role of "English teacher," "history teacher," "science teacher" (and teachers in the other disciplines as well) in ways that would empower teachers to engage their students in discussions of moral and existential issues. As we saw in the example of Ms. Sherman, who referred a question about belief in God to a rabbi, teachers do not necessarily feel authorized or competent to address such issues. Their pre-service education should help them gain this authority and competence.

In some senses, the work that needs to be done could be seen as an elaboration on Shulman's insight that teaching demands knowing more than generalized teaching strategies and subject matter content; it demands what he has called "pedagogical content knowledge," which is greater than the sum of the parts. It is knowing which particular pedagogical strategies will work with which particular subjects with which particular students. Here I seek to extend the notion of pedagogical content knowledge so that it explicitly includes an ability to understand and facilitate exploration of the moral and existential questions that both underlie the disciplines and fascinate students.[6] There is challenging and important work to be done in conceptualizing and enacting teacher education programs that are structured to help new teachers gain this ability.

Listening to Students

Throughout this book I have made an argument that may seem tautological: students will be more interested in school if the curriculum is about things that matter to them. One might protest, in other words, that I am saying that school would be more interesting if it were more interesting. But my argument has been slightly more specific: those things that have mattered to human beings of various cultures and throughout the ages—"the meaning of life, the possibility of gods, birth and parenting, sexuality, death, good and evil, love, happiness"—are those things that will invigorate the curriculum and engage the hearts and minds of students.[7]

I have not based that assumption on pure speculation; rather, it has been reinforced by my interviews with teachers and students and my observations of students' faces, tones of voice, and hands flying up in the air when these matters come under discussion. But much more work could be done in coming to understand the questions and curiosities that truly engage students' passions. The research literature is surprisingly slim in this regard. There is considerable room for new studies that would put students' voices at their center and so provide solid grounding for designing curricula that address students' interests. The point would be not to create curricula that are "relevant" in the most narrow or immediate sense of the term, but to create curricula that help students connect their own lives to the great traditions of human inquiry and to ongoing social needs and dilemmas.

Two Stories

A couple of brief stories—one from a ninth-grade health class I observed (at a school not included in this study) and one from a teacher colleague—help summarize the central claims of this book. The health teacher I observed was lecturing about the circulatory system, drawing on an overhead with red ink to designate arteries and blue ink to designate veins. She explained that the arteries carry oxygen-rich blood from the heart and lungs out to the limbs and the other parts of the body and that the veins carry oxygen-poor blood back from the body to the heart and lungs. She wrote out the names of particular blood vessels, both large and small. After her description of the whole system, a student raised her hand and asked, "So is there something wrong with the blue blood?" The teacher answered that the blue blood needed more oxygen; it was on its way back to the lungs to get it.

The teacher continued to lecture, took a few other questions, and then the same student raised her hand again. "The blue blood is bad blood, right?" The teacher said it was not really bad blood, it was just "deoxygenated." The teacher continued her lecture. It seemed to me as I watched the student's face, though, that despite the teacher's accurate answers, the student still had a question.

After class, I approached the student and said something like, "It sounds like you're really interested in why the blood turns blue." She immediately pulled up her shirt sleeve and showed me her inner arm. "See? I have all of these blue veins. And I have sickle cell, and I want to know if that's the bad blood." Her words nearly bowled me over. She had sickle cell. She wanted to know more about her blood. The lecture had been about the circulatory system. What is there of moral or existential interest in the circulatory system? What personal stake are a bunch of fourteen-year-olds likely to feel in the names and locations of lots of veins and arteries? From a certain perspective, there is nothing personal about it—it is completely standard academic material, easily abstracted into overhead projections and blue and red ink. But for this student, there was nothing standard, academic, or abstract about it.

On reflection, I realize that this student was doing what I believe all students try to do or at least would like to do with the material they study. She asked, "How can I connect this information to what I want and need to know?" She linked the abstract diagram to her concerns about the blood coursing in her own veins. Without classroom norms that encouraged linking subject matter to life, however, she did not know how to formulate her question clearly. And the teacher, focusing on transmitting some fairly rote facts, seemed unaware that what she was teaching—if she could only link it to students' real questions—might actually touch them, help them, give them power to understand and to act. The curriculum has great potential to link to students' lives; the challenge is to carve out the space to discover those linkages, and to seize the teachable moments. We must realize that there is something wrong with classroom instruction if it presents even our own lifeblood as something in which we would not take a personal interest.

Another, similar story comes to mind, shared with me recently via a mutual friend. A teacher was teaching her first-grade students about Rosa Parks and the Montgomery bus boycott, explaining that the law in Alabama at that time dictated that blacks sit in the back of the bus, whites in the front. A little girl of mixed European and Asian descent suddenly raised her hand and asked, "Where would I have sat?"

To me, the little girl's question is a perfect metaphor for students' efforts to make meaning of what they learn. They start by asking, "Given this information, what more do I know about my life? How do I fit into this picture?"

"Is the blue blood bad?" "Where would *I* have sat?" These are wonderful questions to be asking, questions that perhaps come easier to elementary students than to the many high school students who have learned to stop asking. But high school students could learn to ask such questions more frequently, for they are the questions that, to borrow an earlier metaphor, have animated both Adam I and Adam II since the beginning of time: we want to know where we are sitting in this sometimes cruel, sometimes frightening, sometimes beautiful, awe-inspiring world. School could be a place where, wrestling with these questions, we begin to make sense of our lives.

Strategies and Tools for Incorporating Moral and Existential Questions into the Classroom

INCORPORATING MORAL AND EXISTENTIAL QUESTIONS into the curriculum is a very challenging endeavor. It requires learning a lot about the issues themselves and about resources that students might use to research them; it requires a flexible set of instructional strategies very different from those one might use to impart information. Embarking on this work, a teacher might face resistance from students who are being asked to think and express themselves in ways that they are not used to, concerns from administrators who worry about covering material and are shy of drumming up controversy, and fear or anger from parents who believe that teachers should stay out of the moral realm.

Despite these challenges, teachers around the country do grapple with moral and existential questions on a daily basis. This chapter is designed to support teachers in this work with practical suggestions for designing courses and individual lessons as well as ways to shape the professional development work of teachers around moral questions. The suggestions offered here are meant merely to indicate possible directions for this work; they are by no means definitive or all-inclusive. The plans and activities outlined here should be altered to match the needs of particular classrooms and schools. They were developed primarily by teachers and staff from the Coalition of Essential Schools; where possible, I include attributions in the notes.

Designing Units or Courses of Instruction

In devising instruction around moral questions, teachers I have worked with have found it useful to employ one or more large questions as frameworks for units or whole courses, and then to explore that question through investigations of more narrow questions and specific cases. Tables 9.1, 9.2, and 9.3 show some possible framing questions for courses, along with corresponding sub-themes, case studies, and activities or assessments. As much as the particular examples of topics here, these tables, emptied of their content, might serve as a template for planning.

It is worth noting that one might prefer to use a "provocative proposition" in place of a question.[1] The question "Does democracy result in effective, representative, and humane governance?" might

Table 9.1. **AMERICAN HISTORY COURSE**

Course Title	The Conundrums of Democracy (American History)
Framing Question or Provocative Proposition	Does democracy result in effective, representative, and humane governance?
Sub-Question #1 and a Case Study	Should the public vote on complex policy issues? Case study on ballot initiatives in one's state.
Activities/Assessments for Sub-Question 1	1. Create an ad campaign for or against a particular current ballot initiative. 2. Research aftermath of previous ballot initiatives, such as California's Proposition 13.
Sub-Question #2 and Case Studies	What connections are there between wealth and political power? Case studies on the rise of labor unions and on current campaign finance laws.
Activities/Assessments for Sub-Question 2	1. Research the funding sources and policy stances of a favorite politician. 2. Conduct interview with a union representative and research labor history in his or her industry.
Final Activity/Assessment	Create a dramatization of an episode in history that demonstrates the extent to which democracy does or does not result in effective, representative, and humane governance

Table 9.2. **BIOLOGY COURSE**

Course Title	Exploring Life on Earth (Biology 1)
Framing Question or Provocative Proposition	What is the impact of biological discoveries and technological advances on society and on other living things?
Sub-Question #1 and Case Studies	How shall we use what we are learning from the Human Genome Project? Case studies on Huntington's disease and breast cancer.
Activities/Assessments for Sub-Question 1	Reflective writing on potential advantages and dangers of having deciphered the code of the human genome.
Sub-Question #2 and Case Studies	How do human beings and their technologies affect larger ecological systems? Case studies on local marshes, rivers, dam systems, or forest habitats.
Activities/Assessments for Sub-Question 2	Water analyses of local water sources, charting percentages and changes in concentration of particular chemicals.
Final Activity/Assessment	Panel presentation to the county health commission, making recommendations on a range of public health issues including, for example, immunization, prenatal genetic testing, flouridated water, waste management, stem-cell research, etc.

be rephrased, for example, "Democracy results in ineffective and inhumane governance." The question "What does 'success' mean in America?" might be rephrased, "Money is the main measure of success in America." The students' job, then, is to defend or refute the proposition, incorporating evidence from the core texts as they are studied. Whether using questions or propositions, the goal is always to help students deepen their thinking with more information, through discerning nuances and coming to appreciate the power of opposing arguments.

Whatever particular questions one chooses to frame a course, here are a few ideas to keep in mind:

- *What is a provocative question for some will not be provocative for all.* Whether or not a question evokes interest in a particular

Table 9.3. **AMERICAN LITERATURE COURSE**

Course Title	American Identity and Experience (American Literature)
Framing Question or Provocative Proposition	What does it mean to be an American? Is there a set of common American experiences and beliefs?
Sub-Question #1 and Case Studies	What does "success" mean in America? Case studies: *The Great Gatsby; Catcher in the Rye; Beloved; House Made of Dawn.*
Activities/Assessments for Sub-Question 1	1. Final Word Protocol. 2. Discussion based on close reading of selected passages from the core texts.
Sub-Question #2 and Case Studies	What is a "family" in America? How are family relationships structured? *The Bean Trees; I Know Why the Caged Bird Sings; Ordinary People; The Chosen.*
Activities/Assessments for Sub-Question 2	1. Research into the students' family trees, including extended, adopted, blended families. 2. Construction of family trees for the characters in the core texts.
Final Activity/Assessment	Expository or narrative text whose theme revolves around the issue of American identity and experience.

group of students depends on many factors. In classrooms where there are many children from different countries or who speak different languages, for example, the question "What does it mean to be an American?" may be a vital concern. In less diverse classrooms this question, though equally important, may fall flat. In that case, rephrasing the question to speak to students' intrinsic concerns would be crucial.

- *Moral and existential questions are illuminated over time.* A key goal of courses designed around moral and existential questions is to keep coming back to the same big questions, exploring them anew in light of new learning.
- *Information from other disciplines is relevant.* It is in the nature of these kind of questions that answering them well relies on knowing things from several subject areas. It is definitely fair game for teachers and students to bring knowledge from other sources to bear on the questions they are investigating.

As in all instructional planning, and as this template suggests, it is useful to think from the beginning about how the students will be asked to demonstrate their understanding of the concept explored in the unit.[2] What should a student know and be able to do after grappling with the question "What is the impact of biological discoveries and technological advances on society and on other living things?" In the way I have structured the above course outlines, a key strategy is to have students delve deeply into one or more particular issues—for example, immunization—in order to shed light on the larger questions.

Classroom Lessons

Designing courses around key moral and existential questions will help highlight their importance to students and provide them with a framework and rationale for uncovering and remembering specific pieces of information. But even when a course is designed around such key questions, the real teaching challenge lies in structuring day-to-day interactions and activities. The following guidelines may be useful for designing individual lesson plans.

- *Design ways for the least vocal students to participate fully.* So often in open classroom discussions, the students who find it easiest to speak are the ones who get practice expressing their opinions. Below, I give some examples of structures that help to mitigate this.[3] In general, it seems to me that the best way to make sure less vocal students are able to participate fully is to design lessons that move back and forth between writing and speaking, and among individual thinking time, small group discussion, and large group discussion. Often, students who are reticent speaking in large groups will do better if they have had a chance to write down (or draw!) their thinking first, and perhaps to share it with a partner. Similarly, the thinking of students who are quick to talk is often deepened if they have a chance to talk first in a small group and then to write before they face the whole group.
- *Avoid polarization.* Whether it is through police and lawyer programs on television, the rhetoric of politicians, or any of the many other ways we separate the "good guys" from the "bad guys," our society has a tendency to think of all issues in terms of two sides.

A key goal of exploring moral issues is to deepen thinking, not just to choose sides. While debate can be a useful classroom technique, it is also valuable to find exercises that help uncover gray areas, seek common ground, or build consensus. Again, some of the structures below support this goal.

- *Support students in developing an informed opinion.* So often, kids in school get off the hook by saying, "This is what I think; I have a right to my opinion." Of course everyone has a right to his or her opinion. But students should know that even when discussing moral and existential issues, garnering relevant evidence is absolutely crucial.

- *Encourage students to shift their opinions as warranted.* Students may believe that changing opinions is a sign of being wishy-washy. Through explorations of moral issues in class, they can learn that changing opinions can be a sign of courage, of having gained more knowledge, and of deep thinking.

- *Teach the tools of discussion along with the content of the discussions.* Part of what was so impressive about some of the most powerful discussions I have depicted in this book is that the students had sets of tools—that they were conscious of—that facilitated their exploration of tough issues. Students used phrases like "I want to build on what Jessie said," or "I agree with Latisha's first point, but I am not sure I agree with her conclusion." They know how to build on one another and they know how to disagree respectfully. They know that balanced air time matters; they know that lots of issues have important middle grounds. Learning such characteristics of successful discussions and analyzing how any discussion went—aside from its content—is part of the learning.

Sharing First Opinions and Developing a Research Agenda

The structures and discussion formats that follow seek in different ways to address one or more of the above goals. The lesson plan outlined below, using a question about the death penalty as an example, seeks both to find ways for students to share their current opinions and also to help them establish a research agenda so that they can develop a more informed view.

SAMPLE LESSON PLAN. Example prompt: In what cases, if any, is the death penalty warranted?

1. Students do a "free write" in response to the prompt.
2. Students share what they have written, or the gist of it, with a partner.
3. With their partner, students discuss: What do we agree on? What are we uncertain about? What other information do we need? They create a chart that lists "Things we agree on," "Things we disagree on," and "Things at least one of us wants to know more about."
4. With the whole group, collect and chart the various ideas on which different pairs agreed.
5. Invite students to express their opinion to the whole group. Why do you hold the view you do? What ideas inform your opinion?
6. Ask the group: Is there any information that could convince you to change your mind? Is there any information that would help you know that your opinion is, in fact, sound? If you are undecided, is there information you need to help you make up your mind?
7. Develop a "research agenda" to find out more about the issue.
8. Analyze the discussion: How well were you able to share "air time" in your pairs and as a whole group? What feelings arose in you as the conversation proceeded? What suggestions do you have for us as a class for the next time we discuss a controversial issue?

Through discussions such as these, students are likely to generate a new set of questions, the answers to which would inform their opinions, for example: Does the death penalty have a deterrent effect? What are the relevant statistics from states and countries that do and do not practice the death penalty? What is the effect of a criminal's execution on his or her victims? What are the actual goals of the death penalty? To protect society? To punish the criminal? What else? Student research into these questions then may provide rich material for further discussions of this issue and other, related ones.

Final Word Protocols

The Final Word Protocol was originally designed to facilitate discussion around a specific text. This structure and the variation that follows it are especially useful for helping students listen well to a variety of points of view, rather than immediately trying to figure out how to refute them. They also provide comfortable small groups for students to share their views.[4]

METHOD #1: USING A TEXT

1. Everyone is given time to read or reread the text, marking particular passages that seem most meaningful or striking.
2. Form groups of three to five people sitting in tight circles. Each group appoints one person as timekeeper.
3. The first person begins by reading a passage from the text and explaining why he or she chose it as especially meaningful or striking. He or she has three minutes to speak.
4. Proceeding around the circle, each of the other people has one minute to discuss the passage that was selected by the first person. These people may respond to what the first person said or speak to the passage in any other way that extends the group's understanding, including asking questions.
5. The first person has the "final word," responding to what others said or elaborating on his or her original statement.
6. The next person begins by sharing a passage, and the process is repeated.
7. After everyone in the small groups has taken a turn, end with a large group "debriefing," asking questions like these: How did this activity go in your group? Was it easy or hard to stick to the protocol? What did you learn about the text or issue we are studying?

METHOD #2: WITHOUT A TEXT

1. Form groups of three people sitting in tight circles. Each group appoints one person as timekeeper.
2. The facilitator asks a provocative question—for example, Should government money (that is, money collected through

taxes) be used to support people living in poverty? If so, what conditions, if any, should be placed on receiving the money? If not, how should poor people be supported?

3. The first person has two minutes to speak.

4. Proceeding around the circle, each of the other people has one minute to paraphrase what the first person said. The point here is to reflect and reiterate the first person's ideas, not to build on them or challenge them.

5. The first person has the final word, clarifying anything that he or she thinks may have been misunderstood, and elaborating, if desired, on the original statement.

6. The next person begins by responding to the question, and the process is repeated.

7. After everyone in the small groups has taken a turn, end with a large group "debriefing," asking questions like these: How did this activity go in your group? Was it easy or hard to stick to the protocol? What did you learn about the issue we are studying?

Constructivist Learning Groups

"Constructivist Learning Groups" help students delve deeply into a topic through a series of five or so questions or statements. They are structured to promote careful listening and to give everyone a chance to speak in both large and small groups. The example I use does not require reference to a specific text, but questions could be tailored to nurture reflection on particular texts or other content. My example also requires some personal revelation, but questions can be tailored to match the safety level that students feel in the classroom.[5]

PROCESS

1. Form groups of five people. Each person in each group gets a number, one through five.

2. The facilitator presents the first question or problem to all the groups. All the groups discuss the question for five minutes, trying to achieve consensus, if possible, and recording key points of their discussion.

3. At the end of the five minutes, the facilitator calls out a number

from one to five, and the person with that number in each small group reports on that group's discussion.

4. The facilitator charts the responses of all the groups.

5. The facilitator gives the groups another question, and the process begins again until each person has had a chance to report.

6. After the process has been completed, analyze the activity with the whole group: What key ideas are you walking away with? How did this process work for you? How did it feel to know that you might have to report your group's thinking?

EXAMPLE. A series of questions discussed in this way might be:

1. What does it mean to lead a successful life?

2. In your view, is leading a "successful" life the same as or different from leading a "good" life?

3. Would it be possible for everyone in the world to lead a successful life, according to your definition? Or does one person's success rely on someone else *not* succeeding?

4. Are there things in American society that would need to be changed to help more people achieve your definition of success?

5. How close are you personally to achieving your definition of success?

Fishbowl Format

Another technique for fostering large group, in-depth discussions is called the "fishbowl." The fishbowl is especially useful when students have already done some research about a specific topic and have a fair amount of information that they need to synthesize. It allows students to develop listening skills, practice sharing the floor, and build on one another's thinking.

PROCESS

1. Divide the whole group into a small group of two to seven people and a large group of ten to twenty-five people.

2. The small group sits in a circle in the center of the room, with one or two empty chairs in their circle. The large group sits in a

large concentric circle, facing the backs of the small group.

3. The small group begins to discuss its issue. This is a real-time discussion, as the group explores a genuine question that it has been working on.

4. Members of the large group listen. When one of them wants to ask a clarifying question or make a comment, he or she moves into one of the empty chairs. After asking the question or making the comment, he or she moves back out into the big circle.

5. After a predesignated amount of time, the members of the small group stop their discussion. Members of the large group then respond to questions like these: What points were raised that seem most salient? What did you learn about the issue? What did you appreciate about the way the discussion went? Did everyone have a chance to speak?

EXAMPLES FROM VARIOUS DISCIPLINES. After reading the textbook and several primary sources, the fishbowl discussion group might explore one of these questions:

• How are relations between the races in America different in 2001 versus 1955?

• Who or what should be given priority in water allocations in the Southwest: Farmers? Industry? City dwellers? Preservation of natural habitats?

• What does it mean to "come of age"? Use examples from your own experience and the novels we have read.

I want to stress that the questions presented here as examples may meet the criterion of being provocative and relevant in some contexts, with some groups of kids, but not in others. Often it is effective to have the students generate the questions of importance after they have begun studying their topic (and with some practice at ferreting out interesting questions).

Although many teachers have had great success with structured discussions such as the ones outlined here, it may take considerable practice for everyone—teachers and students—to feel comfortable with them. As in all change efforts, the process can be smoother and more enjoyable if it is a group effort. The following section gives some suggestions for how teachers can work together to support one another as they seek to incorporate important issues into the curriculum.

Teacher Collaboration

I have had the opportunity to work with small groups of teachers who are seeking together to revise curriculum and adopt new teaching strategies focusing on moral and existential questions. If one has the luxury of working with such a team, the following four ongoing activities can be very productive: practicing discussing moral issues, collaborative planning, examining student work, and reciprocal classroom observations.

Practicing Discussing Moral Issues

Much of the literature on teaching writing has suggested that it makes sense for writing teachers to write. The theory is not that writing teachers have to be well-known or even published writers, but that both for the sake of credibility and for the sake of truly understanding the challenges they present to their students, teachers should engage in similar challenges.[6] A similar argument applies to the discussion of moral issues. Few of us regularly practice engaging in the sort of discussions that I have argued would be most profitable for students, certainly not in diverse settings with people who may hold extremely divergent views. There is something powerful for teachers in experiencing both the vulnerability and the intellectual excitement of these discussions. Experiencing these discussions as participants has the potential to make us more sensitive and versatile facilitators of students' learning.

But what issues should teachers discuss? The life of the school gives wonderful material for conversations that would be productive to explore for their own sake, not just for the sake of practice. The following sets of questions are just a few examples; the comings and goings of any school could generate many more.

- What is the purpose of giving grades in this school? Are grades a message we send to the outside world or to the students? What effects does our grading system have on our students' motivation to work hard and their ability to recognize high-quality work? Are there ways we should change the system?

- Which students are being served best by the way our school's course offerings and teacher assignments are currently set up? Are there ways in which course offerings and teacher assignments tend to reinforce the achievement gap between different ethnic, racial, and gender groups?
- How do we define cheating here? Are students supposed to work together on assignments? When and how much? Are there ways in which our policies might encourage students to cheat? If we find students cheating, however that is defined, what should we do?

When teachers explore such questions together they are likely to find, just as students do, that emotions run high, so mechanisms need to be found to make sure everyone can be heard. They also are likely to be prompted to gather more information and to seek areas of consensus. They might even decide that some of these same issues are worth exploring with students. All these outgrowths of such discussions have the potential to add richness to the intellectual and moral life of the school and to give teachers practice in concrete skills that may translate to the classroom.

Collaborative Planning

In the examples cited throughout the book, many if not all examples of rich moral and existential questions have been interdisciplinary in nature. For this reason—aside from the fact that working together is invigorating and enriching in general—it makes particular sense for teachers to collaborate when teaching with moral questions. The fragmentation of the intellectual work in high school has been well documented; how powerful it would be for students if they were able to explore a set of similar issues through a variety of disciplinary lenses.[7]

A team of three teachers at Drake High in San Anselmo, California, for example, has taken on this challenge, putting together a course for tenth graders whose overarching question for the year is, "Should limits be put on human behavior?" The three teachers have framed a series of subthemes using provocative propositions, including "the use of force is never justified" and "human beings have the right to use other human beings." Students are exploring these ideas using the tools and content knowledge of their history, literature, and biology classes.[8]

Aside from the exciting potential for interdisciplinary work, planning together can help teachers gain the diversity of perspectives that is so crucial when considering moral issues. As I mentioned in Chapter 7 when discussing my unit on the 1920s in America, my teaching would have been greatly improved if there had been an opportunity to deliberate about curricular choices with colleagues. We can help one another with our blind spots; we can offer new ideas and resources. The Tuning Protocol, developed primarily for use in looking closely at student exhibitions, provides one useful structure for teachers to share plans with one another.[9] The structure allows a group or an individual to receive both supportive and critical feedback without getting caught in needing to respond to all individual comments or questions. Time allotments are suggested as minimums for each task.

TUNING PROTOCOL PROCESS

1. Introduction. Facilitator briefly introduces the protocol's goals, norms, and agenda. Focus is on the presenter getting useful feedback, not on answering all of the reflectors' questions or concerns. (5 minutes)
2. Presenting Group (or Individual) Shares Its Work. In this phase, the presenting group discusses its work without interruption. The reflecting group listens and takes notes. (15 minutes)
3. Clarifying Questions. The reflecting group asks clarifying questions of the presenters, and the presenters respond. (5 minutes)
4. Feedback. The reflecting group engages in a conversation that includes warm (affirming) and cool (pushing) feedback. The presenters listen and take notes, without responding. (15 minutes)
5. Presenters Reflect. The presenters reflect on those comments or questions that they choose to. There is no need to respond to everything mentioned during the feedback phase. (10 minutes)
6. Debrief. The whole group discusses any frustrations,

misunderstanding, or positive reactions that the participants have experienced during the protocol. (10 minutes)

Examining Student Work on Moral and Existential Issues

Part of what makes exploring moral and existential questions with students so challenging is that these questions do not have simple answers. It is hard to construct tests that will measure the students' accomplishments in this realm. So how does a teacher evaluate a student's work? What are the standards? When the goal is deep thinking, what constitutes high-quality work for a ten-year-old? a fifteen-year-old? I know of no better way to grapple with these questions than to analyze collectively real examples of student work. In the past several years, looking at student work has become a fairly widespread practice in the world of teacher professional development, and there are many models used, depending on one's specific purposes.[10]

"Constructing Standards by Examining Student Work" is designed to help teachers jointly develop a sense of what constitutes excellence in the exploration of moral or existential issues.[11]

PROCESS

1. Teachers meet in a group of three to fifteen, all of them bringing an example of what they consider to be among the best work in exploring moral or existential issues that they have received from students.
2. Each teacher looks carefully at the work he or she has brought and creates a list of three or more qualities that contribute to making it outstanding.
3. Meeting in groups of three, teachers swap student work and repeat the process of listing outstanding qualities.
4. The whole group brainstorms the qualities it has found, and then condenses the list to three to five qualities everyone agrees are essential to good work in the realm of exploring moral or existential issues.
5. The group devises a plan for future work, in which teams of teachers will collaborate to develop teaching strategies that will help students master these qualities in their work.

Working together and staying close to the real work that students are producing, teachers will have the opportunity to think creatively about issues of standards and assessment as well as how to push students to continue to develop their powers of thought and expression.

Reciprocal Peer Observations

Much teacher and student work can be shared outside of class. But for teachers fully to work together on creating a school where moral and existential issues are investigated in-depth, observing one another in the classroom seems essential. Observing colleagues at work breaks an extremely strong norm of schooling, for teaching has traditionally happened behind closed doors. But teachers report that one of the most powerful ways for them to get better at their craft is to watch one another and offer feedback.[12] If that is true in general, it is even more important in the context of exploring moral and existential questions, where the pedagogy is so challenging and the stakes are so high.

Observing one another is also crucial in the context of the "whose values" question. As I argued in Chapter 7, if we are going to be actively engaged in exploring moral issues while nurturing democratic and pluralistic values, classrooms and curricular materials must be open—to colleagues, parents, researchers, reporters, and other community members. The Peer Observation Guide provides a simple framework for conducting peer observations whose purpose is to enlist a colleague in helping to understand particular aspects of his or her teaching practice.[13]

PROCESS

1. Pre-observation conference. The teacher who will be observed explains the context of the class period to be observed, and asks the observer to focus on a particular aspect of his or her teaching. For example, a teacher might ask the observer to note how he or she responds to student questions.
2. Observation. The observer focuses on the specific aspect of teaching talked about during the pre-observation conference, taking notes.

3. Debriefing. The observer begins by restating the focus and asking the observee to share his or her thoughts. Example: How did you feel about the lesson? What did you notice about the way you responded to student questions? After the observee talks, the observer may (1) summarize what the observee is saying, (2) supply notes on specific events that corroborate the observee's statements, (3) raise questions related to the focus that arose during the observation, (4) supply notes on specific events that seem to contrast with the observee's comments.

Throughout this book, I have focused on the ways students' lives at school might be invigorated by a deliberate focus on moral and existential questions. I feel equally convinced, though it is a subject for another book, that teachers' lives could be greatly enriched if their role were expanded in the ways suggested here. It's time to transform teaching into work that calls upon our greatest powers of collaboration and creativity, that nurtures our own moral and intellectual development, that takes advantage of the maturity and wisdom we have managed to gain. If we take up the challenge to explore real questions of meaning and purpose with our students and among ourselves, teaching will become that kind of life work.

Appendix: Methods

Observation Schedules

As explained in Chapter 3, I spent approximately four nonconsecutive weeks at each school, observing classes all day. My typical observation schedules at each of the schools were as follows.

PERIOD	FRONTIER	SAINT PAUL	AGNON
1	War and Peace	Biology	World Literature
2	American Literature/ History (two-hour block)	American Literature	U.S. History
3		Morality	Jewish Ethics
4	Biology	Social Justice	Biology
5	Anchor Program	Drama	Jewish Thought
6	various	U.S. History	American Literature
7			Jewish Ethics
8			Psychology/Drama/ other elective

(Agnon had a longer school day with somewhat shorter periods than the other schools, so it had more total class periods.)

Data Collection

Classroom and Interview Data

All students and teachers in the classes I observed were asked for their consent. Early in the study, I distributed "positive" consent forms, requiring parental signatures for the students who agreed to take part in the study. When I had difficulty collecting those consents, I switched to a "negative" consent procedure. Classroom data were collected through the use of field notes and audiotape. I taped classes selectively, recording those sessions that seemed most likely to pertain to moral and existential issues, and where noise and acoustic conditions in the classroom would permit. I later transcribed verbatim from the audiotapes the class sessions that seemed most pertinent to the study.

Interview Data

I interviewed the teachers of each of the core and religion classes at least once for approximately one hour, usually after I had been observing in class for a week or two. I had a short list of questions that I tried to cover at some point with each teacher, but the interviews were open-ended, usually focusing on specific incidents I had observed from that teacher's class. I interviewed a number of the teachers twice, once toward the beginning and again toward the end of my observation period. My overall goal in the teacher interviews was to learn how and to what extent, if any, the teachers saw the subject matter they were teaching as being of moral or existential significance, whether they saw themselves as having roles as moral educators more generally, and what conflicts, if any, they saw in their various roles. All interviews were audiotaped and transcribed.

In addition to the formal interviews, I spoke informally with most of the teachers on several occasions about what they had planned for upcoming classes and about their reactions to particular class sessions or student comments. Although these conversations were instructive, I kept them to a minimum because I wanted as much as possible to get a "student's eye view" of each class, rather than to have inside knowledge of the teacher's intentions. For the most part, I arrived in class with the students a few minutes before the bell and, like them, tucked my backpack under my seat and sat down (toward the back of the room). Being a "fly on the wall" as a researcher is never totally possible, but I tried to keep a fairly low profile in class.

Within each class I observed, I asked for student volunteers to participate in an interview; I also asked for teacher recommendations of students who represented a cross-section of the class in terms of achievement, and invited for interviews individual students whose class participation I had found especially interesting. I interviewed students individually, usually for approximately thirty minutes. On a few occasions I interviewed students in pairs or trios. These interviews, like the teacher interviews, were open-ended, focusing both on particular class sessions I had observed and also on the students' experiences in school more generally. Desiring to test my assumption that students find moral and existential issues particularly compelling, I tried to ascertain which school projects, assignments, or discussions students found most meaningful and important. I interviewed as many students as I could during their free periods and lunch hours. Because Agnon had eight periods a day and students tended to have several free periods during the week, I was able to interview more students and teachers there than at the other schools.

In addition to teachers and students, I also interviewed a few administrators, admissions officials, or counselors at two of the three sites to get a sense of the larger school program and mission. The total number of interviews I conducted at each school were as follows: Frontier, six teachers and nineteen students; Saint Paul, six teachers, sixteen students, and three administrators or counselors; Agnon, ten teachers, twenty-seven students, and three administrators or admissions officials.

Other Observation Data

In addition to regular classroom sessions, I observed other school gathering places and events such as assemblies, athletic practices, the cafeteria, quad, and local fast-food restaurants during lunch, pep rallies, study hall, club meetings, student lavatories, and prayer groups. I aimed throughout the study to get a feel for the rhythm of being in school all day and to find those moments when students' hearts and minds seemed to be engaged. These observations helped provide me with background and a better context for understanding what I saw in the focus of my study, the academic classrooms.

Document Data

At each school and in each classroom I collected and analyzed various documents that had the potential to help me understand the intellectual and moral aims of the school and of individual teachers. Schoolwide documents collected included curriculum guides, student handbooks, and admissions brochures; course-specific documents included syllabi, course requirements and rules, assignments, quizzes, tests, and excerpts from textbooks. I also collected samples of student writing, including course assignments and student-written school newspapers.

Incorporation of Feedback from Teachers

A final source of data collected was the feedback received from teachers on early drafts of my writing. Several months after the observation phase of the study was completed, I scheduled meetings with the teachers I had observed at Frontier and Saint Paul. I shared descriptions of scenarios from all the schools with the teachers who were able to attend the meeting. I thought it particularly important to have teachers critique and add to my analyses of "missed opportunities" in the teaching of moral and existential issues. At both sites, the teachers commented on the scenarios and my analyses; their comments are incorporated into Chapter 4 and Chapter 7. Unfortunately, because of logistic and scheduling difficulties, I was unable to hold this kind of meeting at Agnon.

Validity and Generalizability of the Study

This study joins the relatively new field of empirically based, naturalistic exploration of schools, and so inescapably enters the continuing debates regarding the objectivity and validity of qualitative research methods. Eisner and Peshkin (1990) list some of the questions that remain alive regarding the use of qualitative methods: "Is it possible to talk about 'educational implications' of the research when the situation studied is nonrandom and the method unique to the investigator?... What does one make of an approach to the study of the educational world that depends upon the unique aptitudes and proclivities of the investigator, that possesses no standardized method, that focuses upon nonrandomly selected situations, and that yields questionable generalizations by conventional research criteria?" (p. 10). The questions raised here are relevant to this study, because clearly I cannot base claims for its validity on the criteria traditionally used in experimental research, such as replicability, falsifiability, and generalizability.

Several theorists have suggested alternate criteria for judging the validity of qualitative work in the field of education. Eisner (1991), writing specifically about a form of qualitative inquiry he calls "educational criticism," suggests three: "structural corroboration," the use of multiple sources of data "to support or contradict the interpretation or evaluation"; "consensual validation," a consensus among observers of the same phenomena, or "a consensus won from readers who are persuaded by what the critic has to say"; and "referential adequacy," the extent to which "readers are able to see what they would have missed without the critic's observations" (pp. 112–114). Eisenhart and Borko (1993) paraphrase Howe and Eisenhart (1990) as arguing similarly that "the validity of an educational research study, regardless of the research design used, can be determined by how carefully the study is designed, conducted, and presented, how sensitively it treats human subjects, and how well it contributes to important educational issues, including debates about educational theory and practice" (p. 93).

These sets of criteria differ somewhat. But they share the fascinating notion that a large determinant of a study's validity is whether or not it is useful; whether, in Howe and Eisenhart's word, it "contributes" to debates about educational theory and practice. Whereas experimental research could ostensibly meet validity criteria while still unpublished, in qualitative research, these theorists seem to say, the proof is (largely) in the pudding. Its consumers must judge whether or not it was worth the effort.

It seems to me that while the criteria suggested by Eisner, Howe, and Eisenhart are useful for evaluating the worth of a study, they do not speak to the notion of *validity*, at least not as the word has been understood. It should be noted that "how sensitively one treats human subjects," though supremely important, is irrelevant to validity. Further, the criteria of "referential adequacy" and "contribution" could be used with regard to works of art, for example, and not only academic research. Indeed, Eisner and Peshkin (1990) envision the day when the academy will accept "Ph.D. dissertations in education that are written in the form of novels" (p. 365). Whether or not that comes to pass, it seems to me that the term "validity" fails to capture the senses of verisimilitude or persuasiveness that Peshkin and Eisner—and Howe and Eisenhart—wish to convey. Perhaps the relevant question for qualitative studies will no longer be "Is it valid?" but rather, "Is it worthwhile? Does it provide insight? Does it motivate readers to action?" and the like.

Setting aside the term "validity," then, I will note that I did seek in the course of this study to honor the criteria for quality assurance that Eisner and the others suggest. I attempted to find what Eisner calls structural corroboration (what others call "triangulation") for my claims, both by collecting a variety of kinds of data and by staying in each observation site long enough (approximately four weeks) to discern regularities from anomalous occurrences. Those classroom episodes that I document in the study could easily be shown to represent types I observed rather than being unique or "outliers." I also attempted to achieve a measure of "consensual validity" by incorporating feedback on the work in progress from those I observed and from other teachers, and by citing the work of other researchers whose observations corroborate mine. It remains to be seen whether the study achieves Eisner's "referential adequacy," allowing others to see what they would not have seen or to articulate more fully what they already know, and thereby contributing to the development of educational theory and the improvement of schooling.

Regarding the issue of generalizability, studies like mine, based on a small number of cases, "are generalizable to theoretical propositions and not to populations or universes . . . and the investigator's goal is to expand and generalize theories . . . and not to enumerate frequencies" (Yin, 1984, p. 21). Without any claims to statistical generalizability, this study represents an attempt to gather in-depth data on the everyday life of a number of classrooms across three schools for the purpose of contributing to a broader conceptualization of the kinds of inquiry in which teachers and students might collaboratively engage.

Notes

Chapter 1: The Place of Meaning

1. Coles (1990, pp. 332, 335).

2. Hutchins (1953, p. 70).

3. The study's methods are described in detail in Chapter 3 and the Appendix.

4. In Chapters 2 and 3, I comment further on the choice to use the word "existential" rather than "spiritual" and the different connotations of each.

5. Noddings (1989, p. 243). It is worth noting, too, that while the words enable one to speak and be understood, the distinction between the intellectual and the moral and existential is extremely tenuous as well. Indeed, one of the central arguments of this book is that these categories overlap so significantly that the *intellectual* life of schools is severely impoverished by lack of attention to the other realms.

6. See Wiggins (1993), Meier (2000), and Kohn (1999). For a discussion of what tests can and cannot successfully measure, see Popham (1999).

7. Evenson (1996).

8. Oldenburg and Edmonds (1996).

9. Others who address a similar concern include such diverse thinkers as Stephen Carter (1993) and Stephen Toulmin. Toulmin, a philosopher of science, describes in language quite similar to Havel's the intellectual fragmentation wrought by modern science. He is quoted in *Habits of the Heart:*

> From the early seventeenth century on... the tasks of scientific inquiry were progressively divided up between separate and distinct "disciplines."... Every independent scientific discipline is marked by its own specialized modes of abstraction: and the issues to be considered in each discipline are defined such that they can be investigated and discussed independently—in abstraction from—the issues belonging to other disciplines.... As a result of this first kind of abstraction, the broad and general questions about "cosmic interrelatedness" which were the focus of the earlier debates about nature have been superseded by other, more specialized, disciplinary questions. In its actual content (that is to say) the science of the nineteenth and early twentieth centuries became an aggregate, rather than an integration, of results from its component disciplines. (Bellah et al., 1985, p. 278)

10. Havel (1994).

11. Gray (1994).

12. David Tyack and Larry Cuban (1995) show that the tendency to rely on the schools to solve all social ills has a long history in our country. They also suggest that the attention paid to schools sometimes camouflages the deeper societal roots of the problems schools are called upon to solve:

> In the early twentieth century, educational elites saw themselves as expert social engineers who could perfect the nation by consciously directing the evolution of society. When Lyndon B. Johnson sought to build the "Great Society" and declared war on poverty in the 1960s, he asserted that "the answer to all our national problems comes down to a single word: education."
>
> ...Repeatedly, Americans have followed a common pattern in devising educational prescriptions for specific social or economic ills. Once they had discovered a problem, they labeled it and taught a course on the subject: alcohol or drug instruction to fight addictions; sex education to combat syphilis or AIDS; home economics to lower the divorce rate; driver education to eliminate carnage on the highway; and vocational training or courses in computer literacy to keep the United States economically competitive.
>
> ...The utopian tradition of social reform through schooling has often diverted attention from more costly, politically controversial, and difficult societal reform. It's easier to provide vocational education than to remedy inequities in employment and gross disparities in wealth and income. (Tyack and Cuban, 1995, pp. 2–4)

13. See, for example, Wynne and Ryan (1997).

14. Lickona (1991, pp. 6–12).

15. See, for example, Molnar (1997) and Bradsher (1996).

Chapter 2: What Is Moral Education?

1. For an argument against school being seen only as a means to an end, see Dewey (1938). For powerful and still completely accurate descriptions of the boredom and passivity experienced by most students when they are at school and the "treaties" teachers and students make to avoid discussing matters of substance, see Sizer (1984) and Goodlad (1984); for a more recent treatment of this issue, see Kohn (1999).

2. I do not know how to *ensure* that the products of the educational process will be respectful, reliable, and honest, but then, neither do the proponents of other models of moral education. There is very little reliable evidence that direct instruction in morality such as that promoted by "virtues" education, for

example, actually affects students' behavior. See Sockett (1992), who writes, in the context of sex education: "That the connection between education and behavioral change is negligible is a devastating conclusion in the face of AIDS. Yet failure has been a common theme in the history of moral education in schools" (p. 544). Writing more generally about the absence of research into moral education's effects on behavior, Sockett notes, "While what students learn has been a primary focus of educational research, the student as a moral initiate has not been seen by research as a person with a life outside and between school" (p. 562).

3. See Noddings (1992). Although Noddings' approach appeals to me, even she admits that such a radical restructuring is unlikely to occur (Nel Noddings, personal communication, 1996). As I shall discuss below, Noddings' more recent work stays much closer to the realm of the possible in articulating a vision of how matters of belief could be linked to intellectual pursuits within the academic disciplines.

4. See Lickona (1991), Kilpatrick (1992), and Rosenblatt (1995).

5. Although existential matters are not an explicit focus of her ethic of care, Noddings clearly shares this conviction. In *Educating for Intelligent Belief and Unbelief*, she demonstrates how the academic content of course material—that of mathematics, particularly—can and should be linked to universal moral and existential questions. "I want to challenge the long-standing assumption that mathematics should be taught as a totally separate, isolated set of skills and concepts," Noddings writes. "If I can convince readers that we can educate for intelligent belief or unbelief in mathematics classes, they may be convinced that we can do it anywhere!" (Noddings, 1993, p. 1). This work can in many respects be seen as an empirical extension and elaboration of her idea that existential questions are a key ingredient of genuine academic pursuits.

6. The Character Education Partnership has published "Eleven Principles of Effective Character Education" under the authorship of Tom Lickona, Eric Schaps, and Catherine Lewis (1996), whose own educational works represent differing orientations to curriculum and pedagogy. Included among the eleven principles are many with which I agree. For example, "'Character' must be comprehensively defined to include thinking, feeling, and behavior"; "Character education should strive to develop students' intrinsic motivation"; and "The school staff must become a learning and moral community in which all share responsibility for character education and attempt to adhere to the same core values that guide the education of students."

7. Bennett (1993).

8. Ryan (1989); Wynne (1986, p. 9).

9. Kilpatrick (1992, p. 26).

10. Kilpatrick (1992); Lickona (1991); Wynne (1986).

11. Bennett (1993, p. 701); Noddings (1989, pp. 701 and 231).

12. Noddings (1989, pp. 231 and 232, emphasis in the original).

13. Raths, Harmin, and Simon (1966) and Simon, Howe, and Kirschenbaum (1972).

14. Simon, Howe, and Kirschenbaum (1972, p. 16).

15. Raths, Harmin, and Simon (1966, p. 34).

16. Simon, Howe, and Kirschenbaum (1972, p. 27).

17. Ibid. (pp. 40; 51–53).

18. Chazan (1985, p. 68).

19. Kohlberg (1978, pp. 50–51, emphasis in original).

20. Kohlberg (1980, pp. 78–79).

21. Kohlberg describes the dilemma as follows:

In Europe, a woman was near death from a very bad disease, a special kind of cancer. There was one drug that the doctors thought might save her. It was a form of radium that a druggist was charging ten times what the drug cost him to make. He paid $200 for the radium and charged $2,000 for a small dose of the drug. The sick woman's husband, Heinz, went to everyone he knew to borrow the money, but he could only get together about $1,000, which is half of what it cost. He told the druggist that his wife was dying, and asked him to sell it cheaper or let him pay later. But the druggist said, "No, I discovered the drug and I'm going to make money from it." So Heinz got desperate and broke into the man's store to steal the drug for his wife. Should the husband have done that? Why? (Ibid., p. 27).

22. Kohlberg, 1978, p. 47. See also Power, Higgins, and Kohlberg (1989); Power (1988); and Wasserman (1978).

23. Contrasting the sorts of responses to Kohlbergian-type dilemmas she elicited from eleven-year-old girls with those from boys, Gilligan finds that the boys are willing to "play by the rules" of the hypothetical situation, to wrestle out the conflicts between values like protection of property and protection of life. Girls, on the other hand, try to alter the terms of the dilemma by appealing to human relationships and compassion. Gilligan quotes Amy, for example, when asked if Heinz should steal the drug for his wife: "Well, I don't think so. I think there might be other ways besides stealing it, like if he could borrow the money or make a loan or something, but he really shouldn't steal the drug— but his wife shouldn't die either.... If he stole the drug, he might save his wife then, but if he did, he might have to go to jail, and then his wife might get sicker again, and he couldn't get more of the drug, and it might not be good. So, they should really just talk it out and find some other way to make the money." While eleven-year-old boys would typically weigh the prohibition of stealing against the value of preserving life, Amy, as Gilligan says, sees "not a math problem with humans but a narrative of relationships that extends over time." Amy envisions the wife's "continuing need for her husband and the hus-

band's continuing concern for his wife and seeks to respond in a way that would sustain rather than sever the connection" (Gilligan, 1982, pp. 18–28).

24. Ibid. (see p. 160).

25. Noddings (1984, p. 6; emphasis in original).

26. Ibid. (pp. 11–14).

27. Ibid. (pp. 4, 74).

28. Noddings (1992, pp. xiii, 68–70). Noddings draws on Dewey, who argues that moral education must refer to the conduct of education as well as its product (Dewey 1909 and 1972).

29. Purpel (1989, p. 5).

30. Moffett (1994, p. 31).

31. Genesis 1:28; Soloveitchik (1965, pp. 12–13).

32. Genesis 2:7; Shakespeare, *Hamlet*, Act V, scene I; Soloveitchik uses "I–Thou," clearly echoing Buber (1923/1958).

33. Soloveitchik (1965, pp. 16–17).

34. Noddings (1989, p. 243).

35. Carter (1993, p. 15, ellipses and italics in the original). It is helpful, in the context of considering what is rational, to note Elliot Eisner's instructive distinction between "rationality" and "logic." Eisner defines rationality as "the exercise of intelligence in the creation or perception of elements as they relate to the whole in which they participate. I do not restrict rationality to discursively mediated thought or limit it to the application of logic. Human rationality is displayed whenever relationships among elements are skillfully crafted or insightfully perceived. Poets as well as physicians, painters as well as philosophers, actors and teachers as well as mathematicians and astronomers function rationally. The root of the term rationality is related to ratio—order of relationship. Thus, teachers planning a lesson, evaluators assessing a classroom, and administrators providing leadership to a faculty are all rational actors" (Eisner, 1991, pp. 51–52). Adam II, seeking to understand his or her own relation to the whole of creation, can be seen as quite rational in these terms.

36. See feminist theorists such as Lorde (1984); Noddings (1989); Rich (1976). For the definition of "spiritual" quoted here, see Ehrlich, Flexner, Carruth, and Hawkins (1980, p. 883, emphasis added). The Latin root of the word "spirit," unlike this modern definition, ties that seemingly metaphysical concept to a most physical process, "respiration." So it is, too, in Hebrew, where God brings Adam to life by giving him *n'shamah*, meaning at once "breath" and "soul." Far from being entrapped in or sullied by human bodies, human spirit can be understood to be at one with human physicality.

37. Grumet (1988, pp. 10 and xvi).

38. Peshkin (1986, p. 56).

39. Ibid. (p. 79).

40. Melinda Bollar Wagner has written a fascinating ethnographic account

of several other conservative Christian schools, in which she points out that in these schools Christian doctrine fails to drown out many influences from contemporary American culture: "Inside the schools, competition and materialism coexist or compete with the gentle fruits of the spirit that the conservative Christians identify as 'love, joy, peace, long-suffering, gentleness, goodness, faith, meekness, temperance.' Prayer requests and praise reports of the pupils were much more likely to be concerned with trips to Disney World for themselves, or with teenage relationships, than they were with, for example, healing of others' bodies or souls" (Wagner, 1990, p. 203). Despite these kinds of compromises with popular culture, there is little in Wagner's book to suggest that *intellectual* concerns command as much attention as the school's spiritual considerations.

41. Schoem (1989, p. 64).

Chapter 3: Three High Schools and a Researcher

1. Bryk, Lee, and Holland (1993); Schiff (1966).

2. Pseudonyms are employed for all schools, teachers, administrators, and students named in this study.

3. Catholic schools were first established in North America as early as 1640. At their peak size in 1965, U.S. Catholic schools enrolled 5.5 million students, 12 percent of all elementary and secondary students in the country. Enrollment has dropped since then, to roughly 2.5 million students in 1990, or 5.4 percent of the school-age population (Bryk, Lee, and Holland 1993).

4. Ibid. (1993).

5. See Himmelfarb (1990); Schiff (1966).

6. Reinharz (1979, p. 11).

7. Cuban (1992, p. 8).

8. Wilson, Miller, and Yerkes (1992).

9. I was reluctant to share the teaching files at first, afraid to "contaminate" my results. I realized, however, that if using my files pushed the teachers toward incorporating more attention to moral and existential issues into their units, that would only be for the best: my intention was never to determine how many of these discussions naturally occur in English classes, but to see what happens when they do occur.

10. Jackson, Boostrom, and Hansen (1993) betray the kind of befuddlement in which the discipline finds itself on this score, admitting that they "decided upon the title of [our] project, The Moral Life of Schools, long before we had a firm idea of what we would actually be looking for when our work began or even of what terms like *moral* and *moral life* could possibly mean when they were applied to what goes on in schools" (p. xv; emphases in original).

11. See, for example, Sockett (1992) and Purpel and Ryan (1983). Dewey

unequivocally argues that teachers teach morality "every moment of the day, five days of the week." "It may be laid down as fundamental," he claims, that "the influence of direct moral instruction, even at its best, is *comparatively* small in amount and slight in influence, when the whole field of moral growth through education is taken into account" (Dewey, 1909, pp. 3–4).

12. Jackson (1983).

13. Goodlad (1984); Noddings (1992); Powell, Farrar, and Cohen (1985); Sizer (1999).

Chapter 4: "We Could Argue About That All Day"

1. Purpel (1989), for example, refers to the ways in which students learn "to be obedient and passive, to work at meaningless tasks without complaining, to defer their pleasure, to value achievement and competition, and to please and respect authority figures" (p. 20). Goodlad (1984), in somewhat more neutral language, describes what he calls "the implicit curriculum" as "the ways [schools] present the explicit curriculum—for example, emphasizing acquiring facts or solving problems—through the kinds of rules they impose, and even through the social and physical setting they provide for learning. Thus, they teach students to work alone competitively or to work cooperatively in groups, to be active or passive, to be content with facts or also seek insight, and on and on. In brief, schools implicitly teach values" (p. 30).

2. My findings corroborate those of other researchers, who have argued that teachers of social studies, for example, focus on mastery of content to such an extent that "Standard social studies curriculum has no discernible impact on the socio-moral development of youth" (Leming, 1985, cited in Marker and Mehlinger, 1992).

3. The importance of talking for learning could form the subject of many studies of its own; it is well beyond the scope of this study to prove this point. A prominent source of support for this idea, however, comes from reader-response theory, summarized in Athanases (1993). It posits that there are two crucial stages for coming to understand a literary work—the first, a private response of reading, reacting, and reflecting, and the second, a public response of sharing, discussing, and reflecting. Other documentations of the importance of classroom talk to support and construct learning in math and science include Lampert (1990) and Brown (1994). If talking is a crucial element of coming to understand literature, math, and physics, it seems clear that this would be true of moral issues as well. Aside from the ways discussion fosters learning, discussion itself is a crucial skill for participation in a democracy. For more on this point, see Brookfield and Preskill (1999).

4. Sizer (1992); Shulman (1987a, p. 376).

5. Darling-Hammond (1993, p. 758).

6. Marker and Mehlinger (1992).

7. Turtle, a severely abused infant, had been literally handed to Taylor in a parking lot by a woman who begged Taylor to take the child. Several years later, the state disputed Taylor's right to the child, and Taylor arranged for a fraudulent adoption.

8. It is worth noting that Tom's perception of the nature of discussion in the small groups was significantly different from mine. His sense was that the students did in fact regularly have meaningful discussions in that forum. Here is his description of one moment he found particularly memorable during the study of *The Bean Trees*.

> The moment last week when I was most moved by the kids was in small group discussions over this issue that we were discussing a while ago about the sexual questions that are raised in the novel. And as the kids were talking about the nature of love, and as they were expressing in eloquent, really sophisticated ways what they understand the relationship between two people is really about, and what commitment really means and denial sometimes of drives—that in these kids' minds are the most powerful drives that you can contend with—with their sexual drives at this point in their lives being so strong. Their really sophisticated understanding of the tenderness between the characters at one point really moved me to tears. I mean I had to sort of step away from the group—it's not that I ever hide my tears from the kids, but it was, it was just so touching that a couple of the kids were expressing this in such eloquent terms. I was just sort of overwhelmed in the moment by it. I wouldn't expect it, even though they're articulate kids that I was working with at that moment. I just didn't expect to have kids be able to express something so sophisticated at such a tender age.

I am sure that Tom is accurate in his description of this moment, and his tears demonstrate his own deep connection to his students. My sense, however, is that such moments in small group were relatively rare, at least partly because what clearly "counted" in class—what would translate into a grade—was knowing the answers on the study sheets.

9. Several of the scenarios described throughout this study suggest, with other research in the field, that the way student knowledge is assessed casts a very long shadow on the curriculum as a whole. What ends up "counting," and therefore drawing students' attention, are those things that will be tested. While essay tests are potentially excellent forums in which to have students consider moral or existential issues (which Tom employed at other times), one cannot fault a high school teacher—typically serving 150 students each day—for also devising tests that are easier to score. For more on the effects of assessments on instructional practices, see Wiggins (1989 and 1993) and Kohn (1999).

10. Tom also told me, for example, that one of his students reported in her journal on a very animated discussion she and her classmates had had in the quad after class about a morally charged statement made by Tom in class—that in his experience, most teenage girls were passive, like the character Lou Ann, rather than assertive, like Taylor.

11. This is not to say that the project had no impact on Steve. Indeed, Ms. Morgan mentioned to me that Steve had told her, privately, several weeks after reading the book, that he wasn't going to McDonald's anymore, and Ms. Morgan shared with Steve that she had had the same response. There is something particularly powerful about the private sharing that can go on between individual students and teachers around a journal or a project like this one. But more of that richness could be brought into the central, public core of school. What is more, there are claims in *A Diet for a New America* that have to do with osteoporosis and other elements of human bone structure. Links could be found between the moral issues raised by Robbins and the demand of the current curriculum to teach topics like "bone structure."

12. The textbook they were using was Boyer (1995).

13. Unlike Ms. Gilman, other readers might critique the passage and the history book as a whole for being too much centered on the Anglos, rather than for being too harsh on them. As we are used to seeing in American history textbooks, the protagonists of the story are the "Anglos"; it is their "Westward Expansion" that drives the organization of the chapter. The narrative as a whole is a mostly triumphant story of the Anglos' successful nation-building in America.

14. The ensuing discussion might even have caused Ms. Gilman to reconsider her position, genuinely seeing the problem anew as she explored it with her students. Knowing that their own arguments could carry some weight, could persuade a teacher, would lend even more impetus to students to participate in such a discussion and to support their opinions well.

15. When and if a teacher should "give a right answer" is discussed in Chapter 7.

16. Noddings (1993, pp. 10–11; emphasis added).

17. Linda Darling-Hammond (1993) notes that in most schools, "the press of teaching is 'getting through' the curriculum, even if the students are being left behind (or left numb and unengaged) as the curriculum marches on, page by page and day by day" (p. 756).

18. Dewey (1902, p. 28; emphasis in original).

19. Noddings (1989, p. 243).

20. Deborah Meier (1995) writes convincingly about the phenomenon of teachers striving to cover material, even in the context of a school whose philosophy clearly holds that "less is more," and at the expense of talking about matters of great personal and social significance: "Even at Central Park

East... many new teachers take years before they stop using 'But I thought I had to' as an excuse for curriculum that they otherwise seem alienated from. Asked why they've ignored important social or scientific events rocking the world and their students' lives (the collapse of the Soviet Empire, the California earthquakes), they fall back on worrying about 'covering' the curriculum as though at CPESS [Central Park East Secondary School] that mattered. 'Coverage' remains a word we are all so accustomed to that it lingers long after we have formally abandoned the concept" (p. 143).

21. Ernest Boyer's (1993) comment on the connections between all school subjects, particularly science and art, are quite apt here:

To be truly educated means going beyond the isolated facts; it means putting learning in a larger context; and above all, it means, to return to my favorite word, it means discovering the *connectedness* of things. The Nobel laureate Barbara McClintock wrote on one occasion, "Everything is one. There is no way to draw a line between things." I wonder if Professor McClintock has looked at a school curriculum in recent years with all the separate academic boxes. Frank Press, President of the National Academy of Sciences, said in a recent speech that scientists are in some respects like artists, and to illustrate the point he said that the magnificent double helix, which broke the genetic code, was not only rational, it was beautiful as well. And yet in most schools, science and art teachers live in absolutely separate worlds; they don't communicate with one another. (pp. 6–7)

22. Wiesel (1960). Ms. Sherman's focus on this theme was particularly striking to me because earlier, on the same day, the same group of students had studied in religion class the implications of the commandment "to honor thy father and thy mother"—a precept certainly on Wiesel's mind throughout his experience. No one in class, however, mentioned the connection.

23. The *Science Framework for California Public Schools*, addressing science teachers, explicitly endorses the kind of response given by Ms. Sherman. It advises science teachers: "Every teacher must feel free to say and know when to say, 'Sorry, but that's not a question for science,' and explain why. Such questions should be treated with respect and referred to family or clergy for further discussion" (California State Board of Education, 1990, p. 20).

24. Nel Noddings (1993) writes of the loss involved in subject-area specialization: "Together, teachers and students struggle to find meaning for their lives in [the high school] curriculum. Yet the present reality is that most math teachers cannot help their homeroom students with English or history, and most English teachers turn pale at the mention of math problems. Thus the high school emulates the college with its collection of specialists none of whom is charged with the human responsibility to explore religious and existential questions" (pp. 135–136).

25. Certainly Kohlberg (1980) would recognize the students' comments—that justice and the law do not always correspond—as evidence of higher order moral development.

Chapter 5: "It Makes You Think"

1. For a concise, accessible description of some of these programs, see Bradsher (1996). I have critiqued the tenets of the virtues approach above, and will expand briefly on that critique in Chapter 7. Here, it is sufficient to recall that the approach often reduces the complexities of moral issues, acting as though "right" and "wrong" are always easily discernible and agreed upon by people of good will.

2. Shulman (1992).

3. Applebee (1996). For some examples of exceptional, sustained discussions of moral issues in literature classes, see Athanases (1993) and Haroutunian-Gordon (1991).

4. Small groups and journals are valid venues for the exploration of moral and existential issues. As I noted in Chapter 4, however, the small groups I observed often drifted away from such questions and turned to the more tangible questions on which they would be tested. Even if such small group discussions stay on task, it is significant that they happen only in the relatively private forum of a small group rather than in the large group, where knowledge tends to be recognized, validated, and rewarded. Journals, too, provide room for private reflection, but they do not hold the potential for growth through conversation that discussions can provide. For more on the importance of learning to engage in moral *dialogue*, see Noddings (1994).

5. E. D. Hirsch (1988) has promoted the idea that in order to be "culturally literate," students in each grade level should be acquainted with a fairly long list of texts, historical characters, ideas, and vocabulary.

6. There were various factors that might have mitigated against Larry leading such discussions in U.S. History during the time I was visiting, including his having turned over some of the class time to his teaching partner, Tom Atlas, an English teacher, to work on a novel, and also the presence, in the early fall, of a student teacher, who also took over some of the teaching. Still, in the four weeks I was in Larry's U.S. history class, I saw him lead class more than twelve times, and never saw a discussion of this sort. They were frequent in the War and Peace class.

7. McNeil (1988).

8. For more on the press to teach facts and on the problems with decontextualized facts, see Darling-Hammond (1997, pp. 57–61) and Kohn (1999, pp. 49–50).

9. Because I provide running commentary on this discussion, I refer to everyone's remarks in the present tense.

10. I saw other students cry at school, but only about a social interaction or a teacher-student disagreement—never about anything that was directly related to the topic of a class.

11. Mehan (1979) identifies this structure and refers to it as "IRE."

12. In her powerful and sobering book, Peggy Orenstein (1994) has documented that this is often the case.

13. For an analysis of the limits and possible hazards of the Socratic approach, see Daniel Pekarsky (1994).

14. John Goodlad's (1984) study of thirteen secondary schools found, in social studies classes, a "preponderance of classroom activity involving listening, reading textbooks, completing workbooks and worksheets, and taking quizzes." Tests in social studies "rarely required other than the recall and feedback of memorized information—multiple choice, true or false, matching like things, and filling in the missing words or phrases" (pp. 212–213).

15. The ongoing, extremely controversial nature of questioning the wisdom and justice of dropping the atomic bombs was highlighted by the furor that erupted during the mid-1990s over a proposed exhibit about the *Enola Gay* (the airplane that dropped the bombs) at the Smithsonian Institution. For more on the proposed exhibit and the controversy surrounding it, see DeWitt (1995), Goldberger (1996), and McNulty (1995).

16. This, indeed, captures the sentiment we heard expressed in the previous chapter by Ms. Gilman, with regard to the historical bias of current textbooks.

17. For purposes of simplicity, I have lumped together here the varieties of knowledge implied in "acquiring historical content" or "acquiring scientific content" as if they were one. Of course, they are not. Acquiring scientific content, for example, demands a combination of factual, analytic, synthetic, and procedural knowledge, along with the physical skills of using the tools of the laboratory and the field. It also can require a good deal of creativity and innovation. Here, the point is the distinction between all these ways of knowing and the moral, evaluative function.

18. For additional arguments along these lines, see Noddings (1992).

19. Nixon (1983); many readers will be familiar with this film, as it has been shown on numerous occasions on PBS.

20. For a powerful description of teachers with two very different, but effective, styles of facilitation, see Weinberg and Wilson (1988). One of the teachers they describe plays a very visible, central role, like Larry Carlson; one stays much more behind the scenes, like Angela Rivers.

21. Although the Huntington's example may seem fairly obscure because it is such a rare disease, the widespread availability of amniocentesis—with the power to detect a wide range of genetic abnormalities in utero—makes it routine for prospective parents (in developed countries) to have to grapple with a similar range of questions.

Chapter 6: From the Sublime to the Mundane

1. For a critique of the tendency to address apparent gaps in the high school curriculum by adding more courses, see Powell, Farrar, and Cohen (1985).

2. I shall henceforth in this chapter use the shorthand of referring to these courses collectively as "religion courses."

3. As Lee Shulman (1991b) reminds us, Joseph Schwab stresses the importance of the four "commonplaces" of education, namely, the subject matter, the teacher, the learner, and the milieu. Schwab argues that "no comprehensive statement about education could be offered that did not treat, in some fashion, each of the four commonplaces" (pp. 462–463). Schwab uses these commonplaces for different purposes from mine, but they help highlight the significance of the four areas I have chosen to examine. As Shulman puts it, "education always involved the teaching of something by someone to someone else in some context" (p. 463)—and I have tried, in the categories discussed here, to touch on all these commonplaces. In my scheme, the first category deals with the subject matter, the second with the subject matter as it links with the students, the third with the milieu as it affects the students, and the fourth with the teachers as they affect the milieu.

4. Buber (1923/1958).

5. Matthew 5:44–57 continues: "so that you may be children of your father in heaven; for he makes the sun rise on the evil and on the good, and sends rain on the righteous and on the unrighteous. For if you love those who love you, what reward do you have? Do not even the tax collectors do the same? And if you greet only your brothers and sisters, what more are you doing than others? Do not even the gentiles do the same? Be perfect, therefore, as your heavenly Father is perfect."

6. Again we see how stories, in their power to capture memorably morally complex situations, can serve as moral exemplars and foster deliberation and discussion of moral issues. For me, as always, the interest lies not so much in the stories themselves, but the forum a classroom provides or fails to provide for making sense out of the stories.

7. The first five books of the Hebrew Bible are divided into roughly fifty-two sections, each one corresponding to a given week on the calendar; the cycle is completed and begun anew each year.

8. Highlighting the necessity to interpret and draw possibly divergent meanings from texts would greatly enrich texts like those, for example, in William Bennett's *Book of Virtues*. There, Bennett presents classic stories as though they in some straightforward way exemplify such virtues as "honesty" and "patience." When read with different interpretive lenses, however, these same stories can be seen as validations of such things as materialism and sex-

ism. When we teach these texts, part of the lesson should be about the power and validity of varied interpretations.

9. Another useful pair of terms employed by Rabbi Katz in his Jewish Thought class served as shorthand for the idea that in practicing Judaism, one might lose connection with the power of the religion either by being caught up in details of strict observance while forgetting to invest the practices with meaning, or by focusing on the search for meaning and deep spirituality while neglecting the day-to-day practices that connect one to history and community. The class referred to these two poles as "dying by ice" or "dying by fire." In conversation and in written work, students used the terms to describe their own relationship to religious observance and also in trying to understand the work of such philosophers as Buber and Rosenzweig.

10. For a brief description some of these "virtues" curricula, see Bradsher (1996).

11. See the Babylonian Talmud, *Ketubot* 67a-68a and *Babba Bathra* 9a-11a; also Maimonides, *Matanot Aniyim*, chapters 7-10.

12. Shulman (1991a). Also see Conrad (1991).

13. Another particularly impressive ongoing assignment in Ms. Castle's Social Justice class asked each student to pick some kind of community service work at which they would volunteer at least once a week for the course of the semester. Students worked in homeless shelters, AIDS hospices, day care centers, and nursing homes, among others. They had frequent in-class opportunities to talk and write about both the rewards and the challenges of their work. Several students spoke to me about how much it meant to them to meet people from different backgrounds and different ages; many of them seemed to have developed deep affection for the people with whom they worked.

14. See Sizer (1992) and Cushman (1990).

15. Ahlers, Allaire, and Koch (1992).

16. "I–you statements" here referred to the sort popularized by *Parent Effectiveness Training* (Gordon, 1975), not to Buber's "I–Thou" relationships.

17. The observations of Jackson, Boostrom, and Hansen (1993) support the idea that religion classes resemble other classes in the school more than not. Describing the religion classes they observed in two Roman Catholic schools, they commented: "As far as we could tell as observers, there was nothing unusual about these religion classes from a pedagogical point of view. They were conducted in about the same way as were classes in the other school subjects. Students seemed to approach them with neither more nor less enthusiasm or piety than they did any of their other subjects. Likewise, the teachers in charge taught them with about the same degree of involvement that typified other classes" (p. 5). My findings differ from those of Jackson and his colleagues to some extent—I found rather more excitement regarding the religion classes than other classes. Still, I concur that the content of religion

classes does not *necessarily* affect pedagogy or student attitudes to a significant degree.

18. I will revisit these issues in Chapters 7 and 8 and the Afterword. See also Sizer (1999).

19. Not only the religion classes but almost all the other classes at Saint Paul also began with a moment for the prayers and "intentions" described here, though in other classes time allotted to prayer and intentions tended to be quite brief. Prayer at Agnon was allocated to time outside class, and because of my focus on in-class curriculum I shall not include it in my main discussion. It is worth noting, though, that students at Agnon had the option of attending a brief (seven to ten minute) prayer service every day at the end of lunch, and everyone in the school was required to go to one of several options for extended prayer each Thursday morning. Along with "traditional egalitarian" and "Reform" services, and a few others, a "Doubter's *Minyan*" (*minyan* means quorum, and is used to refer to a prayer group) was offered for students who did not feel comfortable praying. That group met with Rabbi Katz, and students had a chance to talk about such things as how to make sense of being Jewish without believing in God and the difficulty of believing in God given the suffering and evil in the world. Normally, students moved from group to group at their choice from week to week. Because Rabbi Katz wanted to make sure that the "doubters" group remained a safe place for students to express all kinds of feelings and concerns, that group was closed to visitors and "floaters."

20. I have changed the names of the saints invoked, as they are the patron and matron saints of the school, and naming them would thus compromise the confidentiality of the study.

21. For more discussion of this point, see Deiro (1996).

22. To be fair, it must be noted that some students at both schools had very complimentary things to say about the school as a whole and the administration in particular. Sol, for example, clearly had great regard for Dr. Robinson for his moral standards and moral messages. Calling the principal his "favorite thing about the school," he elaborated: "The first day you come to school, there's Dr. Robinson, telling us what we have to know. He tells us not the way we should act, but the way he expects us to act. And he gives us these great speeches. He has these great lines, like, 'If you get an F, you might be an F student, but you're still an A person, and you always have to remember that.' And, it's just—these speeches he gives are just so moving. [You think] 'This is the way I want to be' every time you hear this speech. This guy is just great."

23. Kilpatrick (1992, pp. 238–239).

24. The term "knowledge-out-of-context" is from Applebee (1996, p. 21).

25. David Farrington of Gorham High and Michael Carter and Joanne Dowd of Poland Regional High, both in Maine, for example, teach a course called

"Human Nature and Social Problems," originally developed by John Newlin, now of the Southern Maine Partnership. The course explores such questions as "How do we know what to believe?" "What makes us who we are?" and "What is the right way to live?" and engages students in readings in philosophy, world religions, psychology, fictional literature, and science.

26. As I have suggested above, some other existent courses in addition to the core subject areas, such as those in service learning, peer helping, and leadership, present themselves as logical niches for integration of moral and existential issues.

27. Graff (1992).

Chapter 7: Whose Values Will Get Taught?

1. Noddings (1993, p. 139).

2. The quotation is from Delfattore (1992, p. 140); descriptions of the attempts to ban these books can be found in ibid. (pp. 106, 107, 113, 140).

3. Purpel (1989, p. 68).

4. See Aristotle (1962, pp. 33–34).

5. Bennett (1992, pp. 58–60).

6. Lickona (1991, p. 269; emphasis in original).

7. Kohlberg, too, questions the apparent noncontroversial nature of the list of virtues that the character educators would instill, and finds them much more complicated than they appear at first: "It is easy to get superficial consensus on such a bag of virtues—until one examines in detail the list of virtues involved and the details of their definition.... When one turns to the details of defining each virtue, one finds equal uncertainty or difficulty in reaching consensus. Does honesty mean one should not steal to save a life? Does it mean that a student should not help another student with his homework?" (Kohlberg, 1978, p. 42.) Everyone might agree that honesty is a good thing; but when it comes to figuring out how to act morally, knowing about a particular virtue is not enough to go on. Furthermore, Kohlberg argues, far from being "universal," the virtues listed tend to reify the status quo, and thus are likely *not* valued by those who seek significant social change.

8. Goodlad (1984, pp. 241–242). For much more on the unintended lessons of schooling, see also Sizer (1999) and Pope (2001).

9. Noddings adopts the term "pedagogical neutrality" from Vandenberg (1983). The quotations can be found in Noddings (1993, pp. 139 and 122–123; emphasis in original).

10. Tom (1984) describes these two areas as predominant elements of the teacher's moral role.

11. Alternatively, the teacher might follow the precepts of "universal values" to focus on individual rather than social values, using the lives of the

characters as illustrations of honesty, hard work, generosity, or their opposites. It is hard to know, though, what the "universal values" approach would do with the unfortunate truth that both in fiction and in life, "good guys" often suffer while "bad guys" prosper.

12. See, for example, Eisner (1994, pp. 87–107) and Anyon (1983).

13. The degree of teacher autonomy regarding curricular materials varies considerably from district to district and from state to state. However, even in districts where they have relatively little choice over curricular materials, teachers retain much choice in how the materials will be used, how much time they will be allocated, which sections will be emphasized, what supplementary materials will be used, et cetera. The following example, involving my teaching of a couple of required texts, demonstrates this idea.

14. For a thoughtful discussion of how teachers can and do make curricular decisions, see *The Teacher-Curriculum Encounter* by Miriam Ben-Peretz (1990).

15. Lickona (1991, p. 111).

16. I saw Larry demonstrate his opposition to sharing his political beliefs with students in several contexts in addition to those already described. In one instance, as part of the discussion of Kingsolver's *The Bean Trees*, Larry brought up the point that the United States government in general does not let Guatemalan refugees enter the country. A student responded to this statement by asking Larry if he is a Republican or a Democrat. Larry refused to answer, but the question was particularly telling to me, coming as it did at the very end of the school year, after the students had studied American history with Larry for a whole year. Clearly, none of the discussions of history had made Larry's political affiliation clear to the students.

17. Larry's philosophy is very much like that of Victor Frankl, who, in *From Death-Camp to Existentialism*, reflecting on his experiences under the Nazis, writes: "We who lived in concentration camps can remember the men who walked through the huts comforting others, giving away their last piece of bread. They may have been few in number, but they offer sufficient proof that everything can be taken from a man but one thing: the last of the human freedoms—to choose one's attitude in any given set of circumstances, to choose one's own way" (Frankl, 1959, p. 65).

18. See Buchwald, Fletcher, and Roth (1993). It is also important to note that Milgram would not necessarily find the rape example analogous to the experiments he conducted: he was particularly interested in finding out how people respond to authority even when *no* physical coercion is used.

19. Gerald Graff (1992) writes cogently about the possibility of "teaching the conflicts" and "turning conflict into community."

20. Sizer (1992); Sarason (1990); Darling-Hammond and McLaughlin (1995); Lieberman (1995).

21. Lieberman and Miller (1992).

22. Powerful examples of teachers highlighting moral and existential issues in instructional plans in English can be found in Athanases, Christiano, and Drexler (1992) and Athanases, Christiano, and Lay (1995).

23. I borrow the term "critical friends" from the practice of the Coalition of Essential Schools; see Sizer (1992). For more on mentoring, see Little (1990).

24. For more on learning facts in the context of meaningful explorations, see Kohn (1999, pp. 142, 148).

25. Meier (1995, p. 50).

26. One of the teachers in this discussion, Ed Yearly, appeared in Chapter 6; he teaches Morality at Saint Paul. The others were all interviewed and observed for this study, though excerpts from their classes do not appear here. I use the teachers' pseudonymous first names only in the transcript. Their full pseudonyms and the subjects they teach are Sally Masters, English; Laura Evans, social studies; Ed Yearly, religion, and Dan O'Brian, English. "Kathy" refers to the author.

27. Texts of classroom interactions, like the one I provided to Laura, Dan, Ed, and Sally, might be useful starting places for fostering the discussions that would contribute to the development of such a culture.

28. Noddings' (1996) discussion of the dark side of community is relevant here.

29. Shulman (1995, p. 2).

30. Ibid. (p. 15, emphasis in original).

Chapter 8: The Case for Systemic Reform

1. Although it is beyond the scope of this book to compare in detail teachers' articulated conceptions of the subject matter with their enactment of those conceptions in class, it is worth noting that I found that teachers tended to talk, outside of class, about their subject areas and their instructional goals in very broad terms. In class, however, the practices of information delivery that I have described predominated. This finding corresponds with that of Nystrand and Gamoran's studies of the teaching of literature, summarized in Applebee (1996), who found that "Although teachers claimed to have broad humanist goals for literature instruction (building interest in reading, encouraging creativity and independent thinking), observation of classroom practice found that the teaching of literature tended to be a relatively traditional enterprise" (p. 29).

2. For a discussion of several studies of this trend in textbooks, see Applebee (1996, pp. 21–34), Leming (1985), and Wineberg (1991). For a discussion of the ways in which standardized tests emphasize decontextualized facts, see Darling-Hammond (1997) and Kohn (1999).

3. Applebee (1996, p. 20; emphasis in original). The second quotation is found in ibid. (pp. 51, 52).

4. Dewey (1990, p. 190).

5. Darling-Hammond (1993, p. 755).

6. For a description of pedagogical content knowledge, see Shulman (1987b). Shulman himself, of course, recognizes the moral elements in teaching. See, for example, Shulman (1987c).

7. Noddings (1989, p. 243).

Afterword: Strategies and Tools for Incorporating Moral and Existential Questions into the Classroom

1. My former high school teaching colleague Lee Swenson introduced me to the phrase "provocative propositions" and to the power of organizing instructional units around them.

2. For more on this idea of "planning backward" from assessment to curriculum, see McDonald (1992) and Cushman (1990).

3. For more ideas along these lines, see Cohen (1986).

4. I have adapted these Final Word Protocols from an exercise developed by Daniel Baron of the Harmony School in Bloomington, Indiana, and Patricia Averette, Los Angeles Annenberg Metropolitan Project (LAAMP), Los Angeles, California, and used in workshops by the Annenberg Institute for School Reform.

5. The Constructivist Learning Group protocol is adapted from Garmston and Wellman (1998).

6. See for example, Atwell (1987).

7. For more on the power of interdisciplinary work, see Gardner (1992) and Lear (1993).

8. The team of teachers at Drake is Peter Babb, Nicole Carter, and Adriane Fink.

9. The Tuning Protocol is adapted from Allen (1998). Originally developed by David Allen and Joe MacDonald, the Tuning Protocol is in wide use, with numerous variations.

10. See Lieberman and Miller (2000) and Greenleaf et al. (1999). For a number of additional protocols for examining student work, see also Cushman (1996) and Allen, Blythe, and Powell (1996).

11. This is adapted from a protocol originally designed for students to review their own work, and developed by Daniel Baron of the Harmony School in Bloomington, Indiana. Baron's protocol is cited in Cushman (1996).

12. For more on powerful collegial relationships, see Little and McLaughlin (1993).

13. The Peer Observation Guide described here is slightly modified from one developed by Simon Hole, a teacher from Narragansett, Rhode Island, who has developed a series of ways to do peer observation. For other examples of his peer observation guides, see Cushman (1999).

References

Ahlers, J., Allaire, B., and Koch, C. (1992). *Growing in Christian morality.* Winona, Minn.: Saint Mary's Press.

Allen, D. (1998). The tuning protocol: Opening up reflection. In D. Allen (Ed.), *Assessing student learning* (pp. 87–104). New York: Teachers College Press.

Allen, D., Blythe, T., and Powell, B. (1996). *A guide to looking collaboratively at student work.* Cambridge: Harvard Project Zero.

Alter, J., and Wingert, P. (1995, February 6). The return of shame. *Newsweek,* pp. 20–26.

Anyon, J. (1983). Social class and the hidden curriculum of work. In H. Giroux and D. Purpel (Eds.), *The hidden curriculum and moral education.* Berkeley: McCutchan Publishing Corporation.

Applebee, A. N. (1996). *Curriculum as conversation.* Chicago: University of Chicago Press.

Aristotle (1962). *The nicomachean ethics* (Martin Ostwald, Trans.). Indianapolis: Bobbs-Merrill.

Athanases, S. Z. (1993) *Discourse about literature and diversity: A study of two urban tenth-grade classes.* Doctoral dissertation, Stanford University.

Athanases, S. Z., Christiano, D., and Drexler, S. (1992). Family gumbo: Urban students respond to contemporary poets of color. *English Journal* 81 (5):45–54.

Athanases, S. Z., Christiano, D., and Lay, E. (1995). Fostering empathy and finding common ground in multiethnic classes. *English Journal* 84 (3):26–34.

Atwell, N. (1987). *In the middle: Writing, reading, and learning with adolescents.* Portsmouth, N.H.: Boynton/Cook Publishers.

Bates, S. (1995, January 8). A textbook of virtues. *New York Times Education Life,* pp. 16–19, 43–45.

Bellah, R. N., Madsen, R., Sullivan, W. M., Swidler, A., and Tipton, S. M. (1985). *Habits of the heart: Individualism and commitment in American life.* Berkeley: University of California Press.

Ben-Peretz, M. (1990). *The teacher-curriculum encounter: Freeing teachers from the tyranny of texts.* Albany: State University of New York Press.

Bennett, W. J. (1992). *The de-valuing of America: The fight for our culture and our children.* New York: Simon and Schuster.

————. (Ed.). (1993). *The book of virtues: A treasury of great moral stories*. New York: Simon and Schuster.

Boyer, E. L. (1993). In search of community. Invited address at the Annual Meeting of the Association for Supervision and Curriculum Development. Washington, D.C.

Boyer, P. (1995). *The American nation*. Austin, Tex.: Holt, Rinehart & Winston.

Bradsher, K. (1996, October 23). Putting values in classroom, carefully. *New York Times*.

Brell, C. D., Jr. (1989). Justice and caring and the problem of moral relativism: Reframing the gender question in ethics. *Journal of Moral Education* 18 (2):97–111.

Brookfield, S. D., and Preskill, S. (1999). *Discussion as a way of teaching: Tools and techniques for democratic classrooms*. San Francisco: Jossey-Bass.

Brooks, B. D., and Kann, M. E. (1993). What makes character education programs work? *Educational Leadership* 51 (3):19–21.

Brown, A. L. (1994). The advancement of learning. *Educational Researcher* 23 (8):4–12.

Bruner, J. S. (1960). *The process of education*. Cambridge: Harvard University Press.

Bryk, A. S., Lee, V. E., and Holland, P. B. (1993). *Catholic schools and the common good*. Cambridge: Harvard University Press.

Buber, M. (1923/1958). *I and thou* (Ronald Gregor Smith, Trans.). New York: Scribner's.

Buchwald, E., Fletcher, P., and Roth., M. (Eds.). (1993). *Transforming a rape culture*. Minneapolis: Milkweed Editions.

California State Board of Education (1990). *Science framework for California public schools, kindergarten though grade twelve*. Sacramento: California Department of Education.

Canfield (1994). *Chicken soup for the soul*. New York: Bookpeople.

Card, C. (1990). Caring and evil. *Hypatia* 5 (1):101–108.

Carter, S. L. (1993). *The culture of disbelief: How American law and politics trivialize religious devotion*. New York: HarperCollins.

Chazan, B. (1985). *Contemporary approaches to moral education: Analyzing alternative theories*. New York: Teachers College Press.

Coles, R. (1986). *The moral life of children*. Boston: Houghton Mifflin.

————. (1990). *The spiritual life of children*. Boston: Houghton Mifflin.

Cohen, E. G. (1986). *Designing group work: Strategies for the heterogeneous classroom*. New York: Teachers College Press.

Conrad, D., and Hedin, D. (1991). School-based community service: What we know from research and theory. *Phi Delta Kappan* 72 (10):743–749.

Cuban, L. (1992). Managing dilemmas while building professional communities. *Educational Researcher* 21 (1):4–11.

Cushman, K. (1990). Performance and exhibitions: The demonstration of mastery. *Horace* 6 (3). Providence, R.I.: Coalition of Essential Schools.

———. (1996). Looking collaboratively at student work: An essential toolkit. *Horace* 13 (2). Providence, R.I.: Coalition of Essential Schools.

———. (1999). The cycle of inquiry and action: Essential learning communities. *Horace* 15 (4). Oakland, Calif.: Coalition of Essential Schools.

Darling-Hammond, L. (1993). Reframing the school reform agenda: Developing capacity for school transformation. *Phi Delta Kappan* 74 (10):752–761.

Darling-Hammond, L., and McLaughlin, M. (1995). Policies that support professional development in an era of reform. *Phi Delta Kappan* 76 (8):597–604.

Deiro, J. (1996). *Teaching with heart: Making healthy connections with students.* Beverly Hills, Calif.: Sage.

Delfattore, J. (1992). *What Johnny shouldn't read: Textbook censorship in America.* New Haven: Yale University Press.

Dewey, J. (1902). *The child and the curriculum.* Chicago: University of Chicago Press.

———. (1909). *Moral principles in education.* Carbondale: Southern Illinois University Press.

———. (1938). *Experience and education.* New York: Macmillan.

———. (1972). Ethical principles underlying education. In J. A. Boydston (Ed.), *The early works of John Dewey, 1882–1898: Early essays* (pp. 54–83). Carbondale: Southern Illinois University Press.

———. (1990). *The school and society; The child and the curriculum.* Chicago: University of Chicago Press.

DeWitt, K. (1995, January 31). Smithsonian scales back exhibit of B-29 in atomic bomb attack. *New York Times*, p. 1A.

Doersch, C. (1995, March 10). Bring back the orphanage? *Scholastic Update*, pp. 10–12.

Dole, B. (1996). Republican response to the president's State of the Union Address. Speech delivered in Washington, D.C.: Dole for President, Inc.

Ehrlich, E., Flexner, S. B., Carruth, G., and Hawkins, J. M. (Eds.). (1980). *Oxford American dictionary.* New York: Avon.

Eisenhart, M., and Borko, H. (1993). *Designing classroom research: Themes, issues, and struggles.* Boston: Allyn and Bacon.

Eisner, E. W. (1991). *The enlightened eye: Qualitative inquiry and the enhancement of educational practice.* New York: Macmillan.

———. (1992). The misunderstood role of the arts in human development. *Phi Delta Kappan* 73 (8):591–595.

———. (1994). *The educational imagination: On the design and evaluation of school programs.* New York: Macmillan College Publishing.

Eisner, E. W., and Peshkin, A. (Eds.). (1990). *Qualitative inquiry in education: The continuing debate.* New York: Teachers College Press.

Evenson, L. (1996, December 25). Soul for sale: Authors, publishers latch onto buzzword of the '90s. *San Francisco Chronicle,* pp. 1, 8.

Fineman, H. (1994, June 13). The virtuecrats. *Newsweek,* pp. 30–37.

Frankl, V. (1959). *From death-camp to existentialism: A psychiatrist's path to a new therapy* (Ilse Lasch, Trans.). Boston: Beacon.

Gardner, H. (1983). *Frames of mind: The theory of multiple intelligences.* New York: Basic.

———. (1992). *The unschooled mind.* New York: Basic.

Garmston R., and Wellman B. (1998). Teacher talk that makes a difference. *Educational Leadership* 55 (7):30–34.

Gilkey, L. (1970). *Religion and the scientific future.* New York: Harper and Row.

Gilligan, C. (1982). *In a different voice: Psychological theory and women's development.* Cambridge: Harvard University Press.

Goldberger, P. (1996, February 11). Historical shows on trial: Who judges? *New York Times,* section 2, p. 1.

Goodlad, J. I. (1984). *A place called school: Prospects for the future.* New York: McGraw-Hill.

Gordon, T. (1975). *P.E.T., Parent effectiveness training.* New York: New American Library.

Graff, G. (1992). *Beyond the culture wars: How teaching the conflicts can revitalize American education.* New York: Norton.

Gray, P. (1994, Dec. 26). Man of the year: Empire of the spirit. *Time,* pp. 3; 48–57.

Greene, M. (1978). The artistic-aesthetic and curriculum. In M. Greene, *Landscapes of learning* (pp. 168–184). New York: Teachers College Press.

Greenleaf, C., Schoenback, R., Morehouse, L., Katz, M., and Mueller, F. (1999). Close readings: Developing inquiry tools and practices for generative professional development. Paper presented at annual meeting of the American Educational Research Association, Montreal.

Grumet, M. R. (1988). *Bitter milk: Women and teaching.* Amherst: University of Massachusetts Press.

Guy, E. (1993). America the violent. *Time* 142 (8).

Hansen, D. T. (1993). The moral importance of the teacher's style. *Journal of Curriculum Studies* 25 (5):397–421.

Harmin, M. (1988). Value clarity, high morality: Let's go for both. *Educational Leadership* (May), 24–30.

Haroutunian-Gordon, S. (1991). *Turning the soul.* Chicago: University of Chicago Press.

Hartshorne, H., and May, M. (1930). *Studies in the nature of character.* New York: Macmillan.

Havel, V. (1994, June 8). The new measure of man. *New York Times*, 27.

Himmelfarb, H. (1990). Jewish day schools entering the 1990s. *Private School Monitor* 11 (3):2–5.

Hirsch, E. D., Jr. (1988). *Cultural literacy: What every American needs to know.* New York: Random House.

Hoagland, S. L. (1990). Some concerns about Nel Noddings' *Caring. Hypatia* 5 (1):109–114.

Holy Bible: New revised standard version (1989). New York: Oxford University Press.

Houston, B. (1990). Caring and exploitation. *Hypatia* 5 (1):115–119.

Howe, K., and Eisenhart, M. (1990). Standards for qualitative (and quantitative) research: A prolegomenon. *Educational Researcher* 17 (8):10–16.

Hutchins, R. M. (1953). *The conflict in education in a democratic society.* New York: Harper and Row.

Jackson, P. W. (1983). The daily grind. In H. Giroux and D. Purpel (Eds.), *The hidden curriculum and moral education.* Berkeley: McCutchan Publishing Corporation.

Jackson, P. W., Boostrom, R. E., and Hansen, D. T. (1993). *The moral life of schools.* San Francisco: Jossey-Bass.

Kantrowitz, B. (1994, November 28). The search for the sacred. *Newsweek*, pp. 52–59.

Kilpatrick, W. (1992). *Why Johnny can't tell right from wrong: And what we can do about it.* New York: Simon and Schuster.

Kingsolver, B. (1988). *The bean trees.* New York: HarperCollins.

Kohlberg, L. (1978). The cognitive-developmental approach to moral education. In P. Scharf (Ed.), *Readings in moral education.* Minneapolis: Winston Press.

———. (1980). Stages of moral development as a basis for moral education. In B. Munsey (Ed.), *Moral development, moral education, and Kohlberg: Basic issues in philosophy, psychology, religion, and education.* Birmingham: Religious Education Press.

Kohn, A. (1999). *The schools our children deserve: Moving beyond traditional classrooms and tougher standards.* Boston: Houghton Mifflin.

Kristof, N. D. (1993, April 25). China's crackdown on births: A stunning, and harsh, success. *New York Times*, p. 1.

Lampert, M. (1990). When the problem is not the question and the solution is not the answer: Mathematical knowing and teaching. *American Educational Research Journal* 27 (1):29–63.

Lear, R. (1993). *Curriculum and essential schools*. Providence, R.I.: Coalition of Essential Schools.

Leming, J. S. (1981). Curricular effectiveness in moral/values education: A review of research. *Journal of Moral Education* 10 (3):147–161.

———. (1985). Research on social studies curriculum and instruction: Interventions and outcomes in the socio-moral domain. In W. B. Stanley (Ed.), *Review of research in social studies education: 1976–1983, Bulletin no. 73* (pp. 123–213). Washington, D.C.: National Council for the Social Studies.

Lickona, T. (1991). *Educating for character: How our schools can teach respect and responsibility*. New York: Bantam.

Lickona, T., Schaps E., and Lewis C. (1996). *Eleven principles of effective character education*. Washington, D.C.: Character Education Partnership.

Lieberman, A. (1995). *The work of restructuring schools: Building from the ground up*. New York: Teachers College Press.

Lieberman, A., and Miller, L. (1992). Teacher development in professional practice schools. In M. Levine (Ed.), *Professional practice schools: Linking teacher education and school reform* (pp. 105–123). New York: Teachers College Press.

———. (2000). Teaching and teacher development: A new synthesis for a new century. In R. Brandt (Ed.), *Education in a new era: ASCD yearbook 2000*. Washington, D.C.: ASCD.

Little, J. W. (1990). The mentor phenomenon and the social organization of teaching. In C. B. Cazden (Ed.), *Review of research in education* Washington, D.C.: American Educational Research Association.

Little, J. W., and McLaughlin, M. W. (Eds). (1993). *Teachers' work: Individuals, colleagues, and contexts*. New York: Teachers College Press.

Lorde, A. (1984). *Sister outsider*. Trumansburg, N.Y.: Crossing Press.

Marker, G., and Mehlinger, H. (1992). Social studies. In P. Jackson (Ed.), *Handbook of research on curriculum* (pp. 830–850). New York: Maxwell Macmillan International.

McDonald, J. P. (1992). *Steps in planning backwards: Early lessons from the schools*. Providence, R.I.: Coalition of Essential Schools.

McNeil, L. (1988). *Contradictions of control: School structure and school knowledge*. New York: Routledge.

McNulty, T. (1995, February 5). War of words: What the museum couldn't say. *New York Times*, section 4, p. 5.

Mehan, H. (1979). *Learning lessons*. Cambridge: Harvard University Press.

Meier, D. (1995). *The power of their ideas: Lessons for America from a small school in Harlem.* Boston: Beacon.

———. (2000). *Will standards save public education?* Boston: Beacon.

Miles, M. B., and Huberman, A. M. (1984). *Qualitative data analysis: A sourcebook of new methods.* Beverly Hills: Sage.

Milgram, S. (1974). *Obedience to authority.* New York: Harper and Row.

Moffett, J. (1994). *The universal schoolhouse: Spiritual awakening through education.* San Francisco: Jossey-Bass.

Molnar, A. (Ed.). (1997). *The construction of children's character. Ninety-sixth yearbook of the national society for the study of education.* Part II. Chicago: University of Chicago Press.

Moore, T. (1994). *Care of the soul.* Camp Hill, Pa.: Quality Paperback Books.

News Transcripts, I. (1992, May 19). Excerpts from vice president's speech on cities and poverty. *New York Times.*

News Transcripts, I. (1993, May 21). China's cruelty and women's rights. *New York Times*, p. 26A.

Niebuhr, G. (1993, December 31). U.S. Catholic, Jewish leaders hail Israeli-Vatican accord. *Washington Post*, p. A23.

Nixon, B. (1983). The miracle of life. Paramus, N.J.: Time-Life Video.

Noddings, N. (1984). *Caring: A feminine approach to ethics and moral education.* Berkeley: University of California Press.

———. (1989). *Women and evil.* Berkeley: University of California Press.

———. (1992). *The challenge to care in schools: An alternative approach to education.* New York: Teachers College Press.

———. (1993). *Educating for intelligent belief or unbelief.* New York: Teachers College Press.

———. (1994). Learning to engage in moral dialogue. *Holistic Education Review* 7 (2):5–11.

———. (1995). *Philosophy of education.* Boulder, Colo.: Westview.

———. (1996). On community. *Educational Theory* 46 (3):245–267.

Nucci, L. (1989). Challenging conventional wisdom about morality: The domain approach to values education. In L. Nucci (Ed.), *Moral development and character education: A dialogue.* Berkeley: McCutchan Publishing Corporation.

Oldenburg, A., and Edmonds, P. (1996, August 7). Chasing the values vote: Morals and mixed signals. *USA Today*, p. 4A.

Orenstein, P. (1994). *SchoolGirls: Young women, self-esteem, and the confidence gap.* New York: Anchor.

Pekarsky, D. (1994). Socratic teaching: a critical assessment. *Journal of Moral Education* 23 (2):119–134.

Peshkin, A. (1986). *God's choice: The total world of a fundamentalist Christian school.* Chicago: University of Chicago Press.

Pope, D. C. (2001). *"Doing school."* New Haven: Yale University Press.

Popham, J. (1999). Why standardized tests don't measure educational quality. *Educational Leadership*, March, 8–15.

Powell, A. G., Farrar, E., and Cohen, D. K. (1985). *The shopping mall high school: Winners and losers in the educational marketplace.* Boston: Houghton Mifflin.

Power, C. (1988). The just community approach to moral education. *Journal of Moral Education* 17 (3):195–207.

Power, C., Higgins, A., and Kohlberg, L. (1989). The habit of the common life: Building character through democratic community schools. In L. Nucci (Ed.), *Moral development and character education: A dialogue.* Berkeley: McCutchan Publishing Corporation.

Purpel, D., and Ryan, K. (1983). It comes with the territory: The inevitability of moral education in the schools. In H. Giroux and D. Purpel (Eds.), *The hidden curriculum and moral education.* Berkeley: McCutchan Publishing Corporation.

Purpel, D. E. (1989). *The moral and spiritual crisis in education.* Massachusetts: Bergin & Garvey.

Raths, L. E., Harmin, M., and Simon, S. B. (1966). *Values and teaching: Working with values in the classroom.* Columbus: Charles E. Merrill Books.

Redfield, J. (1994). *The celestine prophecy.* Camp Hill, Pa.: Quality Paperback Books.

Reinharz, S. (1979). *On becoming a social scientist.* San Francisco: Jossey-Bass.

Rich, A. (1976). *Of woman born: Motherhood as experience and institution.* New York: Norton.

Rosenblatt, R. (1995, April 30). Who'll teach kids right from wrong? The character education movement thinks the answer is schools. *New York Times Magazine*, pp. 36–41, 50, 60, 64, 74.

Ryan, K. (1989). In defense of character education. In L. Nucci (Ed.), *Moral development and character education: A dialogue.* Berkeley: McCutchan Publishing Corporation.

Sarason, S. B. (1990). *The predictable failure of educational reform.* San Francisco: Jossey-Bass.

Schiff, A. I. (1966). *The Jewish day school in America.* New York: Jewish Education Committee.

Schoem, D. (1989). *Ethnic survival in America: An ethnography of a Jewish afternoon school.* Atlanta: Scholars Press.

Schwab, J. J. (1973). The Practical 3: Translation into curriculum. *School Review* 81:501–522.

Shulman, L. S. (1987a). The wisdom of practice: Managing complexity in medicine and teaching. In D. C. Berliner and B. V. Rosenshine (Eds.), *Talks to teachers: A festschrift for N. L. Gage* (pp. 369–386).

———. (1987b). Knowledge and teaching: Foundations of the new reform. *Harvard Educational Review* 57 (1):1–22.

———. (1987c). Sounding an alarm: A reply to Sockett. *Harvard Educational Review* 57 (4):473–482.

———. (1991a). *Professing the liberal arts*. An unpublished lecture for the Institute on Integrating Service with Academic Study.

———. (1991b). Joseph Jackson Schwab, 1909–1988. In E. Shils (Ed.), *Remembering the University of Chicago: Teachers, scientists, and scholars* (pp. 452–468). Chicago: University of Chicago Press.

———. (1992). Toward a pedagogy of cases. In J. H. Shulman (Ed.), *Case methods in teacher education* (pp. 1–30). New York: Teachers College Press.

———. (1995). *Communities of learners and communities of teachers*. An unpublished lecture for the Mandel Institute, Jerusalem, Israel.

Simon, S. B., Howe, L. W., and Kirschenbaum, H. (1972). *Values clarification: A handbook of practical strategies for teachers and students*. New York: Hart.

Sizer, T. R. (1984). *Horace's compromise: The dilemma of the American high school*. Boston: Houghton Mifflin.

———. (1992). *Horace's school: Redesigning the American high school*. New York: Houghton Mifflin.

Sizer, T. R., and Sizer, N. F. (1999). *The students are watching: Schools and the moral contract*. Boston: Beacon.

Sloan, A. (1996, February 26). Corporate killers: Wall Street loves layoffs, but the public is scared as hell. *Newsweek*, pp. 44–48.

Sockett, H. (1992). The moral aspects of the curriculum. In P. W. Jackson (Ed.), *Handbook of research on curriculum*. New York: Macmillan.

Soloveitchik, J. B. (1965). The lonely man of faith. *Tradition: A Journal of Orthodox Thought*, 5–67.

Tom, A. (1984). *Teaching as a moral craft*. New York: Longman.

Tyack, D., and Cuban, L. (1995). *Tinkering toward utopia: A century of public school reform*. Cambridge: Harvard University Press.

Vandenberg, D. (1983). *Human rights in education*. New York: Philosophical Library.

Wallis, C. (1996, June 24). Faith and healing: Can spirituality promote health? *Time*, pp. 59–65.

Wasserman, E. R. (1978). Implementing Kohlberg's "just community concept" in an alternative high school. In P. Scharf (Ed.), *Readings in moral education*. Minneapolis: Winston Press.

Weis, L. (1983). Schooling and cultural production: A comparison of black and white lived culture. In M. Apple and L. Weis (Eds.), *Ideology and practice in schooling.* Philadelphia: Temple University Press.

Wiesel, E. (1960). *Night* (Stella Rodway, Trans.). New York: Hill and Wang.

Wiggins, G. (1989). A true test: Toward more authentic and equitable assessment. *Phi Delta Kappan* 70 (9):703–713.

———. (1993). *Assessing student performance: Exploring the purpose and limits of testing.* San Francisco: Jossey-Bass.

Wilson, S., Miller, C., and Yerkes, C. (1992). *Deeply rooted change: A tale of learning to teach adventurously* No. 59. Center for the Learning and Teaching of Elementary Subjects, East Lansing, Mich.

Wineburg, S. S. (1991). On the reading of historical texts: Notes on the breach between school and academy. *American Educational Research Journal* 28 (3):495–519.

Wineburg, S. S., and Wilson, S. M. (1988). Models of wisdom in the teaching of history. *Phi Delta Kappan* 70 (1):50–58.

Wynne, E. A. (1986). The great tradition in education: Transmitting moral values. *Educational Leadership,* 4–9.

Wynne, E. A., and Ryan, K. (1997). *Reclaiming our schools: Teaching character, academics, and discipline* (2d ed.). Upper Saddle River, N.J.: Merrill.

Yin, R. K. (1984). *Case study research: Design and methods.* Beverly Hills: Sage.

Index

abortion, 158, 183, 196, 225; "facts" and, 161, 162; pedagogical neutrality and, 188
Adam I and Adam II, 30–33, 34, 41
advertising, 161
Agnon High School, 41, 42, 43; biology class at, 81–83; English literature class at, 72–75, 87–88; history class at, 58–60, 66–72, 78–80, 92–94, 196; modeling morality at, 174–175; observation schedule at, 249; prayer at, 269n.19; religion classes at, 144, 145–150, 152–158, 166–167, 227; student response to author's research, 44. *See also* Jewish high schools
alcohol, 88–90, 158
amniocentesis, 267n.21
Andrews, Ms. (teacher), 95–97
"Anglos," 66–68, 70, 72, 263n.13
animal rights, 161
Applebee, Arthur, 222
Atlas, Tom (teacher), 60–63, 101, 209, 221
atomic bomb, 7, 95–97, 266n.15; as war crime, 113–130, 131, 132
authority, respect for, 177
Averette, Patricia, 273n.4

Baron, Daniel, 273n.4, 274n.11
Bean Trees, The (King-

solver), 48, 60–62, 209, 262n.8, 271n.16
beauty, 86
Bennett, William, 18, 21, 183, 184, 268n.8
Bethany Baptist school, 34–35
Bible: interpretation of, 154, 268n.7; passages from, 150, 152, 155, 267n.5; teachers' views of, 29–30, 34
biology, 5, 42, 50, 64–66, 223; designing course of instruction in, 233; moral questions in curriculum and, 12, 53; skin trouble discussion, 83–87
Black Boy (Ellison), 191, 210
books, banning of, 181–182
Book of Virtues, The (Bennett), 18, 21, 268n.8
boredom, 130, 224, 256n.1
Boyer, Ernest, 264n.21
Buber, Martin, 27, 148–149, 152, 169–170, 171
Buck, Pearl S., 72

capital punishment. *See* death penalty
"care, centers of," 27–28
care, ethic of, 15, 17, 20, 25–28
Carlson, Larry (teacher), 62–63, 100–102, 151, 153, 166, 167; on existential considerations

of war, 102–113; on morality of history, 113–132; pedagogical neutrality and, 189, 193–194, 197–206; Socratic style of, 131, 138; teaching strength of, 192, 213, 223, 226
Carter, Michael, 270n.25
Carter, Stephen L., 32, 255n.9
Carver, Ms. (teacher), 83–87
Castle, Ms. (teacher), 45–46, 160–162, 163–164, 165, 167–168, 176, 268n.13
Catholic high schools, 5, 40–41, 88, 146, 177, 260n.3. *See also* Saint Paul High School
cells, 83–85
Central Park East High School, 210, 263–264n.20
character education, 15, 18, 99, 155, 157; crumbling of consensus in favor of, 11–12; virtues approach to, 18–21, 256–257n.2
Character Education Partnership, 18, 257n.6
charity, 156–158, 178
cheating, 51, 163–164, 186, 244
childbirth, 137–138, 147–148
Christian schools, 34, 259–260n.40
Civil War, 75–77, 98, 211–216, 226
class background, 40